Frege: An Introduction to his Philosophy

Frege

AN INTRODUCTION TO HIS PHILOSOPHY

GREGORY CURRIE
Assistant Lecturer in Philosophy, University of Otago

THE HARVESTER PRESS · SUSSEX
BARNES & NOBLE BOOKS · NEW JERSEY

First published in Great Britain in 1982 by
THE HARVESTER PRESS LIMITED
Publisher: John Spiers
16 Ship Street, Brighton, Sussex

and in the USA by
BARNES & NOBLE BOOKS
81 Adams Drive, Totowa, New Jersey 07512

British Library Cataloguing in Publication Data

Currie, Gregory
Frege.—(Harvester studies in philosophy; 11)
1. Frege, Gottlob—Criticism and interpretation
I. Title
193 B3245.F24

ISBN 0-85527-826-9

Library of Congress Cataloging in Publication Data

Currie, Gregory.
Frege, an introduction to his philosophy.

1. Frege, Gottlob, 1848-1925. I. Title.
B3245.F24C87 1982 193 81-22880
ISBN 0-389-20268-1 AACR2

Typeset by Alacrity Phototypesetters, Banwell Castle,
Weston-super-Mare and printed in Great Britain by
Mansell Limited, Witham, Essex

To my parents

To bring the dead to life
Is no great magic.
Few are wholly dead:
Blow on a dead man's embers
And a live flame will start.

Robert Graves

Contents

Preface

WHERE POSSIBLE I have cited both an English and a German source of reference to Frege's work. In the notes the page number of a convenient German source is given, followed by the English one in brackets. Where I have identified a passage simply by the number of the section in which it occurs I have not followed the principal of double reference. Also, I give only one page number for references to the *Foundations of Arithmetic* because this is published with the German and English on facing pages. References to letters are given as, e.g. 'letter to Russell, 1902 (p. 247 (164))'. The page numbers refer respectively to the collections Gabriel *et al* (*eds*) [1976], and McGuinness (*ed*) [1980]. Full details of the sources are to be found in the Bibliography of Frege's Writings, at the end of the book (p. 198). Sometimes I have preferred my own translations of Frege's writings to those generally available. Üta Römmermann was kind enough to check some of my translations.

At the end of the book (p. 196) I have included a Glossary of Fregean terms which are used in this book.

A number of people deserve thanks for their advice and criticism. Among them are David Armstrong, George Markus, Alan Musgrave, Graham Oddie (who is responsible for all the remaining errors), Pavel Tichý, and an anonymous referee.

I should like also to thank the staff of the University of Otago, New Zealand, where the greater part of this book was written, for their hospitality to me during my tenure of a University Post-Doctoral Fellowship. The members of the Department of Traditional and Modern Philosophy, University of Sydney, kindly arranged my teaching responsibilities during the first half of 1980 so as to accommodate the completion of this book. For this, together with their encouragement and stimulation, I am most grateful. I am also grateful to David Brosnan who helped construct the Bibliography.

Finally I should like to thank Anthea Bankoff, June O'Donnell and Patricia Trifinoff, who carefully typed various versions of the manuscript.

Introduction

THE AIM of this book is to offer an introduction to the central points of Frege's philosophical programme and to trace the historical development of his views. Frege has very often been discussed from the point of view of later philosophical developments; his views contrasted with those of Wittgenstein, Quine, and other more recent philosophers; and his theories concerning language examined from the supposedly advantaged position of an acquaintance with modern semantics. Such an enterprise is not worthless, but I do not think that it is the best way to grasp Frege's thought in its historical perspective. Instead, I shall examine his philosophy from the point of view of the problems which it was designed to solve. Only in this way, I believe, can we grasp his real achievement.

Many attempts to characterise the general features of Frege's philosophy have suffered from the tendency to interpret his writings in the light of philosophical concerns which were not his own. Some discussions of Frege's work present him as struggling with problems of ontology; the problem, for instance, of categorising the sorts of things that there are and their different modes of existence.[1] Another, initially more plausible, view ascribes to Frege a primary interest in the problem of meaning. On this view Frege was the first analytical philosopher in that he recognised the primacy within philosophy of the problem of meaning.[2]

I do not want to give the impression that there is no evidence for either of these views, or that nothing emerges from Frege's work of significance to either of these problems. But as ways of characterising the real motives and historical significance of his work they seem to me to be quite misleading. What Frege said may well have had interesting and indeed revolutionary consequences for our thinking about meaning and about existence, but once we understand the problems which his programme was an attempt to solve, they both emerge as secondary concerns. What, then, is the best way to approach Frege's philosophy? How can we see its apparently disparate elements as parts of a unified project? His work must, I believe, be seen as a contribution to epistemology, for the problems with which he grappled throughout his philosophical career were the two central questions in the theory of knowledge — the problem of certainty and the problem of objectivity.

Mathematics has always seemed important to those concerned with the question of whether there can be certain knowledge. It has seemed that mathematical knowledge is of a character quite different from our knowledge of contingent matters of fact, and could be rendered immune to the usual arguments about the possibility of error. Frege set himself the task of showing in detail that this was indeed the case. How his programme developed, how he created the conceptual machinery necessary to implement it, and to what extent it was successfully carried out, are questions which will occupy a large part of this book.

Although one can recognise within the history of philosophy many contributions of significance to the problem of objectivity, there is a sense in which this problem was not fully articulated by philosophers until the nineteenth century. Indeed, Frege's own work was one of the first serious attempts to convey the importance of the problem. Since the seventeenth century revolution in philosophy there had been a tendency to see knowledge as something subjective, a certain quality of a person's ideas. That this was so is due partly to the impact of the scientific revolution on philosophy, with its emphasis on sense experience, and partly to the way in which philosophers from that time on had tried to deal with the problem of certainty. It seemed that, for a variety of reasons, greater certainty was to be found in the inner world of a person's subjective experiences than in claims about the objective, external world. Thus the British empiricists claimed that one could have genuine knowledge concerning the relations between one's own ideas, yet be utterly mistaken about their external causes. And Descartes, the founder of European rationalism, claimed to have discovered sufficient certainty upon which to base the whole of his philosophical system by attending to the nature of his own self — not his bodily, outer self but his inner, mental self. The essentially theological outlook which dominated philosophy before Bacon, Descartes and Locke had imposed a certain objectivity on philosophical concepts which was lost when man became the central concern of philosophical thought. Writing on Descartes' philosophy Antony Kenny has said,

The word 'idea' is now at home in ordinary language; but it is a word, like 'quality' and 'intention', that was once primarily a philosophical technicality. Its modern use derives, through Locke, from Descartes; and Descartes was consciously giving it a new sense. Before him, philosophers used it to refer to archetypes in the divine intellect: it was a new departure to use it systematically for the contents of a human mind (Kenny [1968], pp. 96–7).

Frege challenged this subjectivist tradition by disputing its ability to explain the essentially objective character of human knowledge; the fact that knowledge is something which can be shared and communicated. Descartes and Locke had introduced a psychological element into philosophy — and into logic as well.[3] How this subjectivist tradition occupied a central place in nineteenth-century thought, what Frege's criticisms of it were, and how they developed out of his original concern for the justification of our knowledge, is a second group of questions which will concern us here.

We know little about Frege's life or personality. He never wrote about himself and he did not take an active part in public affairs, preferring to devote his energy to philosophy.[4] He was born in 1848 in Wismar, Germany, the son of a school principal. In 1869 he entered the University of Jena where he studied philosophy, natural science and mathematics. After two years' studying at Göttingen he returned to Jena where he obtained his doctoral degree and was admitted in the following year to the post of *Privatdozent* — a lecturing position with no salary attached — in mathematics. He remained at Jena until his retirement from academic life in 1918, by which time he had risen to the position of professor.[5] He died in 1925.

Frege's life was not, it seems, a personally fulfilled one. His wife died in 1905 and he was left to bring up their adopted son, Alfred, alone. A brief but moving personal statement is contained in the note to Alfred directing him to take care of his unpublished papers after his death.[6]

> Do not despise these papers written by me. Even if they are not pure gold, there is gold in them. I believe that one day some of the things in them will be valued more highly than now. See to it that nothing is lost.
>
> In love, your Father
>
> There is a great deal of myself that I leave you in these papers.

Frege was continually disappointed by the poor reception of his work, though his comments on critics and those whose views he opposed display a sharp humour. He once wrote, concerning the failure of logicians to note one of his logical discoveries,

This way academics have of behaving reminds me of nothing so much as that of an ox confronted by a new gate; it gapes, it bellows, it tries to squeeze by sideways, but going through it — that might be dangerous.[7]

In 1903, Bertrand Russell conveyed to him a discovery which showed Frege's work over many years to have been based on error. This must have been a bitter blow, and Frege never resolved the problem which it raised. But Russell had this to say about Frege's response to the discovery:

As I think about acts of integrity and grace, I realise that there is nothing in my knowledge to compare with Frege's dedication to truth. His entire life's work was on the verge of completion, much of his work had been ignored to the benefit of men infinitely less capable, his second volume was about to be published, and upon finding that his fundamental assumption was in error, he responded with intellectual pleasure clearly submerging any feelings of personal disappointment. It was almost superhuman, and a telling indication of that of which men are capable if their dedication is to creative work and knowledge instead of cruder efforts to dominate and be known (Heijenoort (ed) [1967], p. 127).

Frege's political and social views were gloomy and severe. His diaries reveal him as violently opposed to democracy and to civil rights for Catholics and Jews.[8] But perhaps these reflections did not occupy much of his time; Wittgenstein reports that, when he visited Frege in 1920, he could not get him to discuss anything except logic and mathematics.[9] Frege was a clear and conscientious teacher. Carnap, who attended his course in 1914, said that Frege influenced him more than any of his other lecturers, and described his encounter with Frege thus:

Frege looked old beyond his years. He was of small stature, rather shy, extremely introverted. He seldom looked at the audience. Ordinarily we only saw his back, while he drew the strange diagrams of his symbolism on the blackboard and explained them. Never did a student ask a question or make a remark, whether during the lecture or afterwards. The possibility of a discussion seemed to be out of the question ([1963], p. 5).

The extent of Frege's intellectual isolation, so often remarked on now, should not be exaggerated. Frege kept up an energetic correspondence with many of Europe's leading thinkers in the philosophy of logic and mathematics, including Hilbert, Husserl, Russell and Wittgenstein. Much of this was destroyed by bombing during the second world war, but what remains has recently been published, along with a volume of papers which remained unpublished at the time of his death.[10]

Notes

1 See especially Grossman [1969], and some of the essays in Part I of Klemke (ed) [1968]. See the critical remarks in Sluga [1970].
2 See Dummett [1973], especially p. 667.
3 See below, chapter 1, section (b).
4 But see the remarks in a letter to Hugo Dingler in 1918 (p. 45 (30)).
5 He actually occupied the position of 'Honorary Ordinary Professor'.
6 Quoted by Sluga in his [1971], who translated the passage into English.
7 [1906*e*], p. 202 (186). The remark was not intended for publication!
8 See Dummett *ibid*, p. xii. Dummett expresses great shock and sorrow concerning Frege's views. But, distasteful as these views may be, they must have been common enough among German professors of the late nineteenth century. (See the remarks in Ringer [1969], pp. 135-6.)
9 See Geach [1961], p. 129.
10 See Hermes *et al* (eds) [1969], and Gabriel *et al* (eds) [1976].

1 *The Background to Frege's Work*

IN ORDER to appreciate Frege's achievements, it will be necessary to understand some developments which occurred during and before the nineteenth century. It will be convenient to begin with the case of mathematics.

(a) Mathematics

As Frege pointed out at the beginning of *The Foundations of Arithmetic*, there were significant changes during the nineteenth century in the practice of mathematics.

> After deserting for a time the old Euclidean standards of rigour, mathematics is now returning to them, and even making efforts to go beyond them. In arithmetic, if only because many of its methods and concepts originated in India, it has been the tradition to reason less strictly than in geometry, which was in the main developed by the Greeks. The discovery of higher analysis only served to confirm this tendency; for considerable, almost insuperable, difficulties stood in the way of any rigorous treatment of these subjects, while at the same time small reward seemed likely for the efforts expended in overcoming them. Later developments, however, have shown more and more clearly that in mathematics a mere moral conviction, supported by a mass of successful applications, is not good enough. Proof is now demanded of many things that formerly passed as self-evident. Again and again the limits to the validity of a proposition have been in this way established for the first time. The concepts of function, of continuity, of limit and of infinity have been shown to stand in need of sharper definition. Negative and irrational numbers, which had long since been admitted into science, have had to submit to a closer scrutiny of their credentials.
>
> In all directions these same ideals can be seen at work — rigour of proof, precise delimitation of extent of validity, and as a means to this, sharp definition of concepts ([1884 *b*] p. 1).

These remarks require some clarification. The Greeks had achieved a high degree of sophistication in geometry, and Euclid had systematised their results in an axiomatic theory. Starting from a small number of axioms, truths of geometry were deduced with the help of definitions.[1] The development of arithmetic was somewhat different (Frege means to include here elementary algebra as well). Results were known, but no axiomatic basis for them was discovered. The mathematicians of India, who discovered many of these results, did not, it seems, have the concept of an axiom system, and from the Renaissance to the beginning of the nineteenth century very sophisticated developments in arithmetic and algebra were undertaken without there being any attempt to provide a system of axioms for the theory. In fact, a set of axioms was developed during the time of Frege's work by Dedekind and Peano. 'The discovery of higher analysis' refers to the invention of the calculus by Leibniz and Newton in the seventeenth century. The calculus brought with it powerful new methods for the analysis of motion and other kinds of change, but there were grave problems about justifying the techniques to which it appealed (Frege's 'almost insuperable difficulties'). These difficulties had to do particularly with the idea of the infinite in mathematics.

The most obvious problem was that the theory seemed to require the existence of quantities which are smaller than any finite number, yet different from zero (the 'infinitesimals'). It was thought, understandably, that this idea involved a contradiction.[2] Another problem was that certain arithmetical operations, such as addition, could be extended to cover cases where the operation is repeated an infinite number of times to produce a numerical result. Sometimes this seemed to work, but in other cases it was known to lead to absurdity. The 'moral conviction, supported by a mass of successful applications' to which Frege refers is the habit which developed during the eighteenth century of applying these sorts of method without any firm theoretical basis for doing so, and of justifying them pragmatically by their success in particular cases. The work of Cauchy, Weierstrass and others during the first three-quarters of the nineteenth century was in some ways an attempt to reverse these tendencies, and to reintroduce rigour into mathematics. Cauchy's work is perhaps less significant in this respect than has sometimes been suggested; the infinitesimals make appearances in his work, often in an apparently essential way, though he did improve our understanding of the crucial notion of convergence.[3] It was Weierstrass, Dedekind and Cantor who eliminated the infinitesimals, and showed that the number system could be based on concepts from within arithmetic — together, that is, with the notion of set, which was not very well understood at that time.[4]

Another problem with which the movement towards rigour attempted to deal was that of the relation between proofs and theorems. The idea of proof within mathematics seems to be so essential to the enterprise that it is difficult to realise the lack of clarity which surrounded its application at this time. What is to count as an acceptable proof in mathematics? What methods of proof are to be allowed? How can one decide whether a proof establishes the precise result it is intended to establish rather than some subtly different result? These were questions which nineteenth-century mathematicians were in no good position to answer. It was not uncommon for a mathematical result to be 'proved', yet for it to be known that the result is, strictly speaking, false. This was often expressed in terms of the result 'suffering exceptions', or being stated in a 'false generality'. But what, then, was the true generality of the theorem? Exactly under what conditions did it hold? In many cases no precise answer to these questions was forthcoming.[5] Frege seems to have been aware of the problem of the relation between proof and theorem. In the passage just quoted he mentions the increased tendency towards 'precise delimitation of extent of validity', and a little further on he says:

> It not uncommonly happens that we first discover the content of a proposition, and only later give the rigorous proof of it, on other and more difficult lines; *and often this same proof also reveals more precisely the conditions restricting the validity of the original proposition* ([1884*b*], p. 3, my italics).

This point is of some importance to us, since it was Frege who discovered a method for determining whether a proof is valid. Indeed, one of his most remarkable achievements was to have formulated the problem in a precise way. How can we lay down a set of rules for inferring one statement from another, and formulate proofs in such a way that we can definitely decide whether the rules have been properly applied or not? The validity of a proof must not depend in any way upon features of the subject matter about which there can be any dubious element. We do not want the validity of the proof to depend, for example, upon the meanings of the terms which describe the subject matter under discussion, for their meanings will not always be so clear as to afford us grounds for making a definite decision about validity. Errors were known to arise when results were inferred which rely upon the intuitive meaning of such terms as 'function' and 'continuity'. Nor do we want proof to be such that it depends upon features which are hard or impossible to specify precisely; say, for instance, the intuitive acceptability of the steps of the proof. This had been important in geometry where it was traditional to appeal to a drawn figure to render the proof obvious. In analysis, this appeal to visual intuition proved to be disastrously misleading, for it turned out that certain functions could have properties quite contrary to those which would be expected from an inspection of their corresponding graphs.[6] Frege realised this, and sought to avoid the difficulty by formulating the steps of a proof symbolically in such a way that the validity of the proof could be checked by an inspection of its purely structural features. In simple terms, whether or not a proof is valid depends only upon the shapes and juxtaposition of the signs it contains.[7] The problem was to devise a uniform symbolism for mathematics, and to provide a way of connecting symbolic expressions which would indicate precisely the nature of the logical relations between them. It was in the *Begriffsschrift*[8] (1879) that Frege presented the first version of his solutions to these problems, and at the beginning of that work he outlined clearly the conditions which a satisfactory solution must meet.

> So that something intuitive could not squeeze in unnoticed here, it was most important to keep the chain of reasoning free of gaps. As I endeavoured to fulfil this requirement most rigorously, I found an obstacle in the inadequacy of the language; despite all the unwieldiness of the expressions, the more complex the relations became, the less precision — which my purpose required — could be obtained. From this deficiency arose the idea of the 'conceptual notation' presented here. Thus, its chief purpose should be to test in the most reliable manner the validity of a chain of reasoning and expose each presupposition which tends to creep in unnoticed, so that its source can be investigated. For this reason, I have omitted the expression of everything which is without importance for the chain of inference ([1879*a*], p. x (104)).

There is, as we can see, a general sense in which Frege's work is connected with the trend in nineteenth-century mathematics towards improved standards of rigour. There are, however, very important differences between Frege's approach to the problem and the approach of working mathematicians. The difference might be described as the difference between a static and a dynamic viewpoint. Frege's attitude towards mathematics was static in this sense: he was concerned with mathematics as a given body of knowledge, the form of which he hoped to perfect by imposing on it the structure of a rigorous axiomatic theory. He was not concerned with mathematics as a living and growing enterprise, as were mathematicians like Cauchy, Weierstrass, Dedekind and Cantor. Their concern with 'foundational' problems arose out of their concern with intrinsically mathematical problems about, for instance, Fourier series, convergence and divergence, the existence of derivatives and integrals. Their commitment to the idea of rigour was a relative one. They wanted mathematics to be more rigorous in areas where mathematical progress was being hindered by lack of clarity concerning, say, the domain of applicability of a result, or the conditions for the existence of a limit. Where mathematical practice seemed not to be affected by a looseness of expression, say in the definition of what a number is, then they were less inclined to be scrupulous.

As we have seen, Frege's attitude was very different. For him rigour was an all or nothing affair, with no room for compromise.[9] Thus he was inclined to be very critical, especially in his later writings, of the mathematicians who were contributing to the improvement of mathematical rigour. Here I think we see one possible reason why his work was so much ignored. Frege's static approach was of little interest to the working mathematician, who is concerned first of all with the discovery, via informal methods, of new results. As long as it seemed as if new results were not to be expected from Frege's programme, it was bound to be of little interest to them.[10] Of course this situation eventually changed, but it did so because it became evident that foundational studies in mathematics opened up rich new areas of informal research in the subject which we now call 'metamathematics'; the mathematical study of mathematical systems.

Thus, although Frege was trained as a mathematician, his interest in mathematics was a philosophical one. He wanted to substantiate the thesis that mathematics represents certain knowledge, and his attempt to make precise the notion of mathematical proof was a part of this project. Yet rigour in itself was not enough for him. Even the most rigorous proofs can proceed from premises which are false. The other aspect of the problem was to show that arithmetic could be deduced from premises which are absolutely indubitable; from premises, indeed, which are statements of pure logic. The achievement of rigorous standards of proof was something which he realised was a necessary prerequisite for this, for if mathematical proof is imperfectly rigorous, the possibility will always exist that a given proof requires premises other than those actually stated, and that the 'hidden assumptions' might be open to dispute. As long as this possibility existed, one would never be able to say for certain that all the premises necessary for the proof had been clearly stated, so the thesis that those premises were nothing but unquestionable truths of logic would remain doubtful (see Frege [1893], p.vi. (2–3)).

When did Frege's project for the founding of mathematics on logic first become clear to him? It was, on his own account, the earliest motive for his work.

> I became aware of the need for a *Begriffsschrift* when I was looking for the fundamental principles or axioms upon which the whole of mathematics rests. Only after this question is answered can it be hoped to trace successfully the springs of knowledge upon which this science thrives ([1896*a*], p.221 (1)).

Already in the *Begriffsschrift* he distinguished between truths which follow from principles of pure logic and those which depend upon matters of fact, and he says:

> The firmest method of proof is obviously the purely logical one, which, disregarding the particular characteristics of things, is based solely upon the laws on which all knowledge rests. Accordingly, we divide all truths which require a proof into two kinds: the proof of the first kind can proceed purely logically, while that of the second kind must be supported by empirical facts ([1879*a*], p. ix (103)).

It is immediately after this remark that he introduces the idea of a rigorous method of proof. Clearly then, Frege's aim of constructing a method of precise mathematical proof was part of his wider aim of showing that mathematics 'is based solely upon the laws on which all knowledge rests' i.e. the laws of logic.

Thus for Frege 'rigour', 'clarity' and 'sharp delimitation of concepts' were things to be insisted upon, but not for their own sake. Rather they were important in so far as they contributed towards the security of mathematical knowledge. Yet some commentators have written as if these things were Frege's ultimate goal. It has been claimed, for instance, that Frege's purpose was 'to devise an adequate and perspicuous symbolism to express mathematical propositions and deductions . . . It was the effort of devising it that obliged Frege to formulate his revolutionary views about the philosophy of logic'.[11] So on this view Frege's epistemological theses about the logical basis of mathematics emerged as a by-product of his quest for a precise language for the expression of mathematical concepts.

Another writer says that 'The analysis of the concept number is indeed the ultimate goal of Frege's scientific programme' (Angelelli [1967], p.231). This view, according to which Frege's main aim was the clarification of the language and concepts of mathematics, is one of the assumptions underlying the theory that his philosophical programme lies within the philosophy of language. If Frege's early logico-mathematical work is seen as an attempt to make the language of mathematics perspicuous, then it will seem quite reasonable to interpret his later investigations into language as simply the natural development of this conceptual-linguistic programme. The programme starts with an investigation of mathematics, gradually broadening out, via the introduction of the distinction between sense and reference and the later discussion of names and demonstratives, to include the language of ordinary discourse.

Yet I believe that Frege was not fundamentally concerned with the problems of clarity and precision in mathematics. I have already suggested how his project for a logical language and precise specification of mathematical proof emerged from a deeper and more profound concern with the status of mathematical knowledge. Clarification and rigour were, for Frege, important only in so far as they served this more fundamental goal. His interest was not with mathematics for its own sake, but with mathematics as exemplifying an epistemological ideal — a deductive science in which the basic principles and the logical relations between truths are indisputable. He put it thus:

> If you ask what constitutes the value of mathematical knowledge, the answer must be: less in what is known than how it is known, less in the subject matter than in the degree of its intellectual illumination and the insights it affords into logical interrelations ([1898-9], p.171 (157)).

(b) Psychologism

(i) Introduction

The central theme of Frege's philosophy is his objectivism; his insistence that concepts like truth, validity and even knowledge must be characterised in ways which show them to be independent of the means which we have for recognising them. Frege's great philosophical enemy was *psychologism* — the view according to which we are to give a subjective, mental explanation of the nature of these concepts. In the 1830s systematic philosophy of the kind associated with the idealism of Fichte, Schelling and Hegel was criticised from a number of standpoints, and a more 'scientific' spirit began to prevail. One of its manifestations was an intense interest in psychological accounts of philosophical problems, beginning with the work of Fries and Beneke. Fries set about constructing an 'anthropological' critique of reason — a determination of the structure of the mind by methods which were empirical and fallible — while Beneke sought psychological explanations for our ethical and aesthetic judgements. This and related 'naturalistic' movements gained impetus through the middle of the century.

Kolakowski has described these developments as follows:

> In giving up the tradition of German idealism, philosophy gave up its independence from the sciences. It started regarding itself either as a synthesis of the sciences or as a psychological analysis. Even new variants of Kantianism shifted to the psychological standpoint and explained the Kantian *a priori*, not as a set of transcendental conditions for knowledge (valid for any rational being), but as specific qualities of the human psyche, and this led fatefully to generic relativism ([1975], p.6).

Psychologism had its origins in earlier forms of philosophical thought. Locke's 'new way of ideas' was an attempt to give epistemology a naturalistic basis by making it a study of the sources of our knowledge (conceived of as ideas in individual minds) and the mechanism by which that knowledge is acquired. In this way the study of knowledge becomes the study of an essentially natural phenomenon. Also important were the criticisms, due to Locke and Descartes,[12] of Aristotelian logic from a subjectivist point of view. In general Locke, Descartes and other seventeenth-century philosophers saw themselves as associated with a new movement of scientific enlightenment opposed to the Scholastic tradition of reliance upon the authority of Aristotle. Since logic was so much a preoccupation of Scholastic philosophy, the new thinkers were very much inclined to criticise it, which they did on the grounds that the syllogism is incapable of giving us new knowledge. The conclusion of a syllogism only makes explicit what is already implicit in the premises. As Locke puts it:

> [the syllogism] fails our reason in that part, which, if not its highest perfection, is yet certainly its hardest task, and that which we most need its help in; and that is *the finding out of proofs, and making new discoveries*. The rules of syllogism serve not to furnish the mind with those intermediate ideas that may show the connexion of remote ones. This way of reasoning discovers no new proofs, but is the art of marshalling and ranging the old ones we have already ([1700], IV, xvii, 6, vol. 2, p.272. See also Descartes [1628], pp.32-3, [1637], p.91 and [1644], p.211).

Both Descartes and Locke wanted to absorb the activities of logicians into the programme for finding a method of discovery, a method by which reason and observation could be used to make discoveries and to formulate general laws. They both claimed that man has a faculty by which he can make discoveries, a faculty which can work without the help of explicit rules for syllogistic reasoning. Deduction, for Descartes, becomes a relation between ideas; it takes place when the mind passes from one clear and distinct idea to another, a process which leads always from truths to truths.

> ... deduction, or the pure illation of one thing from another, ... cannot be erroneous when performed by an understanding that is in the least degree rational. And it seems to me that the operation is profited but little by those constraining bonds by means of which the Dialecticians claim to control human reason ([1628], II, vol.1, pp.4–5).

Thus Descartes is willing to use the term 'deduction' in contexts where it seems strange to do so: he talks, for example, about 'deducing' laws from factual data — what we would now describe as an inductive inference. But for Descartes the point was that the inference is one which is validated by intuition rather than by formal rules of inference. Thus the 'formal' distinction between induction and deduction begins to lose its significance.

Views such as these gave rise to a practice of treating logic naturalistically, as the science of certain mental processes, rather than as the *normative* discipline of distinguishing (objectively) valid inferences from invalid ones. Clearly part of what made such an interpretation possible was the poverty of syllogistic inference; its inability to pronounce on the validity of inferences of a complex kind. Defences of the objective interpretation of logic were unlikely to succeed as long as the logic which was being defended was as weak as syllogistic logic. It was Frege who not only provided crushing criticism of subjectivism in logic, but who created a logic of the traditional, objective variety — a logic of objective propositions — of infinitely greater power than the Aristotelian logic.[13]

Psychologism in the nineteenth century was not only influential in Germany. Apart from Frege's own work, the most important logical investigations during the nineteenth century were those of Boole, the English mathematician. Frege was not influenced in his own work by Boole, except in so far as he made strenuous but unsuccessful attempts to persuade others that Boole's system was much inferior to his own.[14] Boole's ideas on the philosophy of logic exemplify some aspects of psychologism.

Boole held to the view that the laws of logic are the 'laws of thought'. In his *The Laws of Thought* he said:

The design of the following treatise is to investigate the fundamental laws of those operations of the mind by which reasoning is performed; to give expression to them in the symbolic language of a Calculus, and upon this foundation to establish the science of logic and construct its method (Boole [1854], p.1).

Accordingly, logic must be an empirical science in the sense that we must discover its laws by observation.

Like all other sciences, that of the intellectual operations must primarily rest on observation — the subject of such observation being the very operations and processes of which we desire to determine the laws (*ibid*, p. 3).

But this view created certain difficulties for Boole which he could not ignore. It was difficult for him to give a psychological interpretation to certain parts of his theory. For example, he employed the mathematical notion of division in some of his calculations, but he could not find any interpretation for this in 'ordinary reasoning'.[15]

Psychologism was, for Boole, a way of avoiding the possibility that there could be alternative systems of logic, with the relativism which this seems to entail. For how could we choose rationally between competing logics? His results, he says

are not to be ranked as merely probable or merely analogical conclusions, but are entitled to be regarded as truths of science. The Nature of the evidence upon which they rest, though in kind distinct, is not inferior in value to any which can be adduced in support of the general truths of physical science (*ibid*, pp.401-402).

And because of this logic has a certain objectivity;

It is to be remembered that it is the business of science not to create laws, but to discover them. We do not originate the constitution of our own minds ... And as the laws of the human intellect do not depend upon our will, so the forms of the science, of which they constitute the basis, are in all essential regards independent of individual choice (*ibid*, p.11).

For Boole, then, the objectivity of logic (that the laws of logic are the same for all of us) is due to the fact that logic is a descriptive science rather than a set of conventions, and therefore enjoys the certainty of scientific laws. In chapter 6 we shall see how Frege realised that to accord this sort of status to logic is merely to play into the hands of those who want to criticise logic from a sceptical or relativistic position.[16]

In the later part of the century more traditional philosophical forms reasserted themselves. The most prominent was the Kantian revival, based on a clear-cut separation between facts and norms. Thus Rickert and Windelband argued for the independence of values from the facts of psychological experience, while Cohen and Natorp of the Marburg school argued that the validity of science depended on methodological rather than psychological considerations. Brentano and Husserl both started off by advocating the naturalistic point of view. According to their early work, descriptive psychology is the basis of all science. Brentano argued that philosophy could break out of a cycle of stages leading always from initial progress to eventual degeneration only by adopting for itself the methods of natural science, and becoming absorbed into scientific psychology. Only in this way could the basis of ethics, aesthetics and logic be discovered. But Brentano, like Husserl somewhat later, came to regard this position as mistaken. Questions about the good, the beautiful, and the valid cannot be answered by appeal to contingent facts about our psychological dispositions. In rejecting psychologism Brentano and Husserl opted for a position which might be described as *transcendental* subjectivity. Logical truth must be derived from an investigation of the mind, but not an investigation of *contingent* features of the mind which might be otherwise, but from a transcendental enquiry into how the mind *must* be. The laws of logic are not laws valid only for beings who have the sort of mental make up that we have, but are valid for all consciousness, for they are derived from an examination of the necessary conditions for consciousness.

Notes

1 For further comments on Euclid, see below, chapter 4, section (a) (vi).
2 It has been shown in recent years that a consistent theory of the infinitesimals *is* possible, using methods unavailable to mathematicians in earlier times. (See Robinson [1966].)
3 See Robinson [1967] and Lakatos [1978].
4 See Kline [1972], chapters 40 and 41.
5 See Lakatos [1976] for an interesting discussion of this problem.
6 See Kneebone [1963], p.141ff for an explanation.
7 It is in this sense that Frege described his own logic as 'formal', in a sense distinct from the 'formal' theories of arithmetic to which he was opposed. See Frege [1885*c*], p.103 (141); and below, chapter 6, section (a)(iv).
8 Meaning 'ideography'. In what follows I shall refer to this work by its German title.
9 He would have profoundly disagreed with the dictum of the mathematician E. H. Moore: 'Sufficient unto the day is the rigour thereof' (Moore [1902], p.411).

10 This, of course, is not a reason why his work should not have been of interest to working *logicians*.

11 Geach [1961], p.131. See also Sternfeld [1966], p.40: 'Frege's thought started with his interest in clarifying mathematical symbolism.'

12 It is usual to oppose the *a prioristic* rationalism of Descartes to the empiricism of Bacon and his English successors. But from certain points of view, particularly with respect to the problem of subjectivism, Descartes and Locke have a good deal in common. See Passmore [1953]. I am indebted to Alan Musgrave for discussion of the points in this section.

13 This seems to me one reason why Bolzano's criticism of subjectivism in logic failed. Although Bolzano gave very general definitions of validity and logical truth (see his [1837], section 148), he never provided any way of analysing sentences and arguments which would enable those definitions to be applied. Appreciation of the importance of a logic of valid inference increased only when the methods available to logicians became more sophisticated. (Of course there seems to be more to the quite universal ignorance of Bolzano's logical and mathematical work during the nineteenth century than can be accounted for by this sort of explanation alone.)

14 See below, chapter 3, section (a)(i)

15 Boole's system was improved upon later by Jevons, who eliminated division. See Jevons [1874]. For Boole's psychologism, see Musgrave [1972].

16 See below, chapter 6, section (a)(ii).

2 *The Programme of the 'Begriffsschrift'*

FREGE'S FIRST aim was, as I have said, to show that the truths of arithmetic follow according to logical principles from purely logical axioms. He could not do this without first creating a good deal of auxiliary machinery, for ordinary language was not adequate to the task of representing proofs, even when supplemented by the usual symbols of mathematical notation. Mathematicians usually rely on ordinary language to make the logical connections between their formulae clear. They will use expressions like 'thus', 'therefore', 'but' etc; expressions which are sometimes used in contexts where no genuine logical relations exist. Indeed, Frege reports that his first efforts were undertaken using ordinary language, but that because of the 'inadequacy of language' he had to develop his own 'formula language of pure thought' as a substitute. In his first book, the *Begriffsschrift*, he presents us with a version of that language, together with a system of axioms and rules of inference and some results pertaining, somewhat indirectly, to arithmetic.

In this chapter we shall examine Frege's formal language; how sentences are constructed in it; and how proofs are carried out. We shall also look at some of the philosophical ideas of the *Begriffsschrift*, and try to clarify what Frege was aiming at in the mathematical part of the work.

(a) Frege's Logical Language

(i) Judgements and concepts

An important principle underlies the construction of Frege's logical language. Frege expressed this principle in different ways at different times. In the *Foundations* it appears as 'Only in the context of a sentence does a word have significance', while in his later work he says often that 'Thinking is the grasping of a Thought'. Later, we shall examine these ideas in some detail (see below, chapter 6, section (b)). During the early period which is our present concern Frege was inclined to formulate the principle by saying that

judgements are prior to concepts,[1] or that concepts are obtained by splitting a judgement into parts.

... instead of putting a judgement together out of an individual as subject [footnote omitted] and an already previously formed concept as predicate, we do the opposite and arrive at a concept by splitting up the content of possible judgement [footnote omitted] ([1880-1], p. 18 (17)).

The logic of the syllogism can be described as a logic which embodies the opposite view: that judgements are constructed from concepts by putting them together in different ways. Sentences are constructed by taking a concept as subject and adding to it a predicate concept. Thus the sentence 'All men are mortal' was traditionally analysed as having the subject 'All men' and the predicate 'mortal'. Boole was never able to transcend this kind of analysis and this was one of the reasons why his logic was unable to accommodate certain intuitively valid inferences (see Dudman [1976]). In Aristotelian logic one works through a syllogism by extracting the concepts as distinct separable items within the sentences, and rearranging them in ways sanctioned by the syllogistic rules of inference. Frege, on the other hand, discovered a way of developing inferences which depended upon analysing the sentences concerned as having inner *sentential* complexity; their complexity is the result of their being really composed of several sentences. Thus he construes the sentence 'All men are mortal' as a complex proposition, rather than as a simple proposition with inner conceptual complexity. A rough equivalent of his way of writing it would be

(1) If something is a man then it is mortal.

Here we seem to have two sentences,[2] 'something is a man' and 'it is mortal' corresponding to what would previously have been thought of as two concepts; *being man*, and *being mortal*. Our task is to understand the connection between the two sentences. The first thing to notice is that 'something' in the first sentence and 'it' in the second are clearly related. We can see this more clearly by rewriting (1) as 'If something is a man then that thing is mortal'. We need a way of registering the fact that, loosely put, 'something' and 'it' speak of the same entity or entities. We cannot do this by writing the sentence as 'If something is a man then something is mortal', because no connection is established in this way between the two somethings. The connection that we are concerned with is of such a kind that the following holds: we must be able to replace 'something' and 'it' by the same proper name and get a sentence which is a special case of the general sentence (1). Thus, replacing 'something' and 'it' by 'Plato' we get 'If Plato is a man then Plato is mortal', which is true if (1) is true.

(ii) Functions

It is at this point that Frege draws upon mathematical notions to help formulate his ideas. What he does is to argue that sentences can be thought of as constructed in the same way as certain mathematical expressions. Consider the expression '2.3^2+3'. This expression designates a number, the number 21. If we replace '3' by a variable, 'x', we get the expression '$2.x^2+x$', which is the sort of expression which we typically take to stand for a function. In a complex expression like '$2.3^2 + 3$' we can imagine part of the expression replaced by a variable, and the rest held constant. We shall call the constant part the function-name, and the part replaceable by a variable the name of the argument of the function. An argument is something such that, when we apply it to a function, we get a definite value of that function. Thus the value of the function $2.x^2 + x$ for the argument 3 is 2.3^2+3, or 21.

Clearly, the same expression can be split up into function-part and argument-part in different ways. In the expression '2.3^2+3' we could look upon '2' as the replaceable part (the argument-name), in which case our function would be $x.3^x + 3$. Frege says that the division of an expression into function-name and argument-name is not something inherent in the 'content' of the expression, but simply results from the way we chose to regard it (see Frege [1879*a*], section 9). The distinction within an expression of parts corresponding to function and argument is, at least at this stage of Frege's work, a conventional one.

Frege points out that we can view a sentence in the same way. In 'Socrates is mortal' we can regard 'Socrates' as replaceable by a variable, in which case the sentence is construed as having a function-part, 'is mortal', and an argument-part, 'Socrates'. If we replace 'Socrates' with a variable we get an expression for a function, 'x is mortal'. Now in place of the variable 'x' we can substitute any name that we like to get a new sentence, as in 'Plato is mortal' or 'Aristotle is mortal'.

As Frege points out, the analysis of a sentence into function and argument replaces the traditional subject-predicate analysis. And where the latter demands that every sentence have only one subject — a view which involves difficulties which traditional logic was never able to overcome — the function-argument analysis can easily accommodate relational sentences. 'Plato is younger than Socrates' is analysed into a function-part 'is younger than', which takes *two* arguments, in this case 'Plato' and 'Socrates', just as 'x^2+2y' represents a mathematical function of two arguments.

We can now apply these ideas to the sentence (1). Replacing 'something' and 'it' by a variable 'x' we get

(2) If x is a man then x is mortal.

in which we can substitute particular names for the variable in order to get special cases of our general sentence, as in

If Plato is a man then Plato is mortal.

(1) has now been analysed as a sentence containing two expressions, 'x is a man' and 'x is mortal', which are joined together in a certain way. In fact (1) has the form of a conditional sentence, 'If A then B'. We want a way of symbolising the component expressions and the connections between them. The first task is solved by appealing again to mathematical symbolism, in which we represent functions in the form '$f(x)$', '$g(x)$', etc. We shall represent 'x is a man' and 'x is mortal' respectively as '$f(x)$' and '$g(x)$'. The fact that these are connected as components of a conditional sentence will be represented as

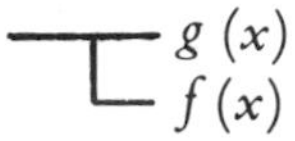

$g(x)$
$f(x)$

In general we shall write a conditional sentence 'If A then B' as

Notice that Frege's symbolism is two-dimensional, and that we read this sentence from the bottom up. This seems strange at first, and was one reason why critics disliked Frege's formal language; but it has definite advantages of perspicuity. It means, for instance, that one can easily distinguish the content of a complex sentence from its logical form. Each sentential part is displayed on a separate line, and the whole is connected together by a number of lines (the full complexity of which is yet to be described) which represent the logical connections.

Our method in this section is one of successive approximation to Frege's actual symbolism. Until now we have used the conventional 'x' is a variable. Frege actually uses italicised letters 'a', 'b' etc, as variables, and from now on I shall do the same. Later we shall introduce a further class of symbols which can replace variables in certain circumstances.

(iii) Generality and scope

If we think about the role of variables in the system, it becomes clear that they actually perform two functions. First they are a way of achieving cross-reference between different parts of a sentence. In formalising the sentence 'If something is a man then it is mortal' we use the same variable for 'something' and for 'it' in order to formalise the idea that these are related pronouns. Secondly, they are a way of conferring generality of a sentence.[3] Thus our sentence (1) could be written

(3) For all a, if a is a man, then a is mortal.

Now there are situations in which it is not possible for the variables alone to indicate generality. These are situations in which considerations of *scope* arise. There is a difference between 'It is not the case that everything has mass', and 'Everything does not have mass'. Both are obtained from the sentence 'Everything has mass' by some operation of negation which we have yet to examine, but they are clearly obtained from it in different ways. The difference is, in fact, the scope of the negation. Let us first introduce a symbol for negation. We symbolise the sentence 'Socrates is mortal' by '$f(\gamma)$' — 'γ' being the symbolic translation of the name 'Socrates'. In the formal language we shall always write a sentence by prefixing to it what is called the 'content stroke' or 'horizontal stroke' thus (see below, chapter 4, section (*d*) (*i*) and [1879*a*]):

$$(4) — f(\gamma).$$

Now for any sentence 'P', we shall call the sentence 'It is not the case that "P" the *negation* of P'. The negation of (4) appears in Frege's symbolism as

$$(5) \top f(\gamma).$$

We call the small vertical stroke the 'negation stroke'. In the case of (4), which is a statement about a single individual, there is only one way to negate the sentence. Ambiguity arises with a general sentence like 'Everything has mass'. In 'It is not the case that everything has mass', we say that the negation has as its scope the whole sentence. In 'Everything does not have mass', we are not negating the whole of the sentence, but rather a part of it. The scope of the negation seems to be 'having mass'. But to attach the negation stroke to the predicate rather than to a whole sentential unit we would have, as it were, to prise the sentence open and insert the negation sign. This would offend against Frege's principle that logical complexity is a matter of sentential complexity; anything that is done to a sentence must be done in such a way that the predicate is not made to stand out on its own apart from its arguments or from the variables which go with it. This means that we are going to rethink the formalisation of (1). What we do is to introduce a new element into the sentence which will take over the function of expressing generality. In place of 'For all *a*, *a* has mass' we shall write

$$-\overset{a}{\smile}-\ f(a)$$

What we have done is to introduce a new symbol (the 'concavity' over which stands a variable) in order to indicate scope. We can now write 'It is not the case that everything has mass' as

$$\top\overset{a}{\smile}-\ f(a)$$

and 'Everything does not have mass' as

$$-\overset{a}{\smile}\top\ f(a)$$

In the first, the negation stroke has large scope, in the second it has small scope.

It then turns out that the symbols for generality themselves can have different scope. To understand this, note first that there is more than one kind of generality. In addition to saying that everything has mass, we can say that something has mass. And this last is clearly not equivalent to the statement that any particular object has mass. One can know that something has mass without knowing that any particular thing has mass. It turns out that we can express this other kind of generality in terms of notions which we have already introduced. If

$$\top\overset{a}{\smile}-\ f(a)$$

says that it is not the case that everything has mass, then

$$(6)\quad \top\overset{a}{\smile}\top\ f(a)$$

says that it is not the case that everything does not have mass, or in other words that something does have mass. In general then a sentence of the form (6) says that there is something which has the property *f*.

Now certain sentences involve what is called 'multiple generality'. It is clear that a sentence like 'Everybody loves somebody' will involve two symbols for generality. Another way to express the same sentence would be as 'For every *a* there is a *b* such that *a* loves *b*'. In Frege's symbols this appears as

$$(7)\quad \overset{a}{\smile}\!\top\!\overset{b}{\smile}\!\top\, L\,(a,\ b)$$

While the sentence 'Somebody is loved by everybody' is written

$$(8)\quad \top\!\overset{b}{\smile}\!\top\!\overset{a}{\smile}\!-\, L\,(a,\ b).$$[4]

Thus the difference between (7) and (8) appears as a difference in the scopes of the symbols for generality; in (7) 'Somebody' lies within the scope of 'Everybody', while in (8) the situation is reversed.

As the medieval logicians were aware, there are relations between sentences such as these which it is important for a logic to capture. (8) implies (7) but not conversely. In Frege's system the rules of inference allow the derivation of (7) from (8) but block the invalid derivation of (8) from (7).

There is a further notational change. Until now we have been using italicised letters for variables whether or not they occur with a symbol for generality. Frege uses different letters to mark these different situations. If a variable is not associated with a symbol of generality, then an italicised letter is used and it is understood that the sentence is equivalent to one where that letter is bound by a symbol of generality prefixed to the sentence as a whole.[5]

If a variable is associated with a symbol for generality then the italic letter is replaced by a letter from the Gothic alphabet, and the same Gothic letter stands over the concavity, as in

$$-\overset{\mathfrak{a}}{\smile}-f\,(\mathfrak{a})$$

(iv) Generality and suppositio

We should notice here a difference between Frege's theory and the medieval theory of *suppositio*. In the earlier theory a term like 'men' was supposed to stand for individual men, such as Socrates and Plato, but to stand for them in different ways determined by the different structures of the sentences in which it occurs. General terms like 'men' and 'mortal' were taken to stand for members of classes; 'men' for the class of men and 'mortal' for the class of things which are mortal. The problem was then to account for the differences between statements like 'All men are mortal' and 'some men are mortal'. Here the 'all' and the 'some' were thought to have their different effects, not by modifying what the terms 'men' and 'mortal' stood for, but by modifying the *manner* in which they stood for them. This way of standing for something was the *suppositio* of a term.[6] A weakness of this theory was that there are, in reality, unlimited ways in which the supposition of a term might vary according to the complexity of the sentence, so the theory was bound to be always an *ad hoc* and incomplete one. But Frege's account gives a perfectly uniform reading to terms like 'men'. It does not stand for individual men in any way at all. Rather, it stands for the concept *man*. A sentence like 'All men are mortal' could be read 'Everything which falls under the concept *man* falls under the concept *mortal*'. The task of accounting for the complexity of a sentence is taken away from the terms which stand for concepts and placed upon variables and quantifiers.

Another weakness of the theory of *suppositio* was this. It makes a general statement such as 'All men are mortal' equivalent to a conjunction of particular statements about the particular men that there are. It says that Socrates is mortal, and that Plato is mortal and that . . . , and so on. But one can understand that general sentence perfectly well without knowing anything about the particular men that there are. One may not be in a position to identify any actual men, and one is never likely to be in a position to identify them all. Indeed, on Frege's analysis, 'All men are mortal' is not *about* particular men at all; it simply says that the following condition holds for every object — if that thing is a man then it is mortal. In saying *this* one is not saying anything about the chief of an African tribe of whom one has never heard, as Frege put it ([1894], p. 188 (332) and [1895*a*], p. 209 (105)).

(v) The logic of sentences

We now have an adequate notation for generality, together with a notation for negation ('not . . .') and conditionality ('If . . . then . . .'). With these devices, together with variables, names, letters for functions and for sentences, we can cope equally well with categorical statements like 'All men are mortal', and with hypothetical statements which are compounds of other statements.[7] Like the Stoics, who were the first to investigate systematically the logic of hypothetical sentences, Frege interpreted the conditional 'If *A* then *B*' so as to be true except in the case where '*A*' is true and '*B*' is false. He then shows how, using conditionality and negation, we can define those other connections between sentences (we now call them 'sentential connectives') which depend for their truth value only on the truth values of their components. Since '*A* or *B*' is true when either '*A*' is true or '*B*' is true, it is equivalent to 'If not *A* then *B*'. We can therefore write '*A* or *B*' as

'*A* and *B*' is equivalent to (i.e. true under exactly the same circumstances as) 'Not-(If *A* then not-*B*)',[8] so we can render a conjunction as:

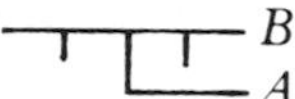

In this way we can build up very complex sentences. 'If *A* and *B* then *C* and *D*' is equivalent to 'If *A* then, if *B*, then *C* and *D*', and so can be written as:

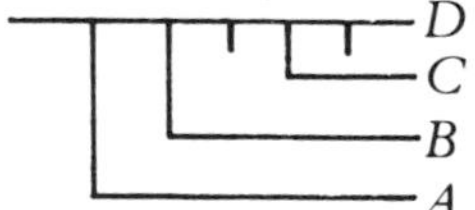

'If not-*A* then (*B* or *C*)' appears as:

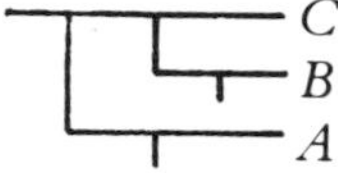

As with the symbols for generality and negation, we can distinguish between conditional connectives with different scope. There is a difference between 'If *A* then (if *B* then *C*)' and '(If *A* then *B*) then *C*'. The latter appears as

Thus Frege's logic has the effect of uniting the traditionally distinct categorical and hypothetical logics into one system by showing how categorical statements can be analysed as hypotheticals governed by variable binding operators. In this way the

hypothetical (or 'secondary' as they were called) propositions appear as logically prior to categorical (or 'primary') ones. Frege saw this, and remarked that his own logic 'avoids the division in Boolean logic into two parts (primary and secondary propositions) by construing judgements as prior to concept formation'.

(b) The Idea of an Axiomatic Theory

(i) An epistemological ideal

Having devised the tools necessary for the presentation of his results, Frege gives us the logical theory which will form the background of his mathematical investigations. Frege was very much influenced by certain epistemological ideas which derive partly from the example of Euclid's geometry. On this view a theory must, if it is to constitute genuine knowledge, be capable of representation by a set of axioms — propositions which do not require any justification themselves because their truth is self-evident. All the other statements of the theory are then justified by being shown to be logical consequences of the axioms. Time and again Frege makes it clear that he thinks that true knowledge must conform to this pattern; that logical deductions are to be carried out only from premises recognised to be true, and that something cannot properly count as an axiom unless it has this property of self-evidence (e.g. [1914], p.221 (205)). For him, the whole point of logic as a means of deduction is its role in justifying the statements of a theory. In other words he saw logic as serving an essentially epistemological purpose; that of making statements certain by showing them to follow from statements whose certainty is already clear. In an early passage he says this about the nature and function of logic:

> Now the grounds which justify the recognition of a truth often reside in other truths which have already been recognised. But if there are any truths recognised by us at all, this cannot be the only form that justification takes. There must be judgements whose justification rests on something else, if they stand in need of justification at all.
>
> And here lies the task of epistemology. Logic is concerned only with those grounds of judgements which are truths. To make a judgement because we are cognisant of other truths as providing a justification for it is known as *inferring*. There are laws governing this kind of justification, and to set up these laws of valid inference is the goal of logic ([1879-91], p.3 (3))

There are several things of interest in this passage, and I shall say more about it later (see below, chapter 4, section (d) (iii)), but for the moment let us note that it clearly illustrates the fact that Frege's interest in logic is part of his general programme for opposing the sceptical doubt which had traditionally plagued the claims of philosophers to genuine knowledge. The sceptic's claim to doubt any given proposition is to be answered by the discovery of propositions which are beyond the possibility of serious doubt. But these propositions, apart from being beyond question, must be such as to provide a derivative justification for all the other propositions of the theory in question. And for this we need a clearly specified machinery of logical deduction which can itself be provided with a non-question-begging justification.

(ii) Rules of inference

Frege saw the need for such a machinery as perhaps no philosopher or logician before him had done, and in addition to providing a set of logical axioms for his theory, he tried to make explicit the rules for inferring one statement from another. These are the 'laws of valid inference' described in the quotation above. In his presentation of geometry, Euclid had discussed in detail the axioms for this theory, but he seems not to have realised the necessity for introducing rules of inference. This may be partly due to the fact that certain steps in his proofs make essential appeal to the visual properties of a drawn figure. Proofs in Euclid's geometry do not proceed exclusively in terms of one *statement* following from another. Thus it would not have been possible for him to have specified rules of inference in the way that we now regard as essential. The subsequent history of Euclidean axiomatics shows a similar tendency to concentrate attention on the truth of the axioms and to leave the underlying logic of inference unexamined. There were, for instance, many attempts to justify Euclid's so-called parallel postulate, an axiom which seemed more doubtful than the rest, and it was on this question that most of the controversy about Euclid's system centred, until Frege's own work highlighted the necessity for a separate specification of rules of inference.[9]

Another difficulty which stood in the way of a clear explication of the notion of a rule of inference is the difficulty of understanding how they differ from axioms. There is a tendency, in fact, to assimilate inference rules to the axioms; to suppose that they can be treated as statements which appear within the logical system itself. There is, indeed, a close relationship within a system of logic between truths of the system itself and the rules of inference which sanction the steps from axioms to theorems. Thus Frege's system has a rule of inference which says that, given premises of the form '*P*' and 'If *P* then *Q*' we may write a conclusion of the form '*Q*'. And this rule corresponds to the logical truth.

'If *P* and, if *P* then *Q*, then *Q*'.[10]

Because of this it is tempting to suppose that there is no need for a specification of rules of inference separate from a specification of the logical truths. And this is exactly the situation in the logical system of Peano, and that of Russell and Whitehead's *Principia Mathematica*, written some time after Frege's work.[11] But this is a mistake, as Frege realised. Although a logical truth may correspond to a rule of inference in the sense described above, it cannot fulfill the function of such a rule. For a rule of inference is not itself something which is true or false; it is a directive which allows us to write down a certain formula in a proof if we have already established certain other formulas; its status is quite different from that of any statement which appears within the system itself.

As has often been noted, Frege, although clear in principle about the nature of the necessity for rules of inference, is still not quite clear about exactly which rules of inference are required by the deductions in his own system. In the *Begriffsschrift* he claims at one point to have reduced all inference to one mode — that sanctioned by the rule which I described in the example above. But he does require several others, and in fact explicitly states one other rule. In the more highly developed system of *The Basic Laws of Arithmetic*, written fifteen years later, he attempted a much more careful analysis of the rules he uses.[12]

Using the rules of inference, proofs can now be carried out in the formal language of the *Begriffsschrift*. The rules of inference allow a certain formula to be written down, given that certain other formulas have been written down. Proofs are, as we would now say, purely *syntactic* items. They are simply sequences of written sentences. What determines whether we may proceed from one sentence to another is the form of the sentence rather than its content. Thus, for example, if we have two sentences of the form[13]

and

$\vdash A$

then a rule of inference allows us to write as a conclusion a sentence of the form

$$\vdash B$$

Proofs would become impossibly long if they always had to be written out in full. Frege therefore introduces a number of devices which abbreviate the procedure but which give us sufficient information so that we could write out the proof in full if we needed to ([1879*a*], section 6).

(iii) The axioms

Frege offers nine axioms as the basis for the deductions which are carried out in the *Begriffsschrift*. The axioms are written in the system as follows ([1879*a*], sections 14 and 16–22);

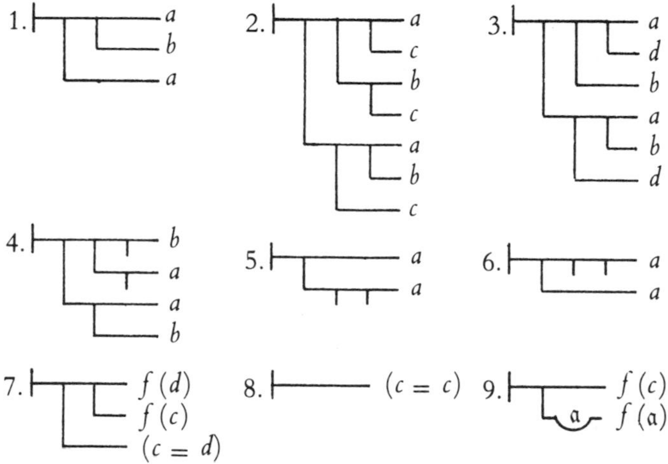

It is clear from Frege's exposition that he intends the letters '*a*', '*b*', '*c*' and '*d*' as variables for which sentences can be substituted. Thus, for instance, Axiom 1 is what we should call an axiom 'schema', since an infinite number of axioms can be obtained from it by substituting propositional letters for the variables. Axioms 7 and 8 assert familiar properties of identity; if *c* is identical with *d*, then anything which holds of *c* holds of *d*, and everything is identical with itself. Axiom 9 says that if *f* holds of everything, then it holds of any given thing, *c*.

With hindsight we can see Frege's presentation of this axiomatic system as a landmark in the history of logic, because the system has a mathematical property which we now consider of the greatest importance. It is *complete* in the sense that, with respect to a certain class of statements called 'first order statements', every logical truth can be proved using the axioms and rules of inference. First order statements are those in which variables bound by symbols for generality may be replaced by names of individuals, but not by predicate letters like '*f*' and '*g*'.

The logical significance of the class of first order statements was not realised until the work of certain logicians in the early part of the twentieth century drew attention to it. For Frege, the differences in kind between what we now think of as first and 'higher order' sentences (i.e. sentences in which generalisation with respect to the predicate occurs) were not such as to make them belong to distinct logical theories. Although Frege makes explicit reference to the possibility of applying a symbol for generality to a function name, he does not provide an axiom which would enable him to deduce the results he needs which involve generality with respect to functions. At one stage he appeals to a result which can be stated as follows ([1879*a*], section 27):

> If, for all $\mathfrak{a}$, $f(\mathfrak{a})$ if and only if b, then if b then $f(c)$

This involves generality only with respect to the arguments of the function f. The principle he ought to appeal to here is the corresponding principle stated in terms of generality for functions:

> If, for all functions $\mathfrak{f}$, M holds of $\mathfrak{f}$ if and only if b holds, then, if b, then M holds of the function f.

Where '$\mathfrak{f}$' is a letter replaceable only by names of functions.

In his much later work, the *Basic Laws*, Frege introduced an axiom to govern generality with respect to functions (see below chapter 5, section (a) (ii)).

(*c*) Our Knowledge of Arithmetic

(i) Mathematical induction

That Frege requires the notion of generality with respect to functions becomes clear when we consider the purpose to which he puts his logical system in the final part of the *Begriffsschrift*. The results he presents there have to be seen in the context of his wider aim of showing that arithmetic can be reduced to logic. Now perhaps the central concept within arithmetic is that of *mathematical induction*. This can be explained in the following way. The natural numbers form an infinite series which can be generated in two stages. First we specify an initial member of the series, usually zero; then we specify a procedure which takes us from any given member of the series to the next member, called the 'successor' of the previous member. The procedure is, obviously enough, to add one to the previous member. In this way we obtain one from zero, two from one, and, in general, the $n+1th$ member of the series from the *nth*. Now the fact that the natural numbers can be generated in this way has important implications for the way that we can prove results about the mathematical properties of the numbers themselves. It means, in particular, that the following principle holds of the series of natural numbers: that if any property P holds of zero, and if, given that P holds of the *nth* member of the series, it then holds of the $n+1th$, then P holds of all the natural numbers. This idea, implicit in mathematical proofs as far back as Euclid, provides us with a powerful method for proving arithmetical results.[14] In order to prove that a certain property P is possessed by all the numbers, we have only to prove that (i) it is possessed by 0, and (ii) if it is possessed by n it is possessed by $n+1$. Frege's aim in the concluding part of the *Begriffsschrift* was to show that this principle, called the principle of induction, could be expressed in such a way that it could be seen to be a quite general truth of logic, with no specifically arithmetical content. Before I describe Frege's procedure, let us look more closely at what Frege saw as the philosophical problem associated with this endeavour.

(ii) Arithmetic, geometry and intuition

Philosophers have often claimed that the epistemological basis of arithmetic — the source of arithmetical knowledge — is a certain intuition which we have of the sequence of numbers. According to Kant we obtain this intuition from our intuition of time. Frege agreed with Kant that geometrical knowledge is based on our intuition of space, and he thought that it was absurd to ask for any justification of geometrical knowledge other than an appeal to the intuitive self-evidence of the geometrical axioms. Certainly, he admitted, we can treat geometry purely formally, and deduce consequences from the axioms without appeal to their content. In this way we can explore the non-Euclidean geometries which contain certain axioms different from the axioms of Euclid's geometry. But these non-Euclidean geometries have no basis in our intuition and so cannot count as knowledge. 'non-Euclidean geometry will have to be counted among the pseudo-sciences, to the study of which we still attach some slight importance, but only as historical curiosities'.[15]

This theory of geometry stands in marked contrast to Frege's philosophy of arithmetic, which began to crystalise in 1874, when he announced that

> There is a remarkable difference between geometry and arithmetic in the manner in which they justify their principles. The elements of all geometrical constructions are intuitions, and geometry points to intuition as the source of all its axioms. Since the axioms of arithmetic have no intuitiveness, its principles cannot be derived from intuition ([1874*a*], p. 50).

And in the *Foundations*, in which he outlined his programme for the founding of arithmetic on logical principles, he emphasised the extent to his agreement with Kant.

> In calling the truths of geometry synthetic and *a priori*, [Kant] revealed their true nature ... If Kant was wrong about arithmetic, this does not seriously detract, in my opinion, from the value of his work. His point was that there are such things as synthetic judgements *a priori*; whether they are to be found in geometry alone, or in arithmetic as well, is of less importance ([1884*b*], pp. 101-2).

Here is something significant from the point of view of the history of logicism — the name given later to the programme for deducing mathematics from logic. The logicist thesis is usually seen as a philosophical position directly opposed to the views of Kant about the justification of mathematics.[16] But Frege's logicism was intended as at most a correction to a part of Kant's view rather than as an attempt to overthrow it. Frege, it seems, had no intrinsic objection to the attempt to base mathematics on intuition; he thought that in geometry this is indeed the correct method. But he thought that there simply is no intuition corresponding to the concepts and procedures of arithmetic, and that, accordingly, arithmetic would have to seek its justification elsewhere.

Why did Frege feel that there is no intuition in arithmetic corresponding to that in geometry? Kant, after all, thought that there was, and that it was the pure intuition of time. In the *Foundations* we get some hint of Frege's reasons. He says that

> We shall do well in general not to overestimate the extent to which arithmetic is akin to geometry ... One geometrical point, considered by itself, cannot be distinguished in any way from any other; the same applies to lines and planes. Only when several points, or lines or planes, are included together in a single intuition, do we distinguish them. In geometry, therefore, it is quite intelligible that general

propositions should be derived from intuition; the points or lines or planes which we intuit are not really particular at all, which is what enables them to stand as representatives of the whole of their kind. But with the numbers it is different; each number has its own peculiarities. To what extent a given particular number can represent all the others, and at what point its own special character comes into play, cannot be laid down generally in advance (*ibid*, pp. 19-20).

We shall understand this better if we turn to what Kant said on the subject. According to Kant, mathematical knowledge is the 'knowledge gained by reason from the construction of concepts'. To construct a concept we need an intuition, which must be a particular object. Yet it must, at the same time, represent all other objects which fall under the same concept. Kant goes on:

Thus I construct a triangle by representing the object which corresponds to this concept either by imagination alone, in pure intuition, or in accordance therewith on paper, in empirical intuition . . . The single figure which we draw is empirical, and yet it serves to express the concept without impairing its universality. For in this empirical intuition we consider only the act whereby we construct the concept, and abstract from the many determinations (for instance, the magnitude of the sides and of the angles) which are quite indifferent, as not altering the concept triangle ([1787], p. 741).

This argument may have struck Frege as being inapplicable in the arithmetical case. Frege may have interpreted Kant to be saying that we are able to see a *particular* figure as the representative of an infinite number of geometrical objects; for example, a triangle of a certain kind. The validity of a proof can be guaranteed by inspection of this single object. As Frege remarked, all points in geometrical space are intrinsically alike, and it is this which enables us to say that the lines and planes which we intuit can stand as 'representatives of the whole of their kind'. In this way we can draw conclusions on the basis of reasoning about particular objects, and for this reason our method of proceeding in geometry is intuitive. But the same thing does not hold for arithmetic. Since numbers lack any intrinsic similarity, particular numbers cannot be taken as representative of all (or many) numbers.

Support for this interpretation of Frege's reasoning can be found elsewhere in his work, where he considers the possibility of there being modes of inference which are specifically geometric. Part of the aim of his *Begriffsschrift* was to refute the contention that every step in a mathematical proof needs to be justified by a pure intuition, in so far as this dictum is intended to apply to arithmetic. But in geometry, Frege accepted that inferences have to proceed by extra-logical means. He says:

There is no such thing as a purely arithmetical mode of inference that cannot be reduced to the general inference modes of logic. If such a reduction were not possible for a given mode of inference, the question would immediately arise, what conceptual basis we have for taking it to be correct. In the case of arithmetic, it cannot be spatial intuition, because thereby the discipline would be reduced to geometry ([1885*c*], p. 104 (142-3). See also [1914], pp. 219-20 (203)).

Thus Frege seems to have thought that arithmetic differs from geometry in *two* important ways: first, its axioms are ultimately reducible to logical truths, whereas the axioms of geometry express facts about our intuition of space; secondly, inference in arithmetic proceeds according to purely logical rules, while geometric inference requires an intuition on our part of the properties of a figure.

Perhaps this insistence that geometric inference is distinct from inference conducted according to purely logical laws reflects Frege's conviction that we are able to verify each step of a geometric argument by inspection of a geometric object; something which is not possible in arithmetic.

Frege offers another argument for the non-intuitive nature of arithmetic; that arithmetic is applicable across the widest possible domain in the sense that everything can be counted.

... the ideal as well as the real, concepts as well as objects, temporal as well as spatial entities, events as well as bodies, methods as well as theorems; even numbers can themselves again be counted ([1885*c*], p. 103 (141)).

From which it follows that:

... the basic propositions on which arithmetic is based cannot apply merely to a limited area whose peculiarities they express in the way in which the axioms of geometry express the peculiarities of what is spatial; rather, these basic propositions must extend to everything that can be thought. And surely we are justified in ascribing such extremely general propositions to logic (*ibid*, p. 103 (142). See also letter to Marty, p. 163 (100)).

We must be careful about what this argument really establishes. From the fact that numbers have application to entities which are not themselves susceptible to examination by intuition it does not follow that the numbers themselves are not intuitive objects. Our basic grasp of the numbers might be an intuitive one, even though the further applications of arithmetic take us beyond the intuitively given.

In conclusion we can say that Frege did not find the Kantian philosophy intrinsically repugnant (as did the other important advocate of logicism, Bertrand Russell). Instead he saw it as an admirable programme which could be carried through for geometry, but unfortunately not for arithmetic. On the Kantian view, a geometrical proof, though it relies upon intuition, will still be something objective, in that the intuition which guides us will be for all men the same; it is not a matter of subjective taste. But if arithmetic possesses no such 'universal' intuition, then we are in danger of falling into subjective preference as the criterion of the adequacy of arithmetical proof. So for Frege it was vital that he be able to show that mathematical proof can be carried through by following a small number of universally recognised rules of inference.

We shall now return to our discussion of the mathematical part of the *Begriffsschrift*.

(iii) Hereditary properties

The mathematical part of the *Begriffsschrift* is not easy to follow, and it is not surprising that contemporary reviewers failed to grasp its importance. Frege is there establishing certain results of a purely logical kind which have great generality yet which can also form the basis of mathematical induction. The generality of the results is very important for Frege. They indicate, he claims, the superior power of logical methods over the appeal to intuition (see [1879*a*], section 23, and [1884*b*], section 91). To understand the sort of generality that Frege was aiming for here we must carefully trace out some of the results of this section of the book.

Suppose that we have a relation — say, the relation of parent to child, or the relation of a number to its successor. In the first case let '$f(a, b)$' mean that b is the child of a; in the second that b is the successor of a. We can turn such a relation into a *sequence* in the following way. We need, first, the idea of an hereditary property. Consider the relation of parent to child and the property of being a human being. Ignoring medically difficult cases, the child of a human being is always a human being. In the same way the successor of a number is itself always a number. Being human, and being a number are hereditary properties. More formally, we say that the property F is 'hereditary in the f-sequence' if, whatever x is, if F holds of x and, whatever y is, y is f-related to x, then F holds of y. In Frege's notation, using Gothic letters, this reads

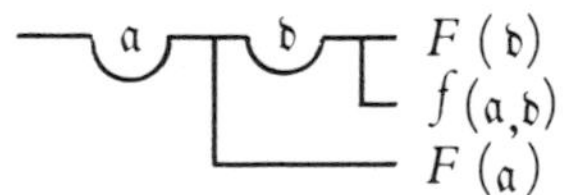

With the aid of this notation we now define the idea of one object following another in the *f*-sequence. Let *F* be any property hereditary in the *f*-sequence, and suppose that for all *x*, if *x* is *f*-related to *a* then *F* holds of *x*. If it follows from these assumptions that *F* holds of *b*, then we say that '*b* follows *a* in the *f*-sequence'; that is, that either *b is f*-related to *a*, or *b* is *f*-related to something which is *f*-related to *a*, or *b* is *f*-related to something that is *f*-related to something that is *f*-related to *a*, or ... Thus if *a* and *b* are numbers and *f* the relation of successor, then *b* follows *a* in the number sequence if *b* is the successor of *a*, or *b* is the successor of something which is the successor of *a*, or ...

Let us now try to grasp the intuitive content of the definition. Suppose that *b* is a number which follows after *a* in the number sequence. Clearly the condition stated in the definition holds, for if *F* is an hereditary property, and if *F* holds of the successor of *a*, then *F* holds of *b*. Conversely, suppose that the condition stated in the definition holds. Does that mean that *b* follows *a* in the number series? Consider the property, *following a in the f-series*, which we shall call *F*. *F* is clearly hereditary and such that it holds of any *x* which is a successor of *a*. But then, since the condition holds, *F* holds of *b*, and so *b* follows *a* in the number series. So we can define the notion of one number following another using the idea of an hereditary property. Some results about sequences and hereditary properties are proved and one of them is what Frege describes as the basis of mathematical induction. It says that if *x* has a property which is hereditary in the *f*-sequence, and if *y* follows *x* in the *f*-sequence, then *y* has the property *F* (theorem 81). To see how mathematical induction is a special case of this, suppose that *f* is the relation of predecessor to successor in the numbers (the relation of the number *n* to the number $n + 1$). The *f*-sequence is thus the sequence of natural numbers. In that case an hereditary property *F* will be such that, if it holds of any member of the series of numbers, then it holds of the successor of that member. Applied to the present case the theorem says that if *x* is a number with an hereditary property *F* and *y* follows after *x* in the sequence of numbers, then *y* will also have *F*. Now the normal way of stating the principle of induction is to say that if *F* holds of zero and if *F* holds of *n* then *F* holds of $n + 1$, then *F* holds of every number. But this can now be proved from theorem 81 in the following way. To say that *F* is such that, if it holds of *n* then it holds of $n + 1$, is just to say that *F* is hereditary in the sequence of natural numbers. Theorem 81 then tells us that if *F* holds of any number, it also holds of any number greater than it (i.e. any number following that number in the series of numbers). But by assumption, *F* holds of zero, so it must hold of every number, since every number is either equal to or greater than zero. Later Frege referred to this method as that by which 'it is possible to reduce the argument from *n* to (*n* + 1) which on the face of it is peculiar to mathematics, to the general laws of logic' ([1884*b*], p. 93).

It is important to realise what we have *not* proved here. In particular, we have not proved, on the basis of logical laws alone, that the natural numbers exist. Our result is a hypothetical one: if there is a sequence of objects constructed from an initial object by applications of the successor operation, *then* mathematical induction will hold of that sequence. Proof of the existence of the natural numbers was not attempted by Frege in this work, though it was what occupied him in his later logical writings. We shall come to this.

Other results follow, including results about a special class of relations — those which are what we call 'many-one' or 'single valued'. From what we have considered so far, the *f*-sequence could be such that an object is *f*-related to more than one object. The relation of parent to child, for example, is such that a parent can have several children. On the other hand the successor operation applied to numbers yields one unique successor for each number.[17] We say that *f* is a many-one relation if, given that *b* is *f*-related to *a* and *c* is *f*-related to *a*, then *b* is identical with *c*. Some general results about *f*-sequences in the case of *f* being many-one follow, though Frege does not try to show that they have any special relevance to arithmetical results.

Notes

1 Notice the Kantian flavour of this formulation. See below, chapter 6, section (e).

2 Strictly speaking it will turn out that neither of these are sentences proper on Frege's analysis. He calls them 'improper-sentences'. See e.g. Frege [1906*e*], p. 207 (190).

3 Frege thought that the expression 'variable' was a misleading one and preferred simply to call the symbols 'italicised letters'. See e.g. Frege [1898–9], p. 173 (159).

4 Strictly speaking (8) would read, for Frege, 'Something is loved by everything'. See below, chapter 4, section (a) (iii).

5 In modern logic we distinguish between free variables and bound variables. A bound variable is one which is associated with a symbol for generality (a 'quantifier'); a free variable is not associated with any such symbol. We do not normally, however, use different kinds of letters to distinguish free from bound variables. In Frege's system there is really no such thing as a free variable, since an italicised letter is assumed to express the same generality as a Gothic letter in conjunction with a symbol for generality having as its scope the whole of the sentence.

6 See the accounts in Boehner [1952], Geach [1962] and Moody [1953].

7 Aristotelian syllogistic logic is a theory of inference for a restricted class of categorical statements; Stoic logic a theory of the ways in which the truth values of simple sentences contribute to the truth values of the complex sentences of which they are parts, and of the patterns of inference between such statements. Boole tried, unsuccessfully, to unite these two programmes into a single logical theory. (See Dudman [1976].)

8 I use brackets to indicate the scope of the negation symbol. In 'Not-(If *A* then not-*B*)' the first 'not' has as its scope the whole sentence 'If *A* then not-*B*', while the second has only the component sentence '*B*' for its scope.

9 For an account of this story see Kline [1972], chapter 36.

10 Rules of inference do not generally correspond to logical truths. Another rule of inference in the *Begriffsschrift* says that from

we can infer

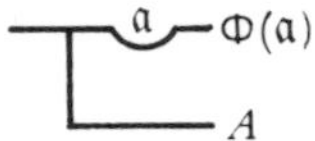

if 'a' does not occur in 'A'. But the corresponding conditional is not a logical truth. (See Frege [1879*a*], section 11.)

11 See Peano [1895], p. 31, and Russell and Whitehead [1910].

12 See below, chapter 5, section (a) (ii).

13 Here I write sentences prefixed by the judgment stroke (the short vertical line). All sentences which appear as independent parts of a deduction in Frege's system require this prefix. For an explanation see below, chapter 4, section (d)(i).

14 See Kline [1972], p. 272. Frege attributes it to Bernoulli, the seventeenth-century Swiss mathematician.

15 Frege [1899-1906], p. 184 (169). See also below, chapter 4, section (a) (vi).

16 See e.g. Russell [1959], pp. 74-5.

17 The successor operation is, in fact, a special case of a many-one relation: it is a one-one relation. It is many-one in so far as a number can have only one immediate successor. It is one-one in that a number can be the successor of at most one number. So while the relation of parent to eldest child is many-one (since a child has two parents) the relation of mother to eldest child is one-one.

3 *The Theory of Number*

IN THIS chapter I shall examine the way in which Frege tried to deduce arithmetic from logic. It would not be practical, however, to follow the details of Frege's deductions as they are carried out in the *Basic Laws of Arithmetic*. That work, the mathematical part of which has not been translated into English, contains the lengthy proofs required to show that the existence of the natural numbers follows from Frege's axioms, together with proofs of some of their most elementary properties. Few readers of Frege will be intending to work through that part of the book; I shall simply indicate the character of the results proved. I have spent correspondingly longer trying to convey the general principles involved in defining the numbers in such a way that their existence could be proved using Frege's methods. The most convenient and instructive way in which this can be done seems to be by following the exposition which Frege gives in the *Foundations* — an exposition which, despite its informality, contains points which require some clarification.

I shall follow Frege in talking about objects, concepts, and the extensions of concepts. These are notions which he explained in detail in later works, and I shall have more to say about them later. For the moment we shall simply proceed at an intuitive level. We can think of an object as a thing of any kind, and a concept as a property of things. Our dog has the property of being black, the number three has the property of being prime. Every concept has an extension, and it turns out later in Frege's work that two concepts have the same extension when the same objects fall under both concepts. It is tempting to regard an extension as a set of things, but Frege was opposed to this conception on the grounds that a set is merely a collection of things, while an extension has an essential unity. We shall avoid, therefore, talking of extensions as sets, as having members, or of one extension being contained in another. The extension of a concept is itself an object. Properties themselves can have properties. The concept *being black* [1] may have the property of being my favourite property. *Being brave* may have the property of being admired by John Smith. *Being an even prime number greater than two* has the property of having no objects falling under it (i.e. there is no even number which is prime and greater than two).

(a) The Foundations of Arithmetic

(i) Introduction

The *Begriffsschrift* was poorly received. As is indicated by the remarks made by reviewers at the time, logicians did not recognise the tremendous advances that it represented. They criticised Frege's symbolism ('a monstrous waste of space' said one),[2] and thought that, in general, it was inferior to the logic of Boole. One reviewer said that, apart from Frege's introduction of a notation for generality, and his treatment of relations, the new logic did not go beyond that of Boole[3] — which is rather like saying that, apart from its solving all the known anomalies of planetary motion and successfully predicting new facts, Einstein's physics is no better than Newton's!

Faced with this rejection, based on misunderstanding, Frege tried to answer some of these criticisms by writing a long paper showing in detail the ways in which his logical system is superior to that of Boole. This, and a similar shorter paper ([1880-1] and [1882*b*]) were both refused publication. (Frege did publish a brief note on the subject in the Proceedings of the Jena Society for Medicine and Science ([1882-3]).)

In his next work, *The Foundations of Arithmetic*, he tried a different approach. He attempted to show, by a critical analysis of contemporary views, that there was no clear understanding of the basic concepts of arithmetic, including the concept of natural number, and he offered a non-technical exposition of his own theory which, he claims, overcomes all the difficulties. The book — perhaps the most important work ever in the philosophy of mathematics — is lively, and for the most part non-technical, while at the same time bringing a previously unknown clarity to its subject.

The *Foundations* begins with a lengthy discussion of some theories of number which Frege rejects, together with a methodological analysis of their failures. In this chapter we are concerned with the development of Frege's logic — which, for him, includes arithmetic — and it will be convenient to treat the general philosophical views presented in the *Foundations* in another chapter.[4] So in this section I shall consider only what Frege says about the definition and construction of the natural numbers.

As I remarked above, the *Begriffsschrift* contains some general results which relate to mathematical induction, but it says nothing specific about the natural numbers, the objects with which mathematical induction is concerned. In the *Foundations* Frege gives us a general definition of what it is for something to be a natural number, and a way of defining each particular number. Some very elementary results are proved which are meant to illustrate the adequacy of the definition. There is, however, no attempt to lay down a system of axioms from which these results strictly follow. In this section I shall try to present Frege's results carefully and simply.

(ii) Numerical identity

Remarking that it is 'only in the context of a sentence that words have any significance',[5] Frege says that we must begin our researches into the nature of number by first determining the meaning of a proposition in which a number word occurs. But until we know what numbers *are*, how do we know what sort of propositions number words can legitimately occur in? According to Frege there is one sort of proposition which we can assert about numbers on the basis of an absolutely minimal knowledge of their properties. That is, if we assume that numbers are *objects* of some kind (rather than properties of objects) we can state a sentence which says that two numbers are identical. For an object is exactly the sort of thing for which the question of identity arises; the general form of an identity being '$a=b$' where 'a' and 'b' are names of objects. Since Frege thinks that numbers are objects, he is then able to consider what it means to say that $a=b$, where 'a' and 'b' are terms designating numbers. He calls such a statement a statement in which we express our 'recognition of a number as the same again' (*ibid*, p. 73). In this way Frege introduced into philosophy a profoundly influential idea: the idea that a class of objects can be regarded as given in some determinate way only if we can give 'identity conditions' or a 'criterion of identity' for the members of that class.

What, then, does a numerical identity assert? Because of certain things that he has already argued for in an earlier part of the book Frege rejects the view that a number is a property of an empirical collection, or 'heap'. Rather, when we say 'the number of cards in the deck is fifty-two', we mean that the concept *card in the deck on the table* is such that there are fifty-two objects which fall under it. To say that the number of objects of a certain kind is the same as the number of objects of another kind is to say that the number of objects falling under the one concept is the same as the number of objects falling under another. For Frege the number of objects falling under a concept is the number which belongs to that concept. So for Frege the paradigm of a statement of identity between numbers is of the form

> The number which belongs to the concept *F* is the same as that which belongs to the concept *G* (*ibid*, section 62).

Our task is then to find another sentence which has the same content as this sentence but which does not contain the expression 'the number which belongs to the concept *F* (or *G*)'. Frege points out that his method involves assuming that we already have an understanding of identity in general, which we apply to this particular case in order to find out about the nature of numbers.

He then notes a systematic connection between certain kinds of relations and identity. For instance, we assert the relation of *parallelism* between lines if and only if the direction of the first line is *identical* with the direction of the second. We say that two geometrical objects are *similar* if the shape of the one is *identical* with the shape of the other. So given that 'line *a* is parallel to line *b*' means the same as 'The direction of *a* is identical with the direction of *b*', we ought to be able, in the case of numbers, to replace the statement 'the number which belongs to the concept *F* is identical with the number which belongs to the concept *G*' by some statement of the form '*F* is *R*-related to *G*', where our task is to find the name of a suitable relation between concepts to replace the '*R*'. The relation which Frege is actually going to employ here is the relation between two concepts of *being in a one-one correspondence* (see *ibid*, section 63).

Consider two concepts answering to the general terms '*X*' and '*Y*'. We say there is a one-one correspondence of the *X*s and the *Y*s if each *X* can be paired off with just one *Y*, and each *Y* with just one *X*, so that there are no *X*s, and no *Y*s either, left over unpaired at the end. To use an example of Frege's, we can tell whether there are just as many knives as forks on the table by pairing off knives with forks in such a way that there is just one fork for every knife, and just one knife for every fork, and nothing remaining unpaired. In that case the knives are in one-one correspondence with the forks.

Our proposal amounts to this: the sentence

The number belonging to the concept F is identical with the number belonging to the concept G

is deemed to be equivalent to (true in exactly the same circumstances as) the sentence

F is in a one-one correspondence with G

And this gives us identity conditions for numbers.

Frege points out what he sees as a fundamental objection to the whole procedure as stated so far: that the most we can hope for from it is an answer to the question 'what are the identity conditions for numbers?' And this is not an answer to the question that we are most interested in: 'What does it take for something to *be* a number?' If we have two number-descriptions like 'the number of the planets' and 'the number of square roots of two', we could use the identity conditions to decide what it would take for them to refer to the same number, but we need a way of deciding in advance whether the objects concerned *are* numbers. (Frege puts the point somewhat obscurely, by remarking that the identity conditions for numbers do not allow us to decide whether Julius Caesar is a number.) To say that numbers are such that their identity conditions depend upon the existence of a one-one correspondence between two concepts does not uniquely determine what numbers are. We can see this by adapting an argument which Frege used later in a different context (see below, chapter 4, section (a)(iv)). Let us call the number that belongs to the concept F, 'a' and the number that belongs to the concept G, 'b'. Then we know that

(1) $a = b$ if and only if F is in a one-one correspondence with G.

Can we then identify a and b as the objects which the condition stated in (1) is true of? We cannot, precisely because (1) may be true of more than just this single pair of objects. We can see this in the following way: Let f be any function which takes objects as arguments and values, and which is such that distinct arguments have distinct values. Thus if $a \neq b$, then $f(a) \neq f(b)$. Also, we stipulate that f is such that $f(a) \neq a$ and $f(b) \neq b$. It is clear then that

(2) $a = b$ if and only if $f(a) = f(b)$.

Then from (1) and (2) we get that

(3) $f(a) = f(b)$ if and only if F is in a one-one correspondence with G.

Suppose now that $f(a)$ and $f(b)$ are given to us in some notational form which does not allow us to recognise them as values of the function f, but simply as objects named 'c' and 'd'. Then we have

(4) $c=d$ if and only if F is in a one-one correspondence with G.

Given the truth of (*4*), together with the assumption that the identity conditions for numbers enable us to pick out the numbers, we would conclude that c is the number of F's and d the number of G's. But by construction of the function f, c and d are not those numbers; indeed they might not be numbers at all. So (*1*) holds of objects other than those it is intended to hold of, and cannot serve to single out the numbers for us.

Under what conditions will there be such a function f? The function will exist if there is a class of objects distinct from the numbers but which have the same *structure* as the numbers. One way of interpreting the failure of (1) to identify the numbers uniquely is as pointing to the possibility that there might be many different structures similar to the natural numbers. Frege's approach to arithmetic may succeed in identifying the type of structure, but it cannot identify one such structure as *the* natural numbers.[6]

(iii) Numbers as extensions

Frege tries another approach. Although he drops the idea of defining numbers through their identity conditions he does use his earlier discussion to motivate the definition that he will eventually give. Reverting to an earlier analogy, suppose that a is parallel to b. Then everything which is parallel to a is also parallel to b and conversely, in which case all the things which fall under the concept *parallel to a* fall under the concept *parallel to b*. Thus the two concepts have the same extensions. And if the two concepts have the same extension in the above sense, then a is indeed parallel to b. So a is parallel to b if and only if the extension of the concept *parallel to a* is identical to the extension of the concept *parallel to b*. The statement

> The extension of the concept *parallel to a* is identical with the extension of the concept *parallel to b*.

has then the same truth conditions (is true in just the same circumstances) as

(5) The direction of a is identical with the direction of b.

This suggests that we might try to define the direction of *a as* the extension of the concept *parallel to a*. A similar method applied to the case of numbers would involve defining the number belonging to F as the extension of the concept *being in a one-one correspondence with F*. With this in mind we can proceed to our definition. We know that the truth conditions of the following sentences are the same:

The number belonging to F is identical with the number belonging to G.

(5) The extension of the concept *being in a one-one correspondence with F* is identical with the extension of the concept *being in a one-one correspondence with G*.

To abbreviate things slightly we introduce the term 'equinumerate' ('*gleichzahlig*') to describe the relation between concepts which have extensions which are in a one-one correspondence. (5) can be rewritten as

The extension of the concept equinumerate with F is identical with the extension of the concept *equinumerate with G*.

According to the reasoning previously suggested, we shall say that the number belonging to the concept F is to be defined as the extension of the concept *equinumerate with F*.

We have said in effect that the number two is the extension of a concept which applies to just those concepts which themselves apply to just two objects. Can we get rid of the expression 'two' on the right hand side of this explanation? We can, for to say that a concept applies just to two objects is to say that it applies to unequal objects x and y and to no other object. So the explanation can be written out in longer terms which involve no circularity.

Thus it turns out that numbers are assimilated to extensions of concepts. It might be argued that this is hardly how we ordinarily conceive of the numbers, but Frege asks us to judge the definition not on grounds of its initial plausibility, but in terms of its ability to conform to the results which are essential to the concept of number. In other words, taking extensions of concepts, can we prove about them the same results as we would be able to prove about numbers? Frege devotes some attention now to showing that this is indeed the case. To highlight the possibility that the definition of numbers as extensions may be inadequate, let us begin by referring to Frege's own version of the numbers as the 'Numbers'. The question is whether we can identify the Numbers with the numbers.

The first thing Frege shows is that one Number is never a 'wider' extension than another Number; that is, that one is never the extension of a concept under which falls all the things that fall under the concept of which the other is the extension. This he thinks would be a counter-intuitive result and he is anxious to show that his definition avoids it.[7] It is easy to see that this is so, for suppose that m and n are distinct Numbers. They are, therefore, the extensions of distinct concepts. If one were wider than the other there would have to be things which fell under both. Suppose that a falls under the concept corresponding to m. Then a must itself be an extension; it is the extension of a concept under which exactly m things fall. But if a also fell under the concept corresponding to n it would be the extension of a concept under which fell exactly n things. Since $m \neq n$, this is impossible. This shows us that no Number is 'wider' in Frege's sense than any other.

The next thing to show is that a desirable property of the Numbers does follow from the definition: if two concepts F and G are equinumerate then the Numbers which belong to F and to G are the same. If this did not hold it would be plain that our definition had failed to capture the intuitive content of the notion of number, since it would imply that two different numbers applied to extensions which were the same in size. Now suppose that F can be put in a one-one correspondence with G. We have to show that the extension of the concept *equinumerate with* F is identical with the extension of the concept *equinumerate with* G. This will be so just in case the same things fall under the concepts *equinumerate with* F and *equinumerate with* G. Let x fall under *equinumerate with* F. So x is a concept equinumerate with F. But by assumption F is equinumerate with G, and so x is equinumerate with G (since *being equinumerate with* is a transitive relation).[8] x therefore falls under *equinumerate with* G. Similar reasoning shows that anything which falls under *equinumerate with* G falls under *equinumerate with* F. These concepts thus have the same extension, which was to be proved.

(iv) Defining the Numbers

Having defined Number in general, Frege goes on to show how each individual Number can be defined. To be a Number now means to be the extension of the concept *equinumerate with the concept* F for some F. First we define the Number zero. Clearly zero will be the Number which applies to any concept which has *no* objects in its extension. One obvious candidate for such a concept will be the concept 'not equal to itself'. Since everything *is* equal to itself, nothing will fall under this concept. So we say that zero is the extension of the concept *equinumerate with the concept (Not equal to itself)*.[9] Frege remarks that it would be wrong of us to reject self contradictory concepts such as this one. We are free to employ them as long as we do not suppose that any objects fall under them. Indeed, since it often takes a difficult proof to show that a concept *is* self contradictory, we could not decide in advance to have no truck with empty concepts ([1884*b*], p. 87).

Frege then shows that any two concepts under which nothing falls are such that they are equinumerate. To show this, consider two such concepts *F* and *G*. We need to make a one-one correspondence between them. This means that for every object which falls under *F* there is a unique corresponding object falling under *G*, and *vice versa*. But since *F* and *G* are empty concepts, there are *no* objects which fall under either, and so the condition is vacuously satisfied. On the other hand, if *F* is an empty concept and *G* is *not* empty, we can show that *F* and *G* are *not* equinumerate. Suppose that *F* and *G* are equinumerate. Then to every object falling under *G* there is a unique corresponding object falling under *F*. Then there must be a unique thing which is *F* to which the thing which is *G* corresponds. But there is no such thing, and so *F* and *G* are not equinumerate. So it turns out that the Number zero consists of exactly those extensions of concepts under which nothing falls. In fact there is only one such extension, for we say that extensions are the same if the same things fall under the corresponding concepts. Since nothing falls under these concepts, then, trivially, the same things fall under them, and so all their extensions are the same.

Having defined the Number zero, Frege goes on to discuss the relations between any member of the series of Numbers and the Number which succeeds it in the series (as, for example 3 succeeds 2).[10] To this end he proposes that we define the sentence 'The Number *n* follows directly after the Number *m*' to mean the same as

(*) There is a concept *F* and an object falling under it *x*, such that the Number which belongs to the concept *F* is *n* and the Number which belongs to the concept 'falling under *F* but not equal to *x*' is *m*.

This can be explained in the following way. Suppose that *m* and *n* are Numbers and that *n* follows directly after *m*. Since *n* is a Number it is the extension of the concept *equinumerate with the concept F* for some *F*. Since *n* is greater than the other Number *m*, *n* is not equal to zero, and so the concept F must be such that it has at least one object falling under it. Let x fall under F. Now consider the concept *Falling under F but not equal to x*. Clearly under this concept there will fall all the things falling under F except x. Now the Number which belongs to the concept *Falling under F but not equal to x* is the extension of the concept *equinumerate with the concept (Falling under the concept F but not equal to x)*. And this is the Number which holds of every concept which has one fewer object falling under it than the extension of any concept which is equinumerate with the concept F. This is clearly the Number which we want to be the immediate predecessor of n; in other words the Number m.

Frege now shows how, starting with the definition of the Number zero and using the relation which holds between Numbers when one is the successor of the other, we can provide definitions for all the Numbers.

Under the concept *identical with zero* falls exactly one object, the Number zero. Clearly the Number which belongs to this concept should be the Number one. To see that this is indeed the case consider the sentence (*). In place of 'the concept F' substitute 'the concept *identical with zero*', and in place of x substitute 'zero'. This special case of (*) now reads

(*) There is a concept *identical with zero*, and an object falling under it, zero, such that the Number which belongs to the concept, *identical with zero* is n and the Number which belongs to the concept *falling under the concept (identical to zero but not identical to zero)* is m.

What are the Numbers m and n? m is the Number which belongs to the concept: *falling under the concept identical to zero but not identical to zero*. Clearly nothing falls under this concept, and so the Number which belongs to it is zero. Now n is the Number belonging to the concept *identical with zero*, under which exactly one thing falls (the Number zero), and so n is the Number one. And since (*) means the same as 'n follows directly after m', we have that one follows directly after zero, which is what we want.

(v) The infinitude of the Numbers

The next thing to show is that every Number has a successor. Frege's strategy in this regard is as follows. If we are given a Number, say n, we know by definition that n is the Number belonging to some concept, say F. Our task is to show that there is a concept F', such that the Number which belongs to F' is the successor of n. In fact we take the concept *Number of the series of*

Numbers ending with n and show that the Number belonging to this concept is the immediate successor of *n*. We do this in the following way.

Let us recall the idea of one object following another in a series, and apply that idea to the special case of one Number following another in the series of Numbers. We say that *n* follows in the Number series after *m* if and only if the following holds.

(1) For any property *F*, if *F* is hereditary in the Number series, and if any successor of *m* has *F*, then *n* has *F*.[11]

We want to use this definition to show that every Number has a successor. If in (1) we set *m* equal to 0 and substitute for *F* the property *having a successor*, we get

(2) If *having a successor* is hereditary, and any successor of 0 has a successor, then *n* has a successor, for any *n* which follows in the number series after 0, i.e. for any Number other than 0.

This is a conditional statement, the consequent of which ('*n* has a successor, for any *n*') is what we are aiming to prove. So all we need to show is that the antecedent is true, in which case the consequent must be true, and to show that 0 itself has a successor. The antecedent says that, (i) having a successor is hereditary and, (ii) any successor of zero has a successor. But a moment's reflection shows that we can simplify our task. A consequence of (1) is that

(3) For any property *F*, if *F* is hereditary in the Number series, and if *m* has *F*, then *n* has *F*.

From which we can get the special case

(4) If having a successor is hereditary and 0 has a successor, then *n* has a successor, for any *n* which follows in the Number series after 0.

So now we have two things to prove. First, that having a successor is an hereditary property. Secondly, that 0 has a successor. As I have already said, to be the successor of a Number *n* is to be the extension of the concept *equinumerate with the concept (member of the series of Numbers ending with n)*, or in other words, the Number which belongs to the concept *member of the series of Numbers ending with n*. For brevity's sake we shall write this Number as *Num*(-*n*). Now showing that having a successor is hereditary in the Number series amounts to proving the following.

(5) If *a* follows in the Number series directly after *d* and *Num*(-*d*) follows directly after *d* then *Num*(-*a*) follows directly after *a* ([1884*b*], pp. 94–5).

And proving that 0 has a successor amounts to proving that

(6) *Num*(-0) follows directly after 0 in the Number series (*ibid*, p. 95).

It then follows from (5) and (6), simply by the meaning that we have attached to the phrase 'following in the Number series', that every Number has a successor. The actual steps of the proof are not given in the *Foundations*: they are given in full detail in volume 1 of the *Basic Laws* ([1893], pp. 144–9).

Assuming now that we can prove that the Numbers form an infinite series in which each member has a unique successor, and that we can prove that they have the other familiar properties of the natural numbers, we shall simply talk about 'the numbers' when we mean 'the Numbers'.[12]

Let us review what Frege has done in this central part of the *Foundations*. Three stages can be distinguished. First, Frege shows how a statement of identity between numbers can be rewritten as a statement to the effect that there is a one-one correspondence between the extensions of two concepts. Using the idea of a one-one correspondence, he then defines a number as a certain type of extension. Secondly, this general definition is shown to generate a specific definition of each individual number, by starting with a definition of zero and providing a method for defining the successor of any number in terms of the numbers which precede it. Thirdly, it is argued (in an admittedly sketchy way) that, on the definition proposed, every number has a unique successor and that there are infinitely many numbers.

In all this Frege has not made precise the assumptions upon which he is drawing. In order to prove the existence of the numbers he has had to make some assumptions about the existence of extensions. He assumes, in particular, that each concept has a unique well defined object corresponding to it; the extension of that concept. At this time Frege thought that the reference to extensions was inessential, and that the numbers could be defined in terms of concepts themselves rather than in terms of the extensions of concepts. He notes that this seems to be open to the objection that to treat the numbers as concepts would contradict his earlier statement that the numbers are objects; number terms like 'two' can be used in sentences where we predicate something of the term, as when we say 'Two is a prime number'. Secondly, to treat numbers as extensions will lead to results different from those which follow if we treat them as concepts, because distinct concepts can have the same extension. Thus the extension of the concept *equinumerate with the concept (not identical with itself)* is the same as the extension of the concept *being a round square*. But the concepts involved are distinct.[13] Frege says, however, that he is 'convinced that both these objections can be met; but to do this would take us too far afield for present purposes. ([1884*b*], p. 80)' When he came to give a more precise account of the natural numbers in the later *Basic Laws* Frege did not try to dispense with extensions; indeed the programme attempted there depends crucially on the assumptions, implicit in the *Foundations*, that every concept has an extension, and that concepts have the same extension if and only if the same things fall under each.

(vi) Infinite Numbers

Frege's approach to the definition of number naturally lends itself to the extension of the number concept from the finite to the infinite. For instance, if we consider the concept *being a finite number*, we can form the extension of the concept *equinumerate with the concept (being a finite number)*, and ask if this extension is a number. It is certainly not a finite (or, as we shall sometimes say, 'natural') number, for if it were equal to some finite number *n*, then *n* would be the number belonging to the concept *being a natural number*, and there would be only finitely many natural numbers. But it is easy to prove (informally) that there are infinitely many natural numbers.

The German mathematician Georg Cantor had shown, in 1883, that we can indeed extend the number concept to embrace a whole series of numbers which are bigger than any finite number. Frege referred warmly to Cantor's work, saying that there is nothing mysterious about these new numbers; they arise quite naturally if we consider numbers as belonging to concepts, since certain concepts, like *being a natural number*, have an infinite extension. Cantor distinguishes between two different kinds of numbers; 'Powers' (what we now would call cardinal numbers) which are used to measure size, and what he calls *Anzahlen* (what we call ordinal numbers) which are used to denote the position of an object in a sequence. Thus in asking a question of the form 'How many candidates in the maths exam were there?' we expect to be given a cardinal number, e.g. '30'; while to the question 'Where did you come in the maths exam?' the appropriate answer would be to cite a position in the series of numbers, e.g. '30th'. In the case of finite numbers the cardinals and ordinals coincide, but they do not coincide in the case of infinite numbers. Frege considers only the cardinal numbers.[14] He remarks also that some of Cantor's concepts are not very precisely defined, and that he appeals to a rather mysterious intuition to substantiate some of his results.

Cantor, like Frege, was opposed to the psychologistic tendencies which dominated the age, referring to them as 'the now dominant academic positivistic scepticism'—a description which Frege heartily endorsed (see [1892*c*], p. 166). The dominance of positivism led to a deep suspicion of the notion of infinity, particularly the so-called actual or completed infinity which forms the base for Cantor's work. More acceptable were constructivistic tendencies which interpreted mathematical objects as essentially human creations. This was the view espoused by the enormously influential mathematician Kronecker, who was at one time Cantor's teacher and later led his persecution by the mathematical community with a virulence not often seen even in academic life.

Unfortunately Cantor and Frege were unable to co-operate against their common opposition. In a review of the *Foundations* (one of only three reviews which it received) Cantor praised Frege's opposition to the psychological-intuitive standpoint, but went on to display a singular lack of understanding concerning Frege's views about number, which in fact coincided very closely with his own (see Cantor [1885]). In particular, he criticised the basing of the number concept on the idea of the extension of a concept, the latter being not, according to him, precisely determined except in certain cases, and therefore unable to serve the required purpose. In a brief reply Frege tried to clear up the misunderstanding and to emphasise again the extent of their agreement (see Frege [1885*b*]). But the matter got no further forward. Some years later Frege reviewed some papers in which Cantor had presented, together with certain philosophical reflections, his theory of the transfinite. He referred again to Cantor's earlier misunderstandings, and accused him of having fallen into the error of giving psychological explanations of facts about the numbers. But he does conclude by emphasising the significance of Cantor's results about the infinite; results which, he thinks, will prove a stumbling block for subjectivism.

Here is the rock they will founder on! It cannot be denied that the infinite has a place in mathematics and it is on the other hand incompatible with epistemological tendencies. Here, so it seems, is a battlefield where a great decision will be reached.[15]

(b) The Basic Laws of Arithmetic

(i) Introduction

The last of Frege's books was the *Basic Laws of Arithmetic* published in two volumes in 1893 and 1903.[16] Interest in his logical system had not significantly increased as a result of the *Foundations*, and Frege had to bear the cost of the new publication himself. Yet the *Basic Laws* is, as scholars now readily acknowledge, a wonderful achievement. The rigour of its proofs, and the attention to syntactic and semantical distinctions, was something that logicians had not previously attained. No other work approached its standards for many years after.

It is remarkable also in another feature: it is a model of lucid and pedagogically sound exposition. Important definitions are preceded by a discussion of the role they are intended to play in the construction of the number system. Sections begin with an 'analysis' in which the results to be proved are explained and the route to a proof is sketched out. In this way the reader understands the purpose of each step in the argument and the nature of the ultimate goal.

The number and complexity of the results proved in the *Basic Laws* preclude a comprehensive discussion here. I can point only to the main results.

Part of the book covers the same ground as the constructive sections of the *Foundations*, the difference being now that the proofs are given formally and a set of axioms is specified. I shall discuss the axioms in the next chapter, when certain relevant notational and conceptual devices have been introduced.[17]

(ii) Results about the Natural Numbers and the first Infinite Number

Here are stated without proof and in a much simplified form some of the arithmetical results which are proved in the *Basic Laws*. Let u be the extension of a concept F. Then '$Num(u)$' refers to the number of things which fall under F.

(1) $Num(u) = Num(v)$ if and only if there is a one-one correlation between the concepts of which u and v are the extensions. (Theorems 32 and 49.)

(2) If u and v are extensions of concepts under which fall exactly the same things then $Num(u) = Num(v)$. (Theorem 96.)
(3) Suppose that u and v are the extensions of concepts F and G respectively and that exactly one more thing falls under F than falls under G. Suppose that $Num(u) = n$ and that $Num(v) = m$. Then n is the immediate successor of m. (Theorem 101.)
(4) The relation of direct succession in the natural numbers is one-one. (Theorem 90.)
(5) $Num(u) = 0$ if and only if u is the extension of an empty concept. (Theorems 94 and 97.)
(6) Every number other than 0 follows directly after another number. (Theorem 107.)
(7) 0 is not the successor of any number. (Theorem 126.)
(8) $Num(u) = 1$ if and only if u is the extension of a concept under which falls exactly one thing. (Theorems 113, 121, 122, 117.)
(9) 1 is the immediate successor of 0. (Theorem 110.)
(10) $0 \neq 1$ (Theorem 111.)
(11) No natural number follows after itself in the number series. (Theorem 145.)
(12) Every number has a successor. (Theorem 157.)
(13) If n is a natural number then n is the number of numbers between 1 and n inclusive. (Theorem 314.)
(14) The number of numbers between any two natural numbers is a natural number. (Theorem 325.)
(15) If $Num(u)$ is a natural number and v is included in u[18] then $Num(v)$ is a natural number. (Theorem 443.)
(16) Suppose that u and w are disjoint,[19] that v and z are disjoint, and that $Num(v) = Num(w)$ and $Num(z) = Num(u)$. Then $Num(v \text{ or } z)$[20] is equal to $Num(u \text{ or } w)$. (Theorem 469.)

Following Frege's discussion of infinite numbers in the *Foundations*, there are some results about the first infinite number, the number of the natural or finite numbers. Following Frege, we will call this number 'Infinite'.

(17) Infinite is its own successor. (Theorem 165.)
(18) If $Num(v)$ is finite and $Num(u)$ is Infinite, then $Num(u \text{ or } v)$ is Infinite. (Theorem 172.)
(19) Infinite is not a natural number. (Theorem 167.)
(20) Suppose that $Num(u) =$ Infinite, that v is included in u and that $Num(v) \neq$ Infinite. Then $Num(v)$ is some natural number. (Theorem 428.)

(21) If v is included in u and $Num(v)$ = Infinite then $Num(u)$ is not a natural number. (Theorem 484.)

(iii) The real numbers

Until now Frege has dealt with a rather restricted class of numbers, those numbers which we use for counting purposes. In addition to these there exist negative numbers, rational numbers, which are ratios of whole numbers, together with an important class of numbers which cannot be represented as such ratios and which are called ‘irrationals’. The rational and irrational numbers go together to make up the *real* numbers. We can think of the real numbers as corresponding to the points on a straight line. If we mark off a zero point, points to the left will be negative, points to the right will be positive, and each positive or negative point will represent a certain distance from the zero. The basic application of the real numbers seems to be for the measurement of *magnitudes*, such as distances, temperatures, masses, etc.

If we think of the natural numbers as belonging to the real numbers we see that they are marked out from the rest of the reals by having a duality of purpose, once for counting and once for measurement. But Frege chooses not to regard them as belonging to the wider class of real numbers. He rejects the idea of defining the real numbers by generalising them from the natural numbers, the method adopted by other workers in the foundations of mathematics.

What Frege does is to treat the real numbers quite separately from the natural numbers. The real numbers are to be based on logic by giving a quite new construction which proves their existence as a set of entities distinct from the natural numbers. The resulting set of real numbers will contain some numbers which seem to be copies of the natural numbers. 0, 1, 2, etc are real numbers as well as natural numbers. But in Frege’s system they will actually be different entities. This is indicated notationally by the fact that Frege uses special symbols for the natural numbers. He writes ‘$\mathfrak{0}$’, ‘$\mathfrak{1}$’, ‘$\mathfrak{2}$’, etc. for the natural numbers, reserving the more usual ‘0’, ‘1’, ‘2’, etc. for those real numbers which are also positive whole numbers ([1903*a*], section 157).

The natural numbers are used for counting, and tell us how many things fall under a given concept. Thus a given natural number is applicable to the extensions of all concepts which have the same number of objects falling under them. The real numbers are used for measuring magnitudes, and Frege wants to define them as ratios between magnitudes. Proving that the real numbers exist amounts essentially to proving that magnitudes exist. But what are magnitudes? Frege remarks that mathematicians often confuse magnitudes with real numbers themselves, and that this is a mistake. There are different kinds of magnitudes, and the real numbers are capable of being applied to all these different kinds. We must have magnitudes available to us before we construct the real numbers, (see *ibid*, section 160).

Frege's idea for introducing magnitudes is that we can call something a magnitude if it belongs to a certain kind of complex structure, which Frege calls a 'magnitude field'. In other words, we cannot tell whether something is a magnitude simply by looking at its intrinsic characteristics; we need to understand its role in a wider theoretical context.

> Instead of asking, what properties must an object have in order to be a magnitude? we must ask, how must a concept be constituted, so as to have as its extension a magnitude field? We can abbreviate 'extension of a concept' to 'class'. We can then put the question, what properties must a class have in order to be a magnitude field? Something is not a magnitude in itself, but only in so far as it belongs, with other objects, to a class which is a magnitude field.[21]

Frege's general strategy is to be the following. First he will define a structure called a 'magnitude field'. Then he will prove that a structure of this kind exists. Then, having magnitudes available to him, he will define the real numbers in terms of them. A magnitude field is to be a class of objects on which are defined certain operations and relations. The objects are to be the extensions of certain non-empty relations. (Here I shall speak simply of 'relations' when I mean extensions of relations.) Since magnitudes can be added and subtracted we introduce operations on these relations which will mirror addition and subtraction. Frege spends the rest of the second volume of the *Basic Laws* showing that this can be done in a satisfactory way. Doubtless he planned a further volume in which the theory of real numbers was to be completed; an idea which the discovery of Russell's paradox caused him to abandon (see below, chapter 5, section (b)). What he hoped to do was this. In order to show that there exists a set of objects which form a magnitude field Frege would draw upon what he had already proved about the natural numbers. I have said that he rejected the idea that the real numbers could be constructed directly from the natural numbers. But what he does do is to use the existence of the natural numbers to prove that a magnitude field exists. The idea is suggested by a mathematical result to the effect that every real number can be regarded as the value of a certain function of two arguments, the first argument being a natural number, the second an infinite set of natural numbers. The relations in a magnitude field will turn out to be relations between these pairs. Though this idea is suggested by a theorem about real numbers we cannot, without obvious circularity, *use* such a result in our construction since, from a formal point of view, we are not yet supposed to know anything about the real numbers. Frege is therefore anxious to point out that the desired relation between pairs can be defined without reference to real numbers at all. In this way

> we will succeed in defining the real numbers purely arithmetically or logically as ratios between magnitudes which are provably available to us. In this way no uncertainty can remain that irrational numbers exist ([1903*a*], section 164).

Notes

1 I shall sometimes italicise an expression to indicate that it is being used to refer to a concept. See below, chapter 4, section (a) (ii) for further discussion.
2 See Bynum (*ed*) [1972], p. 229.
3 See *ibid*, p. 221.
4 See below, chapter 6, sections (a) and (b).
5 For a fuller discussion of the important principle, see below, chapter 6, section (b).
6 This objection to Frege's programme is pursued by Benacerraf in his [1965].
7 Actually this *is* a consequence of a later definition of the numbers due to von Neumann. On von Neumann's definition, if *a* and *b* are distinct numbers, then either *a* is a subset of *b* or *b* is a subset of *a*. See Halmos [1960], p. 45.
8 That is, if *a* is equinumerate with *b* and *b* is equinumerate with *c*, then *a* is equinumerate with *c*.
9 I use bracketing as a way of making complex expressions for concepts easier to read.
10 See above, chapter 2, section (c) (iii).
11 See above, chapter 2, section (c) (iii).
12 For more on the question of whether Frege's extensions are identical with the numbers, see below, chapter 4, section (c)(iv) and above, p. 46 and note.
13 According to Frege's later view concepts with the same extension *are* the same. See below, chapter 4, section (a) (vii).
14 He uses the term 'Anzahl' for cardinals, which is the term Cantor uses for ordinals.

15 Frege [1892*c*], p. 166. Frege is here using the word 'epistemological' [*Erkenntnistheoretischen*] in the sense of 'based on subjective knowledge'. His remarks should not be interpreted as a general condemnation of epistemology. Elsewhere he said that '... knowledge [*Erkenntnis*] does not constitute the object of epistemology in so far as it is a psychic process, and... therefore, psychology must be distinguished sharply from epistemology' ([1885*a*], p. 102).

16 Frege [1893] and [1903*a*]. I shall refer to this work in what follows as the *Basic Laws*.

17 See chapter 5, section (a) (ii).

18 I say that *v* is included in *u* when *v* is the extension of a concept *F*, *u* is the extension of *G*, and everything which falls under *F* falls under *G*.

19 I say that *u* and *w* are disjoint when *u* is the extension of *F*, *w* the extension of *G* and no object falls under both *F* and *G*.

20 If *u* is the extension of *F*, and *v* the extension of *G*, then *Num*(*u* or *v*) is the number of things which fall under the concept *being either an F or a G*.

21 Frege [1903*a*], section 161. This reasoning ties in closely with Frege's 'Context Principle' according to which what we need to know about a mathematical entity is its role in the relevant mathematical theory. See Frege [1884*b*], section 62 and [1893], section 10. See also the discussion below, chapter 6, section (b). Frege is here very close also to the idea which lies behind Hilbert's treatment of axiomatic theories in his work on the consistency and independence of geometrical axioms. See the discussion below in chapter 4, section (a) (vi).

4 *Frege's Philosophical Logic*

AT THE same time that Frege was developing his logical and arithmetical theories, he introduced a number of ideas and distinctions which were intended to shed further philosophical light on logic and arithmetic. Some of these ideas are summarised in the introductory sections of the *Basic Laws*, and are explained at length in two sets of articles. The first consists of three papers published between 1891 and 1892, and the second, again consisting of three papers, appeared between 1918 and 1923, two years before his death.[1] A number of unpublished papers also contain important information.[2] This chapter offers an account of these ideas.

(a) Function and Object

(i) General explanation

We have already seen how Frege distinguished in the *Foundations* between concepts and objects, though he did not explain in detail what the distinction was based on. We also saw how, in the *Begriffsschrift*, Frege viewed sentences as analysable into a part which represents a function, and parts (perhaps only one) which represent objects, which are the arguments of the function. It turns out that the distinction between concepts and objects is just a special case of the distinction between functions and objects. And this latter distinction is of quite fundamental importance for Frege.

Frege introduces us to the distinction between functions and objects via the distinction between the sorts of expression which can be used to represent functions and their arguments. This was something about which there was a good deal of confusion at the time that he was writing, consequent upon a confusion about the nature of functions themselves. (I shall say more about this in the next section.) Functions were typically represented by expressions containing so-called 'variables', as in '$2.x^3+x$', and this led to the view that functions are 'variable numbers'. But, as Frege points out, each number is a definite entity; there are no variable numbers. Functions must be explained in some different way ([1904], p. 274 (108)). According to him the variable x does not represent anything which is a part of the function itself. It is just one way of indicating that the function needs to be completed by supplying a number in order to obtain another number. Thus a less confusing way to write the function would be as '2.( )³+( )'. If in the gaps we insert an expression which designates a number, say '3', we get a complex expression which designates the *value* of the function for the argument 3. That is, we get '2.3^3+3', which designates the number 57.

In fact, because there are functions of more than one variable, and because we need to know what substitutions are appropriate in the different argument places, we do need some notation to fill the gaps. If we write '( )+( )', it is not clear whether this is to represent a function of one variable, in which we have to substitute the same number-designator in both places, as in '2+2', or whether this is a function of two variables in which independent substitutions can be made, as in '2+3'. By using variables, these two different possibilities are represented as '$x+x$' and '$x+y$' respectively. Frege actually uses lower-case Greek letters for variables as in '$\xi+\zeta$', while insisting that such letters do not designate anything, but merely indicate the places at which expressions which do designate numbers can be inserted into the gaps. In what follows I shall normally designate a function or concept by an expression such as '$f(\xi)$', though occasionally I shall use '$f(\ )$'.

Frege now argues that functions are what he calls 'incomplete' (or 'unsaturated') entities. It is from the structure of the expression for the function that we discern the nature of the function itself. In the expressions

'$2.1^3 + 1$'
'$2.4^3 + 4$'
'$2.5^3 + 5$'

we see that the same function, $2.x^3+x$, is being applied to the arguments 1, 4 and 5. The expression for the function itself contains parts, the variables, which do not designate anything.

> Accordingly, the essence of the *function* lies in that part of the expression which is there over and above the 'x'. The expression for a *function* is *in need of completion, unsaturated*... The function is completed by the argument; what it becomes on completion I call the *value* of the function for the argument... Thus the argument is not to be counted a part of the *function*, but serves to complete the function, which in itself is *unsaturated* ([1893], section 1. Italics in the original. See also Frege [1891*b*], p. 128 (24)).

Being complete is the defining characteristic of an object, and whatever is not an object is a function.

It is easy to extemporise an argument as to why anything which is incomplete in Frege's sense must be a function. From the intuitive point of view, a function is something that correlates any given object with another unique object. Consider an incomplete entity. We take any object and complete the otherwise incomplete entity by adding the object to it. The incomplete entity now becomes completed and we have a new, unique object. Thus an incomplete entity gives us a way of going from one object to another; it is, in other words, a function.

Frege gave a variety of metaphorical accounts of the nature of incompleteness. In one place he compares a function to an open interval on a line (that is, an interval which lacks at least one of its end points) (see [1891*b*], p. 128 (25)). In another place he likens the function to a coat 'which cannot stand upright on its own, but to that end requires someone around whom it is wrapped' (see [1918*b*], p. 377 (52)). Yet another account explains incompleteness in the following way:

> An object, e.g. the number two, cannot logically adhere to another object, e.g. Julius Caesar, without some means of connection. This, in turn, cannot be an object but rather must be unsaturated. A logical connection into a whole can come about only through this, that an unsaturated part is saturated or completed by one or more parts. ([1903*b*], p. 270 (33)).

Here Frege is speaking of the incompleteness of a relation, and to understand this we must understand the assimilation of concepts and relations to functions.

(ii) Concepts as functions

Frege remarks upon the extent to which the notion of a function in the mathematical sense has undergone various extensions ([1891*b*] and [1893], section 2). With the development of the calculus in the seventeenth century and its application to mechanics, functions came to have a central place in mathematics. Yet the notion of a function was an obscure one. It would be no exaggeration to say that, while mathematicians in the eighteenth century were well acquainted with examples of functions and could prove certain results about them, they really had no idea what functions were. Sometimes a function was thought of as a graph in the geometrical sense, sometimes it was identified with the expression used to represent the function. Gradually it was recognised that functions could have a very wide and disparate range of properties. Some functions converge to a definite value, others do not; some are continuous, others discontinuous. By the mid-nineteenth century functions were beginning to be thought of in something like the modern sense. Today we say that a function is any kind of correlation between two sets of numbers (the set of arguments and the set of values) such that each argument is associated with at most one value.[3] We call such a thing a 'single-valued correspondence'. In this way the notion of a function was freed both from the constraints of geometric representability, and of expressibility in terms of a single formula.

Still, however, functions were conceived of in a rather narrow sense. Their arguments and values were usually thought of as having to be numbers of some kind. Frege, on the other hand, wanted further to extend the notion of a function by introducing arguments and values which are not mathematical objects in the traditional sense. We have already seen, in fact, that he wanted to analyse sentences and their parts in terms of expressions for functions and arguments. The extension is best explained in two stages. First of all, consider a function which takes numbers as arguments, but the values of which are not numbers. What, for example, are the arguments and values of the function $x^2=1$? For 'x' we can substitute any number we like, obtaining expressions such as

'$1^2 = 1$'
'$2^2 = 1$'
'$3^2 = 1$'

and so on. These expressions are sentences. The first is true, the others false. Frege proposes that we take the values for the function $x^2=1$ to be the truth values of the sentences which result when a name is substituted for 'x'. We shall say more about this when we discuss the distinction between sense and reference.[4] Thus the function $x^2=1$ is a function which always takes truth values as values, and it turns out that a concept is to be defined as exactly this sort of function: a concept is a function which takes truth values as values.

We can give this definition a more intuitive feel if we think of a concept as being something which effects a separation of objects into two classes. The concept *being red* separates objects into those which are red and those which are not. In this way we can interpret the concept *being red* as a function which takes all objects to one of the two truth-values. It takes an object to the value true if it *is* red, and to the value false if it is not. All the ones which get correlated with the value true form the class of red objects, and all those which get correlated with the value false form the class of non-red objects. Returning to our mathematical example, we can express the function $x^2=1$ in other words as 'x's being such that its square is equal to 1', or '*being a square root of 1*'.[5] For the argument 1 the value of the function is the truth-value true ('the true' as Frege calls it) while for the argument 2 the value is the truth-value false ('the false'). In other words, 1 *is* a square root of 1, and 2 is not. If the value corresponding to the argument is the true, we say that the argument *falls under* the concept. If the value is the false the argument does not fall under the concept. Falling under a concept is to be thought of as the same thing as having a property. 1 has the property of being a square root of 1, while 2 does not have this property.

Relations are dealt with similarly. A relation is a function of more than one argument, the values of which are always truth-values. Consider 'x is less than y'. If we substitute pairs of number expressions for 'x' and 'y' we get sentences which are either true or false. Since '2 is less than 3' is true, the pair consisting of 2 and 3 falls under the relation *being less than*. Since '3 is less than 2' is false, the pair consisting of 3 and 2 does not fall under that relation. (This shows, incidentally, that pairs are distinguished by the order of occurrence of their members. A pair with first member a and second member b will be distinct from a pair with first member b and second member a.)

Apart from numbers and truth-values, functions can take other kinds of values. We can treat the expression 'The capital of Germany' as splitting into a functional expression 'The capital of' together with the name 'Germany' filling the argument place. For this argument the value of the function is Berlin. (Or was in the nineteenth century.) For the argument France the value is Paris, and so on.

(iii) What arguments can a function take?

All the functions so far considered seem to have a natural 'domain of definition'. That is, they seem made to accept certain arguments and not others. *Being less than 3* naturally takes numbers for its arguments, while *being the conqueror of Gaul* takes persons, and *being the capital of France* takes cities. It hardly seems to make sense to ask whether Caesar is less than 3, whether Equador conquered Gaul, or whether Gottlob Frege is the capital of France. Yet here Frege demands another radical extension of generality. Every function is to be defined in such a way that it takes a definite value for *any* argument whatsoever. Thus we are to say that it is just false that

Caesar is less than three; for the argument-pair, Caesar and three, the function *less than* takes the value, false. Cases where the function is a concept or relation, that is, where the function takes only truth-values as values, seem easy to deal with. We simply assign to the 'odd' cases the value false. But what about other kinds of functions such as addition? This is a function, $x + y$, of two arguments. What is the value to be in the case where the arguments are Caesar and Berlin? Frege tells us that it is not important in such cases what we choose the value to be. It is important only that there *be* a value. Thus we can define *addition* in such a way that it takes as values all the values that we would expect it to take when both arguments are numbers, and if either argument is not a number the function takes the value zero.

Frege argues for the thesis that functions must be defined for every argument on the grounds that we require concepts to have well-defined boundaries.

> ... it is essential that ... '$a+b$' should always have a reference, whatever signs for definite objects may be inserted in place of 'a' and 'b'. This involves the requirement as regards concepts that, for any argument, they shall have a truth value as their value; that it shall be determinate, for any object, whether it falls under the concept or not. In other words: as regards concepts we have a requirement of sharp delimitation; if this were not satisfied it would be impossible to set forth logical laws about them ([1891*b*], p. 135 (33). See also Frege [1906*c*], p. 194 (179) and letter to Peano p. 182 (114)).

Why would it be impossible to set forth logical laws if we allow functions to be undefined for some arguments? What Frege has in mind is this. Suppose the concept *being a prime number* is undefined for the argument Berlin. Then putting Berlin in the argument place of this function will not give us any value, neither the true nor the false. The sentence 'Berlin is a prime number' will be neither true nor false. But then presumably the same will hold for the sentence 'Berlin is not a prime number'. But one of the laws of logic which Frege wants to preserve says that for every sentence P, either P is true or not-P is true.

It is not, however, impossible to do logic in a precise, regimented way even if we deny this principle in the sense necessary to deny it if we restrict the domains of definition of some functions. The principle can be restated to say that, if a sentence P has a truth-value at all, that truth-value must be either the true or the false. Frege suggests that concepts which are not defined for every argument would be vague. But a concept will presumably be vague only if it is not *clear* what the value is for a certain argument. Frege was right to set himself against the vagueness of concepts in this sense, for if the value for any particular argument is not clearly specified then one person might choose one value and another person another, and there would be no sense in which either one was objectively correct or incorrect. But this situation need not arise just because we admit functions and concepts with limited domains of definition. As long as it is clear what the domain of definition is, and clear what the value for any argument within the domain of definition is, then there can be no question of vagueness. A concept can be used by us in an objective way as long as it is clear which arguments give the true as value, which the false, and which give neither.

(iv) Courses of values and extensions

There is an important correspondence between functions and certain kinds of objects, called 'courses of values' (*Werthverläufe*). Suppose that two functions are such that, where they take the same argument, they also take the same value. In that case Frege says that the courses of values of the two functions are the same. This is the most important and fundamental fact about courses of values in Frege's logic. He takes it to be 'indemonstrable' and a fundamental law of logic. In the *Basic Laws* it appears as Axiom (V).[6]

We now need a way of representing courses of values. If '$f(x)$' is the name of a function, then 'ἐ$f(\varepsilon)$' is the name of the corresponding course of values. If $f(x, y)$ is a function of two variables then its course of values can be written 'ἀἐ $f(\varepsilon, \alpha)$'. Greek vowels like 'α' and 'ε' are always used to construct names for courses of values.

Concepts are special cases of functions, and now Frege tells us that the extension of a concept is to be regarded as the course of values of a function ([1891*b*], p. 133 (31) and [1893], section 3). But what is a course of values? So far we know only that every function has a course of values, that extensions of concepts are courses of values, and that courses of values are the same when the corresponding functions take the same values for the same arguments. But just as the provision of identity conditions for the numbers failed to identify the numbers, so the provision of identity conditions for courses of values does not tell us what objects courses of values are ([1893], section 10).

Now Frege tried to avoid indeterminacy about the identity of numbers by supplementing their identity conditions with an explicit definition which identifies the numbers with certain extensions. But now it seems that extensions are to be regarded as courses of values and we have not yet identified these objects. So the problem of the indeterminacy of numbers was pushed back a step, but not solved. One way out of the difficulty would be to define courses of values explicitly, perhaps as classes of a certain kind; the course of values of the function $f(\xi)$ would then be seen as a class of ordered pairs, (x,y), where y is the value for the function when it takes x as argument. Thus the course of values of the function x^2 would be the set of pairs consisting of (1,1), (2,4), (3,9), etc., while the course of values (extension) of the concept *being German* would be the set of pairs (Frege, the true), (Napoleon, the false), (Plato, the false), etc. Frege's procedure in the *Basic Laws*, where courses of values play an indispensable part in the construction of arithmetic, is to treat them as if they are not determined in any way other than by the provision of identity conditions. There seem to be two reasons for this. First, the reduction of courses of values to classes only invites the further question of how to determine what classes are. Secondly, Frege insists that classes cannot be regarded as sets or agglomerations of things; they cannot, he says, be constituted by their members (letter to Russell, p. 223, (140)). The existence of a class of things depends upon the existence of a concept under which all those things fall. A class, in other words, must be the extension of a concept. But Frege has assimilated extensions to courses of values. It would obviously be circular then to say that courses of values are to be defined as classes. But our intuition of the notion of class seems to be basic. If courses of values are more fundamental, it seems profoundly difficult to give an intuitive account of their natures.

In the *Basic Laws* Frege adopts the following strategy in response to the problem ([1893], section 10).

What, after all, is our reason for wanting to know what courses of values are? Over and above mere curiosity, the reason must be that we need to know what properties courses of values have which are important in the development of the logical system in the *Basic Laws*. What is important to us about courses of values is the power they bestow on us to prove the logical and mathematical results that we want. So the information which we require about courses of values concerns the role that they play in combination with other entities presupposed by the logical system with which we are working. In particular, courses of values are objects; they are complete entities, unlike the functions with which they are associated. Thus their major role in the logical system will be as arguments and values of functions. The only way in which entities in Frege's system combine together is by the application of an argument to a function. So the conclusion is this: what we want to know about courses of values is, what is the result of applying any function in the system to an argument which is a course of values? Since there is a limited stock of primitive functions in terms of which the other functions of the system are defined, we can, says Frege, confine ourselves to a consideration of the values which the primitive functions take for courses of values as arguments. At this stage of the discussion, the only primitive function of the system is the identity function $x = y$, and the only objects introduced so far are the courses of values and the truth values. So the question is to determine the value of this function in all possible cases. We can do this in the following way.

If both the arguments are courses of values, then Axiom (V) tells us that '$a = b$' is the true if and only if the associated functions have the same value for the same arguments, and otherwise the false. If both arguments are truth-values then '$a = b$' has the value the true if a and b are the true, or if a and b are the false. Otherwise it has the value false. The remaining case is that where one argument is a truth-value and the other a course of values. Here the answer is not so obvious. If we could show that the truth values actually *were* courses of values, then this would reduce to the case where both arguments are courses of values, and we would have an answer.

With the help of a brilliantly imaginative argument, Frege then shows that we are free to identify the true and the false with *any* two distinct courses of values ([1893], section 10). Accordingly, Frege chooses to represent the true by the course of values of the concept *being the true*, and the false by the course of values of the concept *being the false*. Now every object so far introduced in the system is a course of values, and it is determinate how we treat courses of values terms in his formal system.

The question of the nature of courses of values had profound implications for Frege's general philosophical outlook. I shall discuss them later. (See below, chapter 6, section (b) (iv).)

(v) The levels of functions

So far we have supposed that functions take only objects as arguments, and we have noted Frege's requirement that functions be defined for every object as argument. But certain functions do not take objects as arguments. Instead their arguments are functions. Those which take functions as arguments are functions of *higher level.* We find an expression for such a function when we consider Frege's way of representing generality in a sentence. Consider the sentence 'For all $\mathfrak{a}$, $P(\mathfrak{a})$', one identifiable sub-component of which is the concept-name (or 'predicate') '$P(\ )$'. If we remove this from the sentence we are left with the expression 'For all $\mathfrak{a}$, $(\ )\,\mathfrak{a}$', an incomplete expression which is the name of an incomplete entity, in other words a function. What are the arguments of this function? Clearly they are concepts. The function—we shall call it, following modern terminology, the 'universal quantifier'—takes a concept P to the true if every object falls under P, and to the false otherwise. Thus P must be a function which takes objects as arguments, or a first level function. The universal quantifier is a function which takes first level functions as its arguments, hence it is a second level function.

It is important to note that the values of this and all other functions are objects. Functions, whatever their level, take values which are objects. Why must this be? The arguments of a function are things which complete an entity which is in itself essentially incomplete. It is when the arguments have completed the function that a value results. Thus the application of arguments to a function can only result in an object as value, never in something which is itself a function.

One function of third level appears in Frege's system. This is a function which represents generality with respect to first level functions instead of with respect to objects. Remember, that we have names of objects such as 'x' and 'y', object-variables, 'a', 'b', 'c', etc., and letters which replace these variables within a sign for generality, such as '$\mathfrak{a}$', '$\mathfrak{b}$', etc. We can make the same accommodation for functions. We have function names 'f', 'g', 'h', etc., function variables 'Φ', 'Ψ', etc., and also, something which we have not introduced so far, letters which can replace function-variables in a sign for generality. Here, as in the case of generality with respect to objects, we use Gothic letters. In fact the only letter that we shall need will be the Gothic '$\mathfrak{f}$'.

Now consider a second level function which takes as arguments first level functions of one variable. In general we can symbolise such a function as follows ([1893], section 25):

$$M_{\beta}\,(\Phi(\beta))$$

Here 'Φ' is a variable which can be replaced by names of first level functions of one argument. Since, for such an argument, we must obtain an object as value, we need a way of binding the variable which goes along with the name of any function that we substitute for 'Φ'. That is why we write 'β' as a subscript on the second order function name '*M*' and in the place where the argument of the first level function will go. Substituting the function name '$f(\xi)$' for the variable 'Φ', and binding the variable 'ξ', we get the object name

$$M_{\beta}(f(\beta))$$

which is an expression without gaps in it. Suppose that *M* always takes truth-values as values. *M* is a second level concept under which first level concepts of one argument fall. Then

$$M_{\beta}(f(\beta))$$

says that the function $f(\xi)$ falls under the concept *M*. Suppose now that we want to say that *all* first level functions of one argument fall under *M*. We replace '*f*' by a Gothic letter '$\mathfrak{f}$' and introduce a sign for generality thus:

$$\smile^{\mathfrak{f}}\; M_{\beta}(\mathfrak{f}(\beta))$$

This says that all first level functions of one argument fall under the concept *M*. If from this expression we remove the name of the second level concept '*M*' we have an incomplete expression

$$\smile^{\mathfrak{f}}\; (\;)_{\beta}(\mathfrak{f}(\beta))$$

which is the name of a third level function. For any second level function *M* as argument, this function takes the value true if every first level function of one argument falls under it, and takes the value false in all other cases. Here we have a third level function which represents generality with respect to first order functions, as before we had a second order function which represents generality with respect to objects.

A function which takes objects as its arguments cannot also take functions. Suppose that $f(\xi)$ takes objects as arguments. If we try also to put a function name in the argument place we shall have a name of the form '$f(g(\;))$', which is still an incomplete expression, and hence not the name of a value of the function. In the case of the second level function *universal quantification*, we can take a function name '$f(\xi)$' and fit it into the gap in the function expression, because that expression absorbs the argument place of '$f(\xi)$' into its structure. The variable becomes bound and is therefore represented by a

Gothic letter. In Frege's symbolism, the quantifier is written

$$—\!\overset{\mathfrak{a}}{\smile}\!—(\ )(\mathfrak{a})$$

If we complete this expression by adding the function name '$f(\ )$' we arrive at the expression

$$—\!\overset{\mathfrak{a}}{\smile}\!—f(\mathfrak{a})$$

which is a complete expression, and names a truth-value.

Another example of a second level function is the function which takes every first level function to its course of values (*ibid*, section 22). We represent this in the following way. Remember that if $f(x)$ is a function, then its course of values is represented by the expression '$\grave{\varepsilon} f(\varepsilon)$'. This is the name of an object. Let 'Φ' be a variable which can be replaced by names of functions instead of by names of objects. If in the expression '$\grave{\varepsilon} f(\varepsilon)$' we replace the function name 'f' by the variable 'Φ' we obtain the name of a second level function. For any first level function as argument of this function we obtain as value the corresponding course of values.

The situation becomes somewhat more complicated when we consider functions of several variables. Functions of the first level can have one or many arguments, each of which is an object, and second level functions can have one or more arguments, each of which is a first level function. But a second level function may take as its arguments first level functions of one variable, or two variables, and so on. We can even consider functions of several variables where the variables are not all of the same level. A function might have two argument places, one of which can be occupied by objects, the other by first level functions of one argument. In this way the complexity of the hierarchy ramifies considerably. But all that we require is a way of telling, from the expression for the function, what kind of arguments can occupy its argument places, and this requirement is satisfied in Frege's system.

(vi) Some applications

Frege regarded his distinction between concepts of different levels as of great philosophical importance. Let us look at two applications of the distinction.

We have seen how, in Frege's system, generality with respect to individuals appears as a second order concept. A statement of the form 'There is an x such that $P(x)$' appears in Frege's notation as

$$\top\!\overset{\mathfrak{a}}{\smile}\!\top P(\mathfrak{a})$$

Within this sentence we can discern a structure consisting of function-name and argument-name. If we remove the name '*P*' from the sentence we are left with the name of a second level function

$$\neg\overset{\mathfrak{a}}{\smile}\neg\,(\ )(\mathfrak{a})$$

which takes a first level concept *P* to the true if there is an object which falls under *P*, and to the false otherwise. This second level concept corresponds to existence. Existence appears here as a concept which applies to first level concepts — in fact to those first level concepts under which at least one thing falls. For Frege this is not simply a matter of notation. He thought it intrinsically absurd to regard existence as a first level concept and to say of individuals that they exist. In the sentence 'There are square roots of four', we cannot, he claims, be talking about the individual that is the square root of four, and saying of it that it exists. Rather, we are saying of the concept *Being a square root of four* that it is instantiated, ([1903*b*], p. 270 (35)).

If what was being referred to in this sentence were the object or objects which are the square roots of four we ought to be able to substitute names of those objects for the expression 'square root of four' and thereby effect a transformation of the sentence which preserves truth (see below, chapter 4, section (b) (iv)). But to say 'There are two' makes no sense; it has no truth value, so the transformation cannot be a truth preserving one. Similarly we can say 'There is (or there exists) a continent directly to the south of Europe', but we are not thereby saying that Africa exists.

> Not only is it linguistically improper to say 'there is Africa' or 'there is Charlemagne', but it is nonsensical [*unsinnig*] (*ibid.*, p. 271 (35)).

Perhaps Frege thought that sentences such as these are not well suited to the attempt to say something informative or contentful. For if we say of an individual that it has a certain property, then to check whether the sentence is true we have to identify the individual and see whether it does have the property in question. But clearly this cannot happen with attributions of existence. We cannot *first* get hold of the individual concerned and *then* check to see whether it has existence, for by having identified the individual we have thereby shown that it exists. Perhaps it was something like this which provoked Kant to claim that existence is not a property of things because to be told that something has existence is not to be told anything informative about it ([1787], p. 628). Against this it will be objected that certain statements which seem at least to attribute existence to an individual are perfectly in order. After all, it may be historically interesting to be told that Charlemagne exists (or rather existed). I think that this and other objections can be dealt with, but we shall not discuss them here. Instead we shall simply note how Frege applied his theory of existence to the so-called 'ontological argument' for the existence of God. Descartes claimed that God must exist because, roughly speaking, the concept of God involves the concept of existence. Among the characteristics of the concept God is that of having every perfection. And one perfection is existence, in the sense that a being who did not exist would be less perfect than a being who did exist.[7]

Frege draws a number of distinctions which are relevant here. We are familiar with the distinction between objects, concepts of first level, and concepts of second level. In addition, Frege makes a distinction between one concept *falling within* another concept, and one concept being *subordinate* to another. A first level concept can fall within one of second level, as the concept *being a prime number* falls within the second level concept of *existence*. One first level concept can be subordinate to another of first level: if we say that all squares are rectangles we mean that the concept *being square* is subordinate to that of *being a rectangle*. Frege says that the concept *being rectangular* is one of the *characteristics* of the concept *being square*; being rectangular is part of what it takes to be square.

According to Descartes' version of the ontological argument, the concept *God*, or *divine being* has as one of its characteristics the concept of existence; existence is constitutive of divinity. In Fregean terms this would mean that existence is subordinate to divinity, and this can happen only if divinity and existence are concepts of the same level. But while divinity is a first level concept, existence, Frege argues, is one of second level. Hence the one cannot be subordinate to the other. Divinity can *fall within* the second level concept of existence; it will do so just in case there is an individual which satisfies the requirements of being divine. To determine whether or not this is the case is exactly to determine whether God exists. But what Frege has shown, if we accept his claim that existence is a second level concept, is that to determine whether or not God exists we cannot, as Descartes suggests, simply examine the concept *divine being* and see whether one of its characteristics is existence. Existence can never be a characteristic of a first level concept.

Frege also applied his distinction of levels to a group of problems concerning the nature of the axiomatic method. Let us look briefly at the way in which these problems had arisen.

It had long been recognised that there were various defects in Euclid's presentation of geometry. It was understood, for instance, that Euclid made use of certain assumptions which he did not state as axioms or postulates. Certain of his proofs require us to accept facts about a drawn figure which are given to us by visual intuition, but which have no justification within the axiomatic system itself. Another difficulty was that it was thought that some of his explicit assumptions were not of sufficient certainty to provide a firm basis for the science of geometry. Euclid postulated that, given a straight line, and a point away from the line, there is one and only one line which can be drawn through the point and which is parallel to the first line.[8] Is this a self-evident truth? Some doubted that it was, and tried to avoid the difficulty by proving the assumption (called the 'parallel postulate') from the other axioms of the theory.[9] If this could be done, the assumption would be justified by being shown to be a consequence of assumptions which are themselves indubitable. In fact no one was able to do this because the parallel postulate does not follow logically from the conjunction of the other basic assumptions in Euclid's system. In the light of the persistent failure to prove the parallel postulate, mathematicians turned to the possibility that there might be some reasonable alternative to the postulate. They set up systems, called 'non-Euclidean geometries', in which some statement which contradicts the parallel postulate is assumed. Various systems of this kind had been investigated by the late nineteenth century.

Other efforts were expended in trying to avoid some further shortcomings of Euclidean geometry. New and more comprehensive axiom systems were devised, most notably by David Hilbert, the great German mathematician, in *The Foundations of Geometry*, published in 1899 and subsequently revised a number of times. The book is also important because it takes up questions which we now recognise as belonging to metamathematics — the mathematical study of mathematical systems. One such question was whether or not the parallel postulate could be proved from the other axioms of the system. The question can be approached in either of two ways. We can try, within the system of Euclidean geometry, to prove the postulate as a theorem: this would be the conventional mathematical way of approaching the problem. The second involves treating the system itself as an object of study, like any other mathematical object, and trying to prove that the postulate is independent of the other axioms by a method to be described in a moment.

Hilbert also undertook the task of showing that the system of axioms for Euclidean geometry is a consistent one. As long as it was thought that Euclidean geometry was simply a representation of the facts about space, the question of consistency could hardly arise. If the axioms are true statements about physical or perceptual space, they must be consistent. But the development of non-Euclidean geometries suggested that there might be some question as to *which* of these systems applies to space. The consistency of Euclidean geometry could no longer be taken for granted.

Frege, as we have seen, adopted an attitude towards our knowledge of geometry which made these kinds of investigation seem pointless. For him, Euclidean geometry simply expressed our intuitions about space — intuitions which are beyond the possibility of serious doubt. The axioms must be true, hence they are consistent. Though Frege expressed this point very forcefully on many occasions, he never gave a detailed defence of the view that our knowledge of Euclidean geometry has, as Kant said, apodictic certainty. Perhaps he thought that Kant's arguments required no further support. In any case, this is not the aspect of his disagreement with Hilbert that I wish to concentrate on here. Instead we shall turn to the question of definitions within an axiomatic theory.

Frege had read Hilbert's *Foundations of Geometry* when it first appeared. He then wrote to Hilbert, putting forward certain objections. A brief correspondence ensued. Dissatisfied with Hilbert's position as clarified by the exchange of letters, Frege published an article in two parts in which he set out his objections. Hilbert did not reply, but Alwin Korselt, a mathematician and school teacher, published a defence of Hilbert's views. It is doubtful, however, whether Korselt's position corresponds very closely to Hilbert's. Frege concluded the debate with a long article in three parts.[10] We shall attempt, not to follow the debate as it unfolded over time, but merely to distill from it the main issue as it relates to Frege's distinction between concepts of different levels.

In an axiomatic system we have to accept certain notions as undefined, just as we have to accept certain statements (the axioms) without proof. One of Hilbert's methodological innovations was to construe the axioms of a theory in such a way as to circumvent this limitation. He presents a set of geometrical axioms which contain terms like 'point', 'line' and 'between'. These terms are undefined primitives in the traditional sense. But, says Hilbert, we can take the axioms themselves as definitions of these terms in the following sense. We shall say that anything is a point, or that something lies between two other things, if it satisfies the axioms taken together. That is, the terms 'point', 'line', 'between', etc., are capable of being interpreted in a number of ways; the axioms do not give them any particular interpretation. All that is important is that they be interpreted in such a way that the axioms come out true under that interpretation. The axioms sum up, as it were, what conditions a set of concepts and relations must satisfy if the objects falling under them are to count as geometrical objects.

From Hilbert's point of view, it was not desirable that we should specify precisely the meanings of the terms occurring in the theory, or in other words specify the *intended* interpretation of that theory. The theory is not supposed to be a theory about objects which are intrinsically points, lines, planes, triangles, etc. Anything can count as a point or a line as long as it bears certain relations to other objects, and it is the task of the axioms to specify what these relations are. One of Hilbert's aims was to eschew an ontology of intrinsically geometric objects in favour of a higher and more neutral viewpoint. On the traditional view, before one can understand an axiomatic theory one has to understand the meanings of the primitive terms which occur in it. But on Hilbert's view this is unnecessary. It simply does not matter what interpretation one gives to these terms, as long as that interpretation renders the axioms themselves true. The only constraints on interpretation are set by the axioms themselves. It is in this sense that the axioms 'define' the primitive terms.

Hilbert then puts the idea of different interpretations of the axioms to use in proving their consistency and independence. Let us look at the notion of independence. Suppose that we have a set Σ of statements, and we are interested to know whether one of them, S, is derivable from the rest. If it turns out that S is not so derivable then we say that S is *independent* of the other statements. If Σ is our set of axioms, we clearly want all the statements in Σ to be independent, since if any one of them is not independent it can be derived as a theorem and the number of axioms reduced. Hilbert's method of proving independence is as follows. The axioms of his system are, as we have seen, statements which contain terms like 'point', 'line' and 'between', which can receive different interpretations. On some interpretations the axioms will be true and on others they will be false. It may also be possible to choose an interpretation which makes one of the axioms, *S*, false and the others true. If such an interpretation can be found, then *S* will have been shown to be independent from the other axioms. If *S* followed logically from the other axioms then it would not be possible to find an interpretation which made *S* false and the other axioms true, for if *S were* a consequence of the other axioms then any interpretation which made those axioms true would also make *S* true.

Frege's first objection to this procedure was to claim that Hilbert's geometrical axioms are not, properly speaking, axioms at all. An axiom, for Frege, is a true Thought, a Thought being the sense of a sentence (see below, chapter 4, section (b)). But Hilbert's axioms are not Thoughts, for they are not complete entities. Rather they are second level concepts and relations. Each sentence expressing an axiom contains terms which can receive a variety of interpretations. Terms like 'point' and 'line' do not refer to concepts but rather act as variables for which terms referring to determinate concepts can be substituted. Thus the expressions used to formulate the axioms are not sentences but names of functions which, when first level concept-words are substituted in them, take truth values as values and thereby *become* sentences. These 'pseudo-axioms' as Frege calls them are not the same as the axioms of Euclidean geometry which are complete Thoughts, and in the expressions for which terms like 'point' and 'line' do have determinate meanings ([1906*a*], p. 305(84)). Thus Hilbert's method does not at all show that the axioms[11] of Euclidean geometry are independent of one another; it shows that the second order 'pseudo-axioms' are independent of one another.

This objection is not a very convincing one, however. It need only be pointed out that in proving the independence of the psuedo-axioms we are thereby proving the independence of any special case of them. Suppose we have two statements *P* and *Q* and we want to show that *P* is independent of *Q*. Suppose that terms '*a*' and '*b*' occur in the statements. We find new interpretations for '*a*' and '*b*' and thus arrive at new statements P_1 and Q_1, where Q_1 is true and P_1 false. We have proceeded in three stages. We started with axioms *P* and *Q*. We then converted *P* and *Q* into pseudo-axioms $P(x)$ and $Q(y)$ by replacing the terms '*a*' and '*b*' by variables. We then substituted new terms for the variables and arrived at expressions for new axioms P_1 and Q_1. In showing that P_1 is false and Q_1 true we have shown that P is independent of Q, and we have done so by means of the pseudo-axioms $P(x)$ and $Q(y)$. But it would be quite wrong to object that we have only proved the independence of the pseudo-axioms themselves. Rather we have shown that any statements which result from the substitution of terms for the variables in the pseudo-axioms $P(x)$ and $Q(y)$ are independent of one another, and hence we have shown that, as a special case of this, P and Q are independent of one another.

In one place Frege gives a much more sympathetic hearing to the idea of independence proofs. He introduces the idea of a translation *within* a language. Such a translation will be a function from words in one grammatical category to different words in the same category. Thus one translation might translate 'is red' into 'is prime', 'lies between' into 'is the sum of', 'Napoleon' into 'Gottlob Frege', etc. Suppose now that we have a set of sentences and wish to see whether some member S of the set is independent of the other members. We look around for a translation that will translate S into a sentence S_1 which is false, and all the other sentences into sentences which are true. Suppose, to take a trivial example, we wanted to show that the sentence 'snow is white' is independent from the sentence 'snow is cold'. We choose a translation which correlates 'snow' with 'rain', 'white' with 'white', and 'cold' with 'cold'. (It simply leaves these two words unchanged.) Under this translation we get two new sentences: 'rain is white' and 'rain is cold'. The first is false, the second true. This shows that there is a way of interpreting the terms of the first pair of sentences which makes the first false and the second true. Hence the first is independent of the second. In essence, Frege has described the method that Hilbert wants to adopt ([1906*a*], pp. 321-3 (108-10)).

Frege raises certain difficulties about this possibility which are of great interest, but he seems to think that if the difficulties can be met, then the method is an unexceptionable one. An important difficulty concerns the limits to translation. For if we can take a pair of distinct sentences and perform translations on *all* the terms that they contain, we shall certainly be able to find interpretations which make the one true and the other false. Thus, intuitively, 'It is raining' follows from 'It is raining and it is cold'. But if we choose a translation which correlates 'and' with 'or' the result will be a pair of sentences the first of which could be false and the second true. Frege says that any translation must be limited by the requirement that those terms which express concepts and relations peculiar to logic itself are not to be translated into other terms.

Just as the concept *point* belongs to geometry, so logic too, has its own concepts and relations; and it is only in virtue of this that it can have a content. Towards what is thus proper to it, its relation is not at all formal. No science is completely formal; but even gravitational mechanics is formal to some degree, in so far as optical and chemical properties are all the same to it. To be sure, so far as it is concerned, bodies with different masses are not mutually replaceable; but in gravitational mechanics the difference of bodies with respect to their chemical properties does not constitute a hindrance to their mutual replacement. To logic, for example, there belong the following: negation, identity, subsumption, subordination of concepts. And here logic brooks no replacement. It is true that in an inference one can replace Charlemange by Sahara, and the concept *king* by the concept *desert*, in so far as this does not alter the truth of the premises. But one may not thus replace the relation of identity by the lying of a point in a plane. Because for identity there hold certain logical laws which as such need not be numbered among the premises . . . One can express it metaphorically like this: About what is foreign to it logic knows only what occurs in the premises; about what is proper to it it knows all (*ibid*, p. 322 (109–10)).

The problem which Frege is trying to deal with has turned out to be one of the fundamental problems of philosophical logic; that of how to specify the purely logical components of a sentence; those which contribute to its logical form rather than to its content. Of course we can simply rule by fiat that certain terms like 'all', 'some', 'not', 'and', are to be treated as logical, and that hence in any translation they will be left unchanged. But this is simply to avoid the problem of how to give a non-arbitrary specification of what it takes for a term to be a logical term. As far as I know, Frege was the first person to pose the problem clearly.

(vii) The paradox of concepts

There is a much discussed difficulty associated with Frege's distinction between concept and object. The difficulty, which has come to be known as 'the paradox of the concept *horse*' from an example which Frege discusses, arises as follows.

Consider a predicate '$f(\xi)$'. This is an incomplete expression, the 'ξ' simply indicating the argument-place of the function. This predicate is the name of some concept. We ought, therefore, to be able to say

(1) '$f(\xi)$' is the name of X

But '$f(\xi)$' is not a complete name. If it were it would be the name of an object, in which case it would not be a predicate. Hence it must be the name of an incomplete entity or function. But then in (1) the expression 'X' must be incomplete. If it were not, it would be the name of an object, and (1) would say that '$f(\xi)$' is the name of an object, which is not what is intended. So (1) must be written in the form

$$(2)\ \text{`}f(\xi)\text{' is the name of } X(\zeta).$$

But (2) is not a sentence. It contains an expression, '$X(\zeta)$', with an unfilled argument-place, and so cannot be an expression which is the name of an object. But a sentence *is* a name of an object (actually a truth value).[12]

More evident still is that we cannot say things like 'the concept *horse* is the name of a concept', since 'the concept *horse*' is a complete rather than an incomplete expression, and so cannot be the name of anything but an object.

Frege also argues that 'The concept *horse*' cannot name a concept because, if it did, it would have to name the same concept that is named by 'is a horse'. As we shall see, Frege has a principle according to which expressions which name the same entity should be intersubstitutable in a sentence without change of truth (see below, chapter 4, section (b)(iv)). So if 'The concept *horse*' and 'is a horse' were names of the same entity, they would be intersubstitutable in this way, but they are not, since 'Dennis is a horse' and 'Dennis the concept *horse*' do not have the same truth-value (the latter having no truth value) ([1892*a*], pp. 173–4 (49–50)).

The point seems to be this. Only an essentially *predicative* expression can be the name of a concept. But we can never use such an expression to refer to a concept, exactly because the expression is predicative. Predicates can be applied to names of things, they cannot be used to name things themselves.

Frege discussed the difficulty in some detail in his article 'On Concept and Object' of 1892 ([1892*a*]). The difficulty, he says, reflects an irremediable deficiency in language; certain things just cannot be said. We must rely on the sympathetic understanding of a listener, someone who does not 'begrudge a pinch of salt' (*ibid* p. 177 (54)).

This explanation of the difficulty is not a very convincing or satisfactory one. There is certainly here a difficulty for Frege's theory of language, but it is far from clear that he can lay the blame on language itself. There is nothing in the phenomenon of language use to indicate that reference to concepts involves a difficulty of this kind. And if we cannot say what we intend to say about concepts, how then is it that we do seem to understand each other? We can be sympathetic to a speaker if we know what he means to say, but realise that he has not used quite the right words. But if, as Frege says, we are dealing with something for which it is not even *possible* to find the right words, how do we know what he wants to say?

In another place, however, Frege tackles the problem in a rather different way. He tries to show, in fact, that we can refer to concepts without becoming involved in the difficulties just described. Michael Dummett has taken this solution up and elaborated it in his book on Frege ([1973], chapter 7). Let us look at Frege's idea.

In an article written a few years after 'On Concept and Object', but not published during his lifetime, Frege returned to the problem of the concept *horse* ([1892-5]). One way in which the difficulty arises concerns statements of equality. Suppose we want to specify when two concepts are equal; to say, in fact, that they are equal just in case their extensions are the same ([1894], p. 184 (80)). It seems that we cannot even formulate this proposition, for we cannot say that two concepts are equal. We cannot write '$f(\xi)=g(\zeta)$' and hope to get a sentence, since this expression contains gaps, and a sentence is a complete expression. But Frege suggests another way of saying the same thing. At this point I must anticipate some material from the next section. We shall say that a predicate *refers to* a concept, and that a concept is the reference of a predicate.[13] We shall now express the identity of two concepts in the following way.

(1) What the concept word '*f*' refers to is the same as what the concept word '*g*' refers to ([1892-5], p. 133 (122))

Now can this be a legitimate way of expressing the identity of two concepts? What Frege seems to have in mind is that an expression like 'what the concept word "*f*" refers to', is both a name of a concept and a predicate. We can use it to refer to the concept *f*, and we can also use it predicatively in such contexts as 'Jesus is what the concept word "man" refers to', which is equivalent to 'Jesus is a man' (*ibid*).

This theory faces several difficulties. First of all it is Frege's view that the copula 'is' forms part of the predicate; it is not a separate part of the sentence left over after the subject and the predicate have been removed.[14] Thus 'Jesus is a man' has 'is a man' as its predicate. So the predicate in 'Jesus is what the concept word "man" refers to', is 'is what the concept word "man" refers to'. And *this* expression cannot be used to refer to a concept. We cannot say 'Is what the concept word "*f*" refers to is the same as is what the concept word "*g*" refers to'. Even if we ignore this difficulty there is another. Frege's solution trades on the fact that expressions like 'what the concept word "*f*" refers to' can act both as proper names and as predicative expressions. But all that this shows is that such an expression is sometimes (in some contexts) a proper name and sometimes a predicate. Which one it is depends on the context, and in no context is it both; an expression cannot fulfill both the role of a subject and a predicate in the same sentence. In 'What the concept word "*f*" refers to is the same as what the concept word "*g*" refers to' two expressions are being used as proper names of concepts. They are not, therefore, predicates. It follows that in (1) we do not have what Frege requires — a predicative expression being used as a name of a concept (see Dudman [1972]).

Although others have elaborated Frege's solution, there is evidence that he abandoned it. He did not publish the paper in which it was contained, nor did he refer to this solution in later work. He often discussed the problem of reference to concepts, but always reiterated his earlier view that the difficulty is due to a deficiency of language that we simply have to accept (see e.g. (1906*e*], p. 210 (193) and [1919], p. 275 (255)).

(viii) A philosophical problem

In view of the difficulties about the unsaturatedness of functions, difficulties which Frege never adequately solved, why did he continue to insist upon unsaturatedness as an essential characteristic of functions? What were the advantages to him of this view?

Frege seems to have thought of the theory as offering solutions to two philosophical problems. The first is one that is most familiar to us as a problem about the relation between things and properties, or, in more traditional terminology, between particulars and universals. Suppose that a thing (a particular) has a property (a universal). Is there then a relation which holds between the particular and the universal, and in virtue of which the particular partakes, as it were, in that universal? Further, must there also be a relation between the relation, the particular and the universal in virtue of which the relation relates the particular and the universal? Once we start down this road it seems that we can never stop introducing new relations.[15] According to Frege, however, we do not have to undertake the journey at all. We need say only that the unsaturated nature of the property (concept) is such that the property and the object which has this property fit together naturally and without the intervention of any third element.

In the sentence 'Two is prime' we find a relation designated: that of subsumption. We may also say that the object falls under the concept *prime*, but if we do so, we must not forget the imprecision of linguistic expression we have just mentioned. This also creates the impression that the relation of subsumption is a third element supervenient upon the object and the concept. This is not the case: the unsaturatedness of the concept brings it about that the object, in effecting the saturation, engages immediately with the concept, without need of any special cement. Object and concept are fundamentally made for each other, and in subsumption we have their fundamental union ([1906*c*], p. 193(178)).

The second problem is a little more difficult to describe, because it presupposes some material which we have not yet introduced. It concerns the explanation of the fact that sentences and what they express — Thoughts — have a kind of unity. I shall defer discussion of it until a later section.

(b) Sense and Reference

(i) Introduction

So far I have talked about expressions representing or designating functions and objects without discussing in detail the relations between language and the world which language describes. Until the 1890s Frege used the terms 'reference' (*'Bedeutung'*), 'sense' (*'Sinn'*), and 'content' (*'Inhalt'*) when he talked about the relations between language and the world, without distinguishing clearly between the meanings of these terms. At the same time that he argued for the distinction between concepts and objects (in the early 1890s), he proposed another important distinction of a rather different kind. This is the distinction between *Sinn* and *Bedeutung*. No special problems arise concerning the translation of '*Sinn*' — its English equivalent is 'sense' (though, as I shall argue later, there are serious problems about understanding what Frege meant by it). Difficulties have arisen, however, over the translation of *Bedeutung*; I shall say something more about this later. In this section I shall use 'reference' for '*Bedeutung*' and 'to refer' for the verb '*bedeuten*'. This is a translation which, though somewhat unsatisfactory, has become sufficiently entrenched to make a new choice seem odd. Recently 'meaning' has been canvassed as an alternative to 'reference'.[16] For reasons which will become clear only later, I think that this word has misleading connotations.

From the standpoint of much contemporary philosophy, Frege's theory of sense and reference appears to be his most enduring achievement. It is not that the theory is universally accepted; there is an important literature devoted to criticising it.[17] But Frege's characterisation of the dual notions of sense and reference is taken to be the basis for modern semantical investigations. In this chapter my concern is not with later developments of the theory, but solely with the theory as it was developed and presented by Frege himself. I shall start by outlining the major points of the theory, then I shall give a brief account of the way in which it emerged from Frege's early logical investigations. I shall then try to examine and clarify what Frege says about sense, reference, and the problem of identity in his famous paper 'On Sense and Reference'. Only in a later chapter shall we try to answer the question 'What kinds of things are senses?'

(ii) The distinction

According to Frege, every entity is either a function or an object, and every linguistic expression (unless it is a variable, a bracket, or something called the 'judgement stroke', to be explained later) is either the name of a function or the name of an object. Names of objects are proper names, names of functions are function names. Proper names include those which are proper names in the ordinary sense, like 'Napoleon', 'Venus', etc., together with descriptive phrases like 'the greatest military leader of France', 'the second planet from the sun', etc. More surprisingly, sentences are proper names. A sentence is the name of a truth-value. Truth-values are objects, so sentences are proper names. What an expression names is the *reference* of that expression. The thing named is what the expression refers to.

Every expression has a *sense* as well as a reference. Roughly speaking, the sense of an expression is the information which it conveys. Every true sentence refers to the truth-value true. But two true sentences can say different things, and have different contents. The content of a sentence is the Thought expressed by it—its sense.[18] Frege draws the same distinction for all other expressions. 'The author of *Waverley*' and 'The author of *Guy Mannering*' are proper names which have the same reference (Sir Walter Scott), but different senses; the expressions convey different information about Scott. Now we shall discuss the reference and the sense of a function name.

(iii) Sense, reference and functions

While Frege's view that proper names have both a sense and a reference, and that both are objects, is so clearly expressed as to be beyond doubt, the corresponding doctrine for functions is a little harder to locate, particularly in his published works, and many writers on his philosophy have doubted that he held it. But a careful examination of his work shows, I think, that he did hold the doctrine. In an unpublished paper written probably as an appendix to 'On Sense and Reference', Frege says '[there] I distinguish between sense and reference in the first instance only for the case of proper names... The same distinction can also be drawn for concept words' ([1892-5], p. 128 (118)). First of all let us consider the references of functional expressions. In the *Basic Laws* Frege says

> If, from a proper name we remove a proper name that forms part of it . . . then I call that which we obtain by this means a name of a first level function of one argument ([1893], p. 43 (81)).

Thus functional expressions have reference, and what they name are functions. In an essay written in 1906 we find Frege discussing reasons why we should treat function names as having reference ([1906*e*], p. 209 (192)). He offers us three arguments: that if both a sentence and the proper names occurring in it have reference, it is implausible that the function names should be so different from these as to lack reference; if a relation holds between objects which belong to the realm of reference then the relation itself ought to belong to that realm; a proper name with reference can form part of a function name (as in 'is the wife of Socrates'), which makes it plausible that the rest of the function name also has reference.

These arguments are far from being conclusive, as those opposed to the notion of reference for function names have been quick to point out (e.g. Dudman [1972], p. 70). Like most plausibility arguments, they lend plausibility to the doctrine only for those already favourable to it. But they do indicate how firmly committed Frege was to the notion of reference for function names. Now to the question of sense. In his last published articles Frege placed great emphasis on the idea that Thoughts (the senses of sentences) have a structure like the structure of sentences.

> If, then, we look upon Thoughts as composed of simple parts, and take these, in turn, to correspond to the simple parts of sentences, we can understand how a few parts of sentences can go to make up a great multitude of sentences, to which, in

> turn, there correspond a great multitude of Thoughts. But the question now arises how a Thought comes to be constructed, and how its parts are so combined together that the whole amounts to something more than the parts taken separately ([1923], p. 378(55). See also [1918*b*], p. 367(38)).

Frege discussed Thoughts which are constructed from other Thoughts, such as ⌜not-A⌝, ⌜A and B⌝, ⌜if A then B⌝, etc. These, he says, consist of a complete sense, the original Thought, together with an incomplete part, such as is expressed by 'not' or 'and'. Now of course simple sentences are structured as well. A sentence like 'Mont Blanc is over 4000 m high' consists of the parts 'Mont Blanc' and 'is over 4000 m high', the latter being a name of a concept, something incomplete. 'Mont Blanc', in addition to having a reference, has a sense. What about 'is over 4000 m high'? This also has a sense, which, like its reference, is incomplete (see e.g. [1892*b*], p. 156 (71) and [1906*e*], p. 209 (192)). It is clear, then, that function-names have a sense as well as a reference. Indeed Frege at one point suggests that incompleteness applies more naturally to senses than to references ([1892-5], p. 129 (119)). Two of Frege's arguments for the reference of function names can be translated into arguments for sense. If both a sentence and a proper name have sense, it is implausible that function names should be so different as to lack it. If a function name can contain a proper name having sense, surely the rest of the function name has a sense also? Perhaps most important, Frege's dual principle for the determination of a sentence's reference (sense) by the references (senses) of its parts demands that all the expressions which go to make up a sentence have both a sense and a reference.

We now have two distinctions which cut across one another. Expressions are names, either proper names or function names, and every name has a reference and a sense. Both the reference and the sense of a name are entities, and accordingly they must be either objects or functions. If a name is a proper name then both its sense and its reference are objects. If a name is a function name its sense and its reference are both incomplete. The reference of a function name like 'is red' is a function which takes objects as arguments and truth-values as values. What is the sense of a function name? Frege never explicitly describes them as functions, though he insists that they are incomplete. Since they are incomplete they cannot be objects, and Frege often speaks as if the function-object distinction is ontologically exhaustive: everything is either one or the other. And if Frege were impressed by the argument I gave as to why an incomplete entity must be a function, he would have allowed that the senses of incomplete expressions are functions. If we do take these senses to be functions, what are their arguments and values? The sense of 'is red' would most naturally be construed as a function which takes the sense of a name like 'Napoleon' as argument, giving as value the sense of the sentence 'Napoleon is red'. The sense of a concept word would thus be a function from the senses of proper names to Thoughts.

(iv) The relations between sense and reference

In the course of this section I discuss some important theses which Frege held about sense and reference. First, sense determines reference in so far as with each sense there is associated at most one reference, while a given reference may have many senses associated with it. The expressions 'Sir Walter Scott' and 'The author of Waverley' have the same reference — they are names of the same person — but each has a different sense. Frege says

> The regular connexion between a sign, its sense and its reference, is of such a kind that to the sign there corresponds a definite sense and to that in turn a definite reference, while to a given reference (an object) there does not belong only a single sign ([1892*b*], p. 114 (58)).

In the case of sentences this means that the sense, the Thought expressed, determines the truth value of the sentence. We must assume here that the state of the world is something given. If the facts were other than they actually are the truth-value of a Thought might be other than it actually is. When Frege says that sense determines reference he means that someone who knew which Thought a certain sentence expressed, and also knew the facts about the world, would then know whether the sentence was true or not. But, clearly, if one knew the facts about the world together with the truth-value of a sentence, one could not deduce from that what the sense of the sentence was.

So far we have left open the possibility that an expression may have sense but no reference — that there may be no entity of which it is the name. And indeed, as Frege notes, not every expression in our ordinary language has a reference (see [1892*b*], p. 145 (58)). But on Frege's view this is a deficiency to be avoided in a 'logically perfect' language, an ideal to which he often appealed. It is to be avoided by stipulating that, in the case of failure of intended reference, the expression is to have an entity associated with it by convention which will then count as its reference. Thus we might decide to stipulate that 'the least rapidly converging series' has the number zero as its reference, because it is a mathematical fact that there is no least rapidly converging series in the ordinary sense.

This theory has some strange consequences. On Frege's view if a sentence contains an expression without reference then the whole cannot have reference; it must be a sentence without a truth-value. But in avoiding names without reference, and thereby sentences without truth-values, he has to admit as true certain sentences which are intuitively false. Thus if 'the least rapidly converging series' has conventional reference the number zero, it will be true, for example, that there is a least rapidly converging series, that the least rapidly converging series is not a series (unless we redefine 'series'), etc.

I said that on Frege's view, if a component of a sentence lacks reference, the sentence itself will lack reference (truth-value).[19] This is a consequence of Frege's dual principle that the sense (reference) of a complex expression is a function of the senses (references) of its parts. Given the sense and the reference of each component expression it is determined thereby what is the sense and the reference of the whole. And as in the case of a many place function in mathematics, if any of the argument places is left empty (if any of the component expressions has no sense or reference) the function itself will not take on a value. (The sentence will have no sense or reference.) Frege uses the idea that the whole is a function of its parts to argue that the sense and the reference of a sentence are, respectively, the Thought expressed and its truth-value. His method is to ask what aspect of the sentence as a whole is sensitive to changes which take place in the senses (references) of its parts, but insensitive to other kinds of change. Consider for instance

(1) The Evening Star is a body illuminated by the sun.

(2) The Morning Star is a body illuminated by the sun.

(2) is obtained from (1) by substituting the expression 'the Morning Star' for the expression 'the Evening Star'. But these two expressions are both names of the planet Venus, so the difference between (1) and (2) is not a difference at the level of reference. Accordingly, whatever reference is, it must be such that (1) and (2) have the same reference. But 'the Morning Star' and 'the Evening Star' have different senses. We can allow therefore that (1) and (2) have different senses.[20] Intuitively, (1) and (2) differ in their cognitive value, or information content. A person can believe one without

having to believe the other. One could know the one, and yet still learn something new by being told the other. Thus it seems reasonable to say that the sense of the sentence is the Thought, or cognitive content which it contains.

We know that the reference of (1) must be the same as that of (2). What important property do these two sentences share? They share the same truth-value. If the Morning Star *is* the Evening Star then anything true of the one must be true of the other, so (1) is true if and only if (2) is true. Frege concludes that the reference of a sentence is its truth-value. He gives another argument. Sometimes we are concerned with the reference of the parts of a sentence, as when we ask whether there really was an individual such as is described in the sentence 'Odysseus was set ashore at Ithaca while sound asleep'. But the reason that we are interested in the references of the parts of the sentence is because we are interested in whether or not the sentence is true. If we are not concerned with truth or falsity we can read Homer's story without wondering whether the characters described really existed. Thus there is a natural connection between the references of words and the truth values of sentences ([1892*b*], p. 149 (63)).

In 'On Sense and Reference', Frege concludes from this that 'We are therefore driven into accepting the *truth-value* of a sentence as constituting its reference', but in a letter to Russell of 1904 he concludes (more reasonably) only that the reference of a sentence must be 'most intimately connected with its truth' (see [1892*b*], p. 149 (63) and [1914], pp. 250-1 (232) and letter to Russell, p. 247 (165)).

Why treat sentences as names? Surely there is a very great difference between sentences and names in that one can use a sentence to say something, while one cannot use a name to the same purpose? We shall return to this when we discuss assertion (see below, chapter 4, section (d) (ii)). It has been suggested that Frege's theory that sentences are names derives from his view according to which sentences are to be analysed into function and argument names (Dudman [1970]). A sentence is constructed by filling the empty place of a function name with the name of an argument. This line of thought originated in the *Begriffsschrift* (see above, chapter 2, section (a) (ii)). Now when we consider a functional expression '$f(\xi)$' together with an expression 'a' for its argument we regard the resulting expression '$f(a)$' as a name of the value of the function for that argument. For example '2^2' is a name of the number four. Similarly, we might regard a sentence formed from a function name (concept word) and the name of an object as a name of the value of that function for the given argument. And since the value of a concept is always a truth-value, the sentence appears as a name of a truth-value. Since a sentence results from the completion of a function-name with an argument, it must be something complete itself. So what it names, a truth-value, must be an object.

(v) Indirect reference

I have said that the sense (reference) of a sentence is a function of the senses (references) of its parts. There seem to be important exceptions to this. Consider the following.

(3) Copernicus believed that the Morning Star has an elliptical orbit.

(4) Copernicus believed that the Evening Star has an elliptical orbit.

(3) could be true and (4) false, or *vice versa.* But (4) is obtained from (3) by a substitution which preserves reference. Moreover,

(5) Copernicus believed that Venus is a planet

(6) Copernicus believed that 2+2=4

need not have the same truth-value, for obvious reasons. But again (6) is obtained from (5) by substituting one expression ('Venus is a planet') for another ('2+2=4') where the one has the same reference (truth value) as the other. Frege's response to the difficulty was to say that the failure of the principle is only an apparent failure ([1892*b*], p. 152 (66)). In such contexts as these, words do not have their ordinary reference. When we report someone's beliefs by saying 'John believes that . . . ' the expression after 'that' does not signify a truth-value, but rather the content of John's belief, the thought expressed by the embedded sentence. In other words, what is normally the sense of an expression has become its reference. 'The morning star' and 'the evening star', though they normally have the same reference, normally have different senses. But in a case such as the one we are now considering, the ordinary sense has become the reference, and so we are no longer dealing with a substitution which preserves reference. A difference in truth-value between (3) and (4) and between (5) and (6) is therefore to be expected.

Frege's theory of 'indirect' reference faces many difficulties.[21] I shall briefly describe one of them. Consider

(7) Copernicus thought that Venus is a planet, and it is a planet.

This seems to make perfectly good sense. But it does so only if 'it' refers to the same thing that 'Venus' refers to, and on Frege's theory this is not the case with (7). 'Venus' is part of an embedded sentence, the component parts of which must have indirect reference. The reference of 'Venus' here is what we ordinarily take its sense to be. But 'it' cannot signify the ordinary sense of 'Venus', for then the latter part of the sentence would be equivalent to 'The sense of "Venus" is a planet' which is not at all what is intended. This suggests that if (7) is to be made sense of then, contrary to Frege's theory, 'Venus' has its usual reference here (see Linsky [1967], chapter III).

(vi) The unity of Thoughts

We are now in a position to discuss the second of the two problems that Frege's doctrine of the unsaturatedness of functions was intended to solve. We have seen that a sentence like 'Two is even' has a double aspect. 'Two' refers to an object, the number two, and 'is even' refers to a concept, *being even*. Here the object and the concept go together as complete and an incomplete entity to give a complete entity, a truth-value. But 'two' also has a sense, which is an object, and 'is even' has a sense which is incomplete. The sense of 'two' and the sense of 'is even' are related as are their references, and go together to give the sense of 'Two is even'. This is an object, actually a Thought.

Sometimes Frege speaks as if the Thought and the truth-value were *made up of* the concept and the object; that they are its parts.[22] This is a view which seems to have more intuitive appeal when we are considering senses than when we are considering references. It seems quite natural to say that a Thought has an internal structure that is given by its component parts. The relations between Thoughts, including logical relations, seem best explained by saying that they share certain structural features, and, perhaps, that they share certain common parts. The Thought that two is prime and the Thought that three is odd seem to share a common structure, while the Thought that two is prime and the Thought that two is even share in addition to structure a common part, the sense of 'two'.

A truth-value, on the other hand, does not seem to require this explanation in terms of constituent parts. There does not seem to be any intuitive sense in which the true is composed of parts such as the number two and the concept *being prime*. Also, difficulties arise if we extend the idea of composition to functions and arguments in general. The value of the function *being the capital of* for the argument Denmark is Copenhagen. But does that mean that Copenhagen is composed of parts, one of which is Denmark? How can Denmark be a part of Copenhagen?[23]

Ignorning these general difficulties for a moment, it is clear that Frege saw the natural fitting together of concept and object as offering an explanation of the phenomenon which he called the 'unity of the Thought'. The phenomenon itself is not easy to describe in detail. What seems to be meant is that a Thought is, in some intuitive sense, a unit rather than an agglomeration of parts. Something similar seems to be the case with sentences. Sentences are not just lists of words. The words that make up the sentence go together in such a way as to make a unified whole. Frege wants to explain this unity in terms of the unsaturatedness of a function. The function is not simply juxtaposed with its arguments, it fits naturally together with them by virtue of the gaps it contains.

> ... the sense of the phrase 'the number 2' does not hold together with that of the expression 'the concept *prime number*' without a link. We apply such a link in the sentence 'the number 2 falls under the concept *prime number*'; it is contained in the words 'falls under', which need to be completed in two ways — by a subject and an accusative: and only because their sense is thus 'unsaturated' are they capable of serving as a link ([1892*a*], p. 177 (54). See also [1918*b*], p. 375 (48-9)).

I noted earlier that Frege never explicitly says that the senses of concept words are functions, though I argued that there is a natural way to characterise them as such. But our discussion of the unity of Thoughts suggests the possibility that there exists a rather deep ambiguity in Frege's conception of an incomplete entity. Perhaps he had two paradigms of incompleteness; the first, suitable for the treatment of the (ordinary) references of words and sentences, was that of a function. On this view the truth value of a sentence is a function of the truth values of the references of the parts of the sentence, without thereby the references of the parts of the sentence being *parts* of the truth value. The second paradigm of incompleteness would be that applicable to senses; the sense of a concept word would be a part of the sense of the sentence, and its incompleteness would be such as to explain propositional unity: the sense of the concept word is completed by the sense of a proper name to produce a united whole rather than simply a juxtaposition of entities. Exactly what this incompleteness is of course Frege was never able to explain in satisfactory terms.

If Frege had been clearer about the distinction between functions and incomplete entities which are not functions he might have avoided altogether the dubious claim that a truth value is composed of the references of the parts of a sentence. But he would have had to complicate his ontology by allowing for a category of entities which are neither objects nor functions; such entities as, for instance, the senses of concept words.

(vii) Concepts and properties

Now that we understand the distinctions between concepts and objects and between sense and reference we can say something about the relation between concepts and the more familiar notion of a property. Can an object's having a property be the same thing as an object's falling under a concept? Frege's answer is yes.[24] Let us concentrate first on concepts as the references of concept words or predicates. The concept *having a heart* is a function from objects to truth-values which takes an object to the true if it has a heart and to the false if it does not. But suppose that all the objects which have hearts are objects which have kidneys, and *vice versa*. Then *having a heart* and *having kidneys* will be concepts with the same extensions. Now Frege tells us that a relation corresponding to the relation of identity between objects holds for concepts just in case two concepts have the same extension. Putting it bluntly then, and in a way that, as we have noted, involves difficulties for Frege, *having a heart* and *having kidneys* will be identical concepts. But, intuitively speaking, having a heart and having kidneys are not the same property. If these properties are always co-instantiated that is just an accident which tells us nothing about the relations between the properties themselves. So here at least the idea of a concept seems not to work as an explication of the idea of a property.

Of course, expressions like 'having a heart' and 'having kidneys' may have, on Frege's view, the same references, but different senses. Perhaps we should look to the senses of concept-words for an account of properties. Here at least we do not get unwanted identities between concepts. Can we identify the property of having a heart with the (ordinary) sense of the expression 'having a heart'? Here again there are difficulties, for the sense of a concept-word appears not to be related to the right kind of objects in order for it to do the work of a property. The (ordinary) sense of the concept-word is something which relates the sense of 'Dennis' to the Thought expressed by 'Dennis has a heart'. To use a terminology to which Frege sometimes appealed, the property of having a heart belongs to the realm of reference, while the corresponding sense (the sense of 'having a heart') belongs to the realm of sense.

Now there are students of Frege's work who never tire of telling us that this sort of talk of a realm of sense and a realm of reference is illegitimate, since the distinction between sense and reference is a relative rather than an absolute one. The ordinary sense of 'Dennis' can be referred to by an expression like 'the sense of "Dennis"', and hence is the reference of that latter expression, so what is a sense can also be a reference. There are, however, important differences between sense and references of an absolute kind. If, for the sake of simplicity, we confine ourselves to a consideration of physical objects, it is clear that what is a reference cannot also be a sense. Dennis the dog belongs to the physical world. Yet anything which is a sense belongs, on Frege's characterisation, to the realm of the objective, non-physical. A sense is an abstract piece of information which goes with an expression. Dennis the dog cannot be a sense even though the sense of 'Dennis' can be a reference — the reference of the expression 'the sense of "Dennis"'. Dennis is, as it were, stuck in the realm of reference for life, and a relation between objects which are senses cannot be a relation that he enters into. In that case the sense of 'having a heart' cannot be the same as the property of having a heart.

Frege's theory of concepts does not seem to be an adequate explication of the notion of a property.

(c) The Development of the Theory of Sense and Reference

In the previous section I presented the theory of sense and reference as a relatively complete and self-contained entity which could be subjected to a fairly precise logical analysis. But the theory has a history as part of the development of Frege's thought; a history which is important for an understanding of the character of Frege's views. In this section I say something about this development.

(i) The contents of a judgement

Frege's formal language was intended as a device which would help to establish mathematical knowledge in a satisfactory way. The language was designed to make proofs perspicuous, and to enable the theorems of mathematics to be expressed in such a way as to do justice to their contents. Thus there is in the early *Begriffsschrift* some discussion of the way in which expressions of the language represent a 'content'.

It quickly becomes clear that, from the point of view of his later theory, the account which Frege offers here is a confused one. An expression which can be used to make a judgement, that is, a sentence, has a 'content' (*Inhalt*) which may or may not be asserted in any particular instance. Other kinds of expression have a content, but an unassertable one. Frege uses the words 'sense' (*Sinn*) and 'reference' (*Bedeutung*) for the content. The content of an expression is also said to be an 'idea' (*Vorstellung*), or combination of ideas ([1879*a*], sections 1 and 2). It seems as if Frege is here implicitly identifying the sense of an expression, its reference, its content, and the ideas which are in some way associated with it. Our problem is to try to make sense of these terms and to understand the theory which Frege expressed in the *Begriffsschrift* by means of them.

I shall argue that the *Begriffsschrift* does not contain a single identifiable theory of content, but that two different strands of thought corresponding to the later notions of sense and reference are present, one of which dominates the discussion of sentential content, while the discussion of naming and identity exhibits the influence of both.

At the beginning of the *Begriffsschrift*, in sections 2 and 3, Frege's concern is particularly with sentences. Indeed, the fact that the book beings with a discussion of judgement, the content of a judgement and the logical relations between sentences, underlines what I have already said about Frege's reversal of the traditional approach to language and knowledge whereby we start with concepts and arrive at propositions as things which are complex constructions from more basic material (see above, chapter 2, section (a) (i)). Frege starts with sentences and then goes on to show how they can be broken up into sub-sentential units.

What is the content of a sentence? Frege says that

> . . . the contents of two judgements can differ in two ways: first it may be the case that the consequences that can be derived from the first judgement combined with certain others can always be derived also from the second judgement combined also with the same others; secondly, this may not be the case . . . Now I call the part of the content which is the same in both the conceptual content. Since only this is significant for our 'conceptual writing' we need not distinguish between sentences which have the same conceptual content ([1879*a*], section 3).

At other times when Frege uses the word 'content' it is often clear that he means just this *conceptual* content. We see Frege using here a method that was to be characteristic of his later work (see above, chapter 4, section (a) (iv)). He does not tell us what conceptual content is, but under what circumstances two sentences have the same conceptual content.

It seems reasonable to suppose that what Frege is aiming at here is some notion of the *informative* content of a sentence, for it would be natural to say that two sentences which have the same logical consequences convey, or are capable of conveying, the same information. If we now take into account Frege's use of the expression 'combination of ideas' to describe the content of a sentence we might be inclined to suppose that he took the information conveyed by a sentence to be a subjective entity; the ideas arising in the mind of the person who reads it (see e.g. Resnik [1976], p. 37). Though this view receives encouragement from Frege's remark that an unasserted sentence 'should simply invoke in the reader an idea' ([1879*a*], section 2), I believe that we should not interpret Frege in this way. First of all, in the course of his remarks on conceptual content he makes a distinction (though perhaps not an entirely clear one) between objective and subjective aspects of what a sentence conveys, placing conceptual content clearly on the objective side.[25] Secondly, the term which Frege uses here, and which is often translated as 'idea', is the German word *Vorstellung*. We should, therefore, take a moment to look at Frege's use of the word.

(ii) Representation

In the *Foundations* Frege remarked that it was largely because of Kant's use of the term *Vorstellung* that his (Kant's) philosophy was mistaken as a version of subjective idealism. And that

> An idea [*Vorstellung*] in the subjective sense is what is governed by the psychological laws of association; it is of a sensible, pictorial character. An idea in the objective sense belongs to logic, and is in principle non-sensible although the word which signifies an objective idea is often accompanied by a subjective idea, which nevertheless is not its reference ([1884*b*], p. 37).

Frege then says that he intends to use the term *Vorstellung* always in the sense of a subjective idea. It is plausible to suppose that, prior to noticing the likelihood of a confusion about its meaning, he was using the term in an objective sense. Thus we should not conclude that Frege's use of the term 'idea' in the *Begriffsschrift* indicates that he was presenting a theory of content with psychologistic overtones.

Let us try to clarify the objective meaning of *Vorstellung*. Kant used *Vorstellung* to cover two rather different kinds of thing; things which he otherwise distinguished as *intuitions* and *concepts*. He says:

All modes of knowledge, that is, all representations [*Vorstellungen*] related to an object with consciousness are either *intuitions* or *concepts*. The intuition is a singular representation, the concept a *general* or *reflected* representation ([1800], section 1 italics in the original).

Intuitions are sense experiences, while concepts are what our intellectual faculties possess and which enable us to *interpret* our experience; something which Kant summed up in his famous dictum that 'thoughts without content are empty, intuitions without concepts are blind' ([1787], pp. 71-2).

Sometimes Kant speaks of representations in general as if they have the status of private mental experiences:

All *my* representations . . . must be subject to that condition under which alone I can ascribe them to the identical self as *my* representations ([1787], p. 138).

But this doctrine of privacy is really meant to apply to intuitions rather than concepts. Frege himself insisted upon privacy as a truth about ideas in the subjective sense, as we shall see (see below, chapter 6, section (b)(vi)). When Frege talks about ideas (*Vorstellung*) in the subjective sense he has in mind something like Kantian intuitions. What I would also like to suggest is that Frege's *objective* ideas derive from Kant's theory of concepts, and that it is these objective ideas which eventually crystallise into *senses*. Concepts, for Kant, are rather like items of objective knowledge or information. The concept *man* is something which many people can have, and for the application of which there are intersubjective rules. Having a concept means having a link between ourselves and the objective world. And this, as I shall argue later, is exactly the important feature of Fregean *senses*.[26]

When Frege says that the content of a sentence is a combination of ideas (or 'representations') we should, I believe, regard this as the beginnings of the theory of sense.

(iii) The content of a name

When we turn to section 8 of the *Begriffsschrift* a rather different theory of content emerges. There Frege discusses identity statements, and the role of proper names in such sentences. As before, he does not tell us what content is, but rather the circumstances under which two proper names have the same content — when they are names of the same object. We might conclude from this that the content of a name *is* the object which it names. This much seems to be the beginnings of a theory about the references of expressions, for in his later work the reference of a name is taken to be the thing its names.[27]

Frege then says that identity is unusual in that it is a relation between names rather than between the things named. A statement of identity such as 'Gottlob Frege is the author of the *Begriffsschrift*' says that the names 'Gottlob Frege' and 'the author of the *Begriffsschrift*' are names of the same object ([1879*a*], section 8; [1885*c*] p. 108 (150)). Frege does not explain here in full detail why he holds this view, (though the discussion which follows indicates that it has something to do with the informativeness of identity statements). But at the beginning of the later 'On Sense and Reference' Frege says that what forced him to the view which he took in the *Begriffsschrift* was the necessity of distinguishing between informative and uninformative identity statements. The problem seems to have been this. Suppose that the content of a name is the object which it names. Then two names of the same object have the same content, and two sentences which differ only in that the one is obtained from the other by substitution of one name for another where both name the same object will presumably not differ in content. But often they do seem to differ. We all know that Dr Jekyll is Dr Jekyll, but to be told that Dr Jekyll is Mr Hyde may be to acquire an important piece of factual information. Frege tries to solve the problem by denying, in the case of identity, that the content of the name is the object named. Rather it is the name itself. Thus it can happen that two names, which would otherwise stand for the same thing, give different content to the sentences in which they occur. 'Dr Jekyll' and 'Mr Hyde' are different names, and since, in an identity sentence, names stand for themselves, 'Dr Jekyll' has here a different content from 'Mr Hyde'. In this way the content of 'Dr Jekyll is Mr Hyde' can differ from that of 'Dr Jekyll is Dr Jekyll'.

All this proceeds, quite clearly, on the assumption that the content of a name is, normally, the object named. In 'On Sense and Reference', Frege began by recalling his views of this earlier period, and in particular the theory that identity is a relation between names. Later, we shall examine his objections to this earlier view in detail. But in this way Frege was not quite doing justice to his own earlier self, because the rest of section 8 of the *Begriffsschrift* proceeds along quite different lines. It reverts in fact to the epistemic notion of content which had informed the earlier sections on sentential content and which laid the basis for the later theory of sense.

As Frege remarks, the theory according to which identity is a relation between names of things makes it 'appear as though it were here a matter of something pertaining only to the expression and not to the thought [*Denken*]' ([1879*a*], p. 14 (124)). But he goes on:

> ... the necessity for a symbol for identity of content rests upon the following fact: the same content can be fully determined in different ways; but, that the *same content*, in a particular case, is actually given by *two modes of determination* is the content of a *judgement*. Before this [judgement] can be made, we must supply two different names, corresponding to the two modes of determination, for the thing thus determined. But the judgement requires for its expression a symbol for identity of content to combine the two names. It follows from this that different names for the same content are not always merely an indifferent matter of form; but rather, if they are associated with different modes of determination, they concern the very heart of the matter. In this case, the judgement as to identity of content is, in Kant's sense synthetic ([1879*a*], pp. 14-5 (125-6), italics in the original).

All this sounds very much like the later theory, based on the distinction between sense and reference, and according to which the informativeness of an identity statement depends upon the same object being determined by expressions with different senses, or which contain different 'modes of determination'.

(iv) Two problems about the reduction of mathematics to logic

In the *Begriffsschrift*, then, Frege had the notion of the informative content of a sentence, and that of the mode of determination of an object via its name or description. Both of these are important aspects of the later theory of sense. As Frege began to reflect more deeply on the relations between logic and arithmetic, there arose for him two problems which made the notion of sense an important one.

Of the two problems that I shall discuss, the first and most urgent was a result of Frege's rejection of the view that we have synthetic *a priori* knowledge of arithmetic. Frege agreed with Kant that our knowledge of geometry is based on an intuition of space, but he denied that there is any intuition corresponding to number. He argued that numbers, unlike spatial and temporal points, are intrinsically dissimilar from one another. Proof in geometry can proceed with the help of our intuition of a concrete geometrical figure which stands as representative of all figures of its kind; we cannot carry out proof in arithmetic by taking a single number as representative of a whole class of numbers.[28] But he did not want to abandon the view that we know mathematics with apodictic certainty. How, then, do we know it? His answer is that our knowledge of arithmetic is really a species of logical knowledge. The truths of arithmetic are truths of logic and, in Kant's terms, analytic. This raises a difficulty connected with the way in which Kant distinguished between analytic and synthetic judgements. A statement is analytic, according to Kant, if the concept of the predicate is contained in that of the subject.

Now there is a sense in which such a statement will be trivial or uninformative. Someone who has grasped the subject of an analytic statement will not learn anything from it. To hold, as Frege did, that arithmetical truths are analytic, and to accept Kant's criterion of analyticity imposes on us the view that the truths of arithmetic are trivial in this sense. Yet Frege seems to have had a strong intuition to the effect that arithmetical truths are (mostly) non-trivial. In his logical system arithmetical truths are consequences of axioms which he took to be purely logical. Of that system he says

> ... the conclusions we draw from it extend our knowledge and ought therefore on Kant's view to be regarded as synthetic; and yet they can be proved by purely logical means, and are thus analytic ([1884*b*], section 88).

It seems clear from this and certain other passages that Frege understood Kant's criterion of analyticity as offering also a criterion of epistemic triviality. For his own purposes then he was obliged to effect a separation between the two distinctions, and allow for statements to be at once analytic and non-trivial.

A statement is now to be regarded as analytic if it follows according to purely logical modes of reasoning from purely logical truths (see *ibid*, section 3); otherwise it is synthetic. Given this definition there is no reason to suppose in advance that an analytical truth will be uninformative. The definition tells us nothing about the notion of informative content;[29] this must be introduced in some other way. In the *Foundations of Arithmetic*, Frege is content simply to point out that 'sentences which extend our knowledge can have analytic judgements for their content' (section 91). He does not offer a precise explanation of what the content of a sentence is, or how it is determined.

I suggest that the theory of sense was designed exactly to make such an explanation possible. The theory tells us that what determines the sense (content) of a sentence is the senses of its parts, and that expressions with the same references can have distinct senses. Consider identity statements. A statement of the form '$a=a$' is analytic and uninformative; it follows from purely logical laws, and the expressions which flank the identity sign have the same sense (since they are, in fact, tokens of the same expression type). An expression of the form '$a=b$' may be informative, if 'a' and 'b' have different senses, but it may yet be a logical truth. '2+2=4' would be an example. This is analytic, since it is a theorem of Frege's logical theory, yet non-trivial, since '2+2' has a sense distinct from that of '4'.

It is perhaps unfortunate that when Frege introduced the first full discussion of sense in 'On Sense and Reference' he used an example not from mathematics but from more ordinary discourse — the example of the identity of the morning star and the evening star. This example, together with the extended discussion of oblique contexts later in the same paper, has given plausibility to the idea that Frege's interests were in the general workings of language and with associated problems about meaning.[30] Yet this idea is unattractive if only because it gives Frege's excursions into the theory of sense no connection with what was his major philosophical concern — the epistemological status of mathematics.

That his actual motive for introducing senses was closely connected with this sort of problem about arithmetic is suggested by a letter to Peano of 1896. Without the distinction between sense and reference we would have to conclude that

> ... the whole content of arithmetic ... would be nothing more than boring instances of this boring principle [the principle of identity]. If this were true mathematics would indeed have a very meagre content. But the situation is surely somewhat different. When early astronomers recognised that the evening star (Hesperus) was identical with the morning star (Lucifer) ... this recognition was incomparably more valuable than a mere instance of the principle of identity ... even though it too is not more than a recognition of an identity. Accordingly, if the proposition that 233+798 is the same number as 1031 has greater cognitive value than an instance of the principle of identity, this does not prevent us from taking the equals sign in '233+798=1031' as a sign of identity (Letters, p. 195 (126-7)).

Now to what I take to be Frege's second problem. I shall introduce this via a brief discussion of the relations between formal and informal mathematics.

It commonly happens in the history of mathematics that an

intuitive notion has been employed for some time, but that we eventually feel the need to replace it by some more precise notion. In algebra the notion will often be a structural one, and will receive its precision from its place in an axiomatic theory. This has happened in a number of other areas as well, and the definition of a function in terms of an arbitrary set theoretic correspondence is perhaps the best known example. These theoretical replacements often attract the attention of mathematicians because they are required in order for further mathematical progress. Problems about the existence of integrals and Fourier series representations could not be solved within the existing rather vague, understanding of what is to count as a function (see Lakatos [1976], Appendix 1). Frege's reason for wanting to replace the intuitive notion of natural number by the precise notion of what he calls 'logical objects', or the extensions of concepts, was philosophical rather than mathematical. He thought that there was simply no acceptable account of what numbers are ([1884*b*], part 2).

All these replacements of intuitive concepts by precise ones involve a difficulty. How can we tell whether the precise notion is a good explication of the intuitive one? In a rather late paper Frege discussed this problem, ([1914], pp. 227-9 (210-12)). For him it is a matter of showing that the intuitive expression and the precise one have the same sense. Since the intuitive expression already has a sense (though not a completely clear or unambiguous one) it cannot be a case of stipulating its sense by means of a definition. What, then, will be the status of sentences like

(1) A function is a single valued correspondence between sets; or

(2) A natural number is a class of equinumerate classes?

Frege had this to say.

We have a simple sign with a long established use. We believe that we can give a logical analysis of its sense, obtaining a complex expression which in our opinion has the same sense. We can allow something as a constituent of a complex expression if it has a sense we recognise. The sense of the complex expression must be yielded by the way in which it is put together. *That it agrees with the sense of the long established simple sign is not a matter for arbitrary stipulation, but can be recognised only by an immediate insight.* No doubt we speak of a definition in this case too. It might be called an 'analysing' definition to distinguish it from a constructive definition.[31] But it is better to eschew the word 'definition' altogether in this case, because what we should here like to call a definition is really to be regarded as an axiom. In this second case there remains no room for an arbitrary stipulation, because the simple sign already has a sense ([1914], p. 227 (210). (My italics)).

But if 'analysing definitions' are not definitions at all, what are they? Frege says that they must count as axioms, but there are problems about this. For Frege, something can count as an axiom only if it is self evidently true ([1899-1906], p.183 (168); [1914], p.221 (205)). Indeed, he says in this passage that the truth of an 'analysing' axiom can be recognised 'only by an immediate insight'. But what intuitive insight tells us that, for example, 'function' has the same sense as 'single-valued correspondence'? That the two terms have, from the mathematical point of view, the same content is something which we can come to know, if at all, only as the result of working with the set theoretical notion and seeing that it performs satisfactorily — that is, that we can prove all the intuitive results about functions. In other words the question is one which can be decided by experiment (in an extended sense of that term) but not by 'intuitive insight'. And such a statement would, for that very reason, have to be discounted as an axiom by Frege. So analysing definitions seem to have an embarrassingly indeterminate status for Frege.

Frege was, I think, worried by the inadequacy of what he says here, as is evidenced by his immediately going on to suggest a way in which analysing definitions (axioms?) can be eliminated altogether. His suggestion is this. Suppose that we invent the notion of single-valued correspondence to explicate the idea of a function. (This example is not Frege's.) In other words, we analyse the notion of a function into the complex notion of a correspondence between two sets such that to each member of the first set there corresponds at most one member of the second, and say that the sense or content of the word 'function' is the same as that of 'single-valued correspondence'. We are not sure that this claim is true, however; perhaps some result will turn up later which will convince us that 'single-valued correspondence' will not do as an analysis of 'function'. Our statement (1) cannot therefore serve as an axiom. Our recourse, according to Frege, is to drop the original, intuitive notion of a function and work with the new notion of a single-valued correspondence. We can then introduce a short-hand expression to replace 'single-valued correspondence' as this is an unwieldy expression. We could use some new term, or even the familiar term 'function', as long as we now understand that that term has none of its old, intuitive meaning. It is simply a short-hand for 'single-valued correspondence'. Our theory will then be a theory about single-valued correspondence, rather than an attempt to capture, in a precise way, our historically-shaped intuitions about functions. In this way (1) becomes an ordinary stipulative definition. Frege concludes:

In constructing the new system we can take no account, logically speaking, of anything in mathematics that existed prior to the new system. Everything has to be made anew from the ground up (*ibid*, p. 228 (211)).

What Frege is suggesting here will hardly solve any of the problems raised earlier. The whole point of subjecting a notion such as that of number or of function to analysis was to give us a better understanding of an informal concept which has seemed to be an important and worthwhile one. The success of such an analysis depends very much on its being faithful to the intuitive content of the old term. If we then say, as Frege apparently encourages us to say, that we are no longer interested in what that intuitive content is, and simply introduce a new notion as part of a formalised axiomatic theory, we shall have turned our backs on the purpose of the whole enterprise. For instance, it would hardly have been acceptable for Frege to have said that his logical theory was not a theory about numbers in the intuitive sense, but about certain precisely defined objects called extensions whose relation to numbers was incidental and of no interest to his enquiries. In that case the logicist programme would lose much of its epistemological force.

I take it then that Frege had no real solution to the problem of how to decide whether the translation of an informal theory into a formalised one is adequate, that is, a translation which preserves the content or sense of the informal statements. But my aim here is merely to establish his concern with the problem.

The passage just discussed was written in 1914. It is, I believe, Frege's only explicit discussion of the problem. But there is evidence that the problem itself arose at a much earlier stage of his work. I suggest, in fact, that the idea that two apparently rather different expressions can yet share an important relation of *having the same content* was a second reason why Frege required the notion of sense. Some of the evidence for this is to be found once again in the *Foundations of Arithmetic*. There Frege did not yet distinguish sharply between sense and reference, but his use of the word 'content' (*Inhalt*) is often close to his later use of 'sense'. And in later works Frege often continued to talk about content when clearly he was thinking of sense (e.g. [1918*a*], p. 346 (7), and [1924-5*a*], p. 290 (271)). Now let us recall briefly the problem with which Frege was dealing in the *Foundations*. Frege was trying in that book to establish (perhaps only provisionally) that the truths of arithmetic are really logical truths. This involved showing that a statement of numerical identity, such as 'the number of *F*'s is the same as the number of *G*'s', depends for its truth upon the existence of a one-one correlation between the extensions of the concepts *F* and *G*. Frege described the problem thus. We have to

> ... explain the sense [*Sinn*] of the sentence
>
> The number which belongs to the concept *F* is the same as that which belongs to the concept *G*.
>
> That is to say, we must reproduce the content of this sentence in other terms... ([1884*b*], p. 73).

Frege goes on to argue that 'The number of *F*'s is the same as the number of *G*'s' has the same content as the statement '*F* and *G* are in a one-one correspondence'. For illustrative purposes he considers an example of this kind of procedure. The sentence 'Line *a* is parallel to line *b*' is reformulated as an identity: 'The direction of line *a* is identical with the direction of line *b*'. Frege says

> Thus we replace the symbol // by the more generic symbol =, through removing what is specific in the content of the former and dividing it between *a* and *b*. We carve up the content in a way different from the original way, and this yields us a new concept [the concept of direction] (*ibid*, pp. 74-5).

So Frege thinks it possible for two different sentences—sentences which differ considerably—to convey the same information, or have the same content. And it was clearly important for the success of his programme for the reduction of arithmetic to logic that this should be so. For, written in the primitive notation of his logical language, statements which he claims to be arithmetical ones appear as quite different from the statements of intuitive arithmetic. The possibility then arises that someone could object to Frege's method along the lines already suggested. Frege's system, so the objection runs, is sufficient to show that a certain theory can be deduced from logical principles, but this theory whatever its interest to us, is not arithmetic, because the sentences which appear in Frege's theory are quite different from the sentences of arithmetic. Thus Frege wanted to claim that his theory does capture the real content of the arithmetic with which we are familiar. It is, of course, one thing to claim this, it is another to be able to substantiate the claim. Notice how difficult it would be to prove it. For presumably a proof, in order to be conclusive by Frege's own standards, would have to be expressed within an adequate system of formal logic, and the statements of intuitive arithmetic would have to be translated into that system. And the question would arise again as to whether the statements which appeared in the formal system were the same in content as those in the informal theory. But this difficulty aside, it seems clear that the notion of sense is appearing here in the form: that which distinct expressions share in common when they 'say the same thing'.

I shall conclude this section with two comments. The first concerns the problem of sense identity. As has been noted elsewhere, Frege was not able to give a precise and satisfactory account of the circumstances under which two expressions have the same sense (Heijenoort [1977]). Yet Frege insists that all objects have clear-cut identity conditions, and the senses of certain expressions are objects. But in view of what I have said here it is not surprising that Frege encountered difficulty in specifying a criterion of identity for senses. The two problems which I have discussed require quite different identity conditions for senses. The problem about the informativeness of analytic truths makes it necessary that expressions like '2+2' and '4' have different senses. In that case it would follow naturally that, for example, '2+2=4' and '2+2=$\sqrt{16}$' would be sentences with different senses ([1891*b*], p. 132 (29)). A fine discrimination between the senses of sentences is called for. But for the purposes of Frege's second problem — the problem of assessing conceptual change in mathematics — we need quite a coarse-grained notion of sense identity. Sentences which, from an intuitive point of view, differ quite considerably are said to have the same sense. Thus for example

The number of *F*'s is identical with the number of *G*'s

is to have the same sense as

The concepts *F* and *G* are equinumerate.

It is not surprising that Frege was not able to reconcile these two demands in a single criterion of sense identity.

My second point is this. We have seen that Frege introduced the notion of sense for reasons connected with his programme for reducing arithmetic to logic, and particularly with problems about our mathematical knowledge. Thus the theory of sense seems to be intended as a contribution to mathematical epistemology. Yet the theory is most often described as a contribution to the theory of meaning. If this is meant as a claim about Frege's own understanding of the theory it seems to be based on an historical misconception. I shall discuss this issue again in a later chapter.

(v) The mature theory and the problem of identity

In 1892, Frege published his paper 'On Sense and Reference'—an article which is now regarded as one of the most important pieces of writing in the philosophy of language. I have already outlined the theory that he presented, and mentioned some of the problems to which it gives rise. I now want to look at the opening passage of the paper, because in it Frege links up his theory to his earlier views, as expressed in the *Begriffsschrift*. The passage is not an easy one to understand. Commentators have disagreed about it. I shall therefore start by presenting the relevant text, and then try to analyse it in some detail. I shall conclude with some comments on the argument.

> Equality gives rise to challenging questions which are not altogether easy to answer. Is it a relation? A relation between objects, or between names or signs of objects? In my *Begriffsschrift* I assumed the latter. The reasons which seem to favour this are the following. $a = a$ and $a = b$ are obviously statements of differing epistemological value [*Erkenntniswert*]; $a = a$ holds *a priori* and according to Kant is to be labelled analytic while statements of the form $a = b$ often contain very valuable extensions of our knowledge and cannot always be established *a priori*... Now if we were to regard equality as a relation between that which the names 'a' and 'b' signify it would seem that $a = b$ could not differ from $a = a$, provided that $a = b$ is true. A relation would thereby be expressed of a thing to itself, and indeed one in which each thing stands to itself and not to any other thing. What is intended to be said by $a = b$ seems to be that the signs 'a' and 'b' signify the same thing, so that these signs themselves would be under discussion; a relation between them would be asserted. But this relation would hold between the names or signs only in so far as they named or designated something. It would be mediated by the connection of each of the two signs with the same designated thing. But this is arbitrary. Nobody can be forbidden to use any arbitrarily producible event, or object as a sign for something. In that case the sentence $a = b$ would no longer refer to the subject matter, but only to its mode of designation; we would express no proper knowledge by its means. But in many cases this is just what we want to do. If the sign 'a' is distinguished from the sign 'b' only as object (here, by means of its shape), not as sign (i.e. not in the manner in which it designates something), the cognitive value of $a = a$ becomes essentially equal to that of $a = b$, provided that $a = b$ is true. A difference can arise only if the difference between the signs corresponds to a difference in the mode of presentation of that which is designated. Let a, b, c be the lines connecting the vertices of a triangle with the mid-points of the opposite sides. The point of intersection of a and b is then the same as the point of intersection of b and c. So we have different designations for the same point, and these names... likewise indicate the mode of presentation: and hence the statement contains actual knowledge ([1892*b*] pp. 143-4 (56-7)).

First Frege states his problem. Is identity a relation between things, or between the names of things? Suppose that it is a relation between the things themselves. In that case there would be no difference in cognitive value between the statements '$a=a$' and '$a=b$'. But sometimes there is such a difference, so the theory must be wrong (lines 1-11).

What principles is this argument based on? The first principle seems to be that we can know, *a priori*, what the extension of the identity relation is; for we know that everything is identical to itself, and that nothing is identical to anything else (lines 9-11). But how does it follow from this that we can know *a priori* that an identity statement of the form '$a=b$' is true? What Frege has in mind can, I think, be brought out by contrast with the case of some relation other than identity, such as *is taller than*. What do we have to know in order to know that '*a* is taller than *b*' is true, if it is true? First we need to know what objects *a* and *b are*, then we need to know what relation *is taller than* is, and finally we need to have some way of determining whether *a* is taller than *b*. But the case of identity is different. If we know what objects *a* and *b* are, and if we know what relation identity is, then we know already that *a* is identical with *b*. We do not need any way of determining it. This, then, is the sense in which the truth value of an identity statement can be determined *a priori*. Now this argument does not establish what Frege needs; that there is no difference in cognitive content between '$a=a$' and '$a=b$', for we can establish that '$a=a$' is true without first having established what object *a* is, and this is not true for '$a=b$'.[32] So there still seems to be a difference between their epistemological status. What seems likely is that Frege was conflating this argument with another that is not actually stated by him here, but which is easy to articulate given the principles with which he was working in the earlier *Begriffsschrift*. We have stated the argument already (see above, chapter 4, section (a)(iii)). If the content of a proper name is the object which it names, and if the contents of the parts of the sentence determine the content (what Frege here refers to as the 'epistemological value') of the sentence, then '$a=a$' and '$a=b$' would have to have the same content if *a* is the same as *b*. And if we start by assuming that '$a=a$' has no content in the sense that, as Frege puts it, it does not express any proper knowledge, then '$a=b$' will not have any content either (see letter to Peano, pp. 194-8 (125-9)).

Lines 11-15, then, outline another theory (the theory which

appears in section *8* of the *Begriffsschrift*) which is designated to overcome the difficulty; identity is a relation between the names of things rather than between things themselves. It is then argued that this theory leads to the same unacceptable consequence as the first theory — that a sentence of the form '$a=b$' could not express any 'proper knowledge' (lines 13-23).[33] What is the argument for this?

The key premise of the argument is that the relation between a sign or name and the thing it names is 'arbitrary' (lines 13-19). We can use whatever signs we like to designate whatever objects we like, and in that case '$a=b$' would express no proper knowledge. It would merely record an arbitrary linguistic stipulation; that 'a' was to be used to designate the same thing as 'b' is used to designate.

The difficulty of Frege's text is that it is not always easy to see what is being asserted and what is merely put forward for dialectical purposes.

Now I suggest that the function of the argument just referred to is not so much to discredit the claim that identity is a relation between names, but to discredit the presupposition that the relationship of a name to what it names is arbitrary (see Coder [1974], pp. 339-40). Thus, when Frege says 'Nobody can be forbidden ... for something' (lines 16-17) he is merely putting forward a view which he later rejects. The argument has been that if an identity statement is an assertion about names, *and* if the relation of name to thing named is arbitrary, then '$a=b$' can express no proper knowledge. Since the conclusion is false, at least one of the premises must be false. Frege goes on (lines 23-25)

> A difference [in cognitive value between '$a=b$' and '$a=b$'] can arise only if the difference between the signs corresponds to a difference in the mode of presentation of that which is designated.

What Frege seems to be questioning here is the first premise — that the relation between a sign and the thing signified is arbitrary. For if the difference between signs for the same object corresponds to a systematic difference in the 'mode of presentation' of the object, the use of different signs may reflect more than just an arbitrary choice on the speaker's part. It may correspond to a difference in the nature of things. This difference is the different ways in which the same object can be given to us. As Frege's geometric example (lines 25-9) showed, the same object can be given to us in different ways. He concludes:

> It is natural, now, to think of there being connected with a sign ... besides that

which the sign designates, which may be called the reference of the sign, also what I should like to call the sense of the sign, wherein the mode of presentation is contained. (*ibid*, p. 144 (57)).

Thus, what Frege seems to end up by rejecting is not the claim that identity is a relation between names, but the claim that the relation of name to thing named is always an arbitrary one. The relation can reflect a difference in the ways in which things are given to us. We use certain expressions which are complex and which are dependent for their sense on the sense of their parts, in order to describe objects as they are given to us. We may know that a certain point is the point of intersection between a pair of lines, without knowing also that it is the point of intersection between another pair of lines. We can describe it as 'the point of intersection between lines *a* and *b*' — an expression which has parts which already have senses, and which confer a sense on the whole — while not yet knowing that it is also truly describable as 'the point of intersection of lines *b* and *c*'. We discover this by discovering the truth of an identity statement.[34]

Thus the burden of Frege's opening remarks in 'On Sense and Reference' is to establish a relation between signs and what they signify other than the relation of reference or naming. The relation in question is that whereby an expression describes an object from one point of view rather than from another. Different expressions can contain a different mode of presentation of an object. How should this affect our approach to the theory of identity? Our original question is unanswered, for the objection to both theories of identity — that they lead to the consequence that no identity statement can be informative — collapses once we introduce the notion of sense. One can say either that identity is a relation between objects named, and explain the difference in content of '$a=a$' and '$a=b$' by appealing to a difference of sense between 'a' and 'b', *or* we can say that identity is a relation between names of things, and explain differences of content in exactly the same way. Which did Frege choose? It has often been assumed that he opted for the view that identity is a relation between things named. This is certainly the view which is most often adopted in modern semantics. But it is possible to find in Frege's work after the *Begriffsschrift*, and even after 'On Sense and Reference', explanations of identity which make it a relation between signs. In an essay of 1891 Frege says

What is expressed in the equation '$2.2^3+2=18$' is that the right hand complex of signs has the same reference as the left-hand one ([1891*a*], p. 126 (22)).

And in the second volume of the *Basic Laws* he says

> We use the equality sign to express that the reference of the group of signs on the left hand side coincides with the reference of that on the right hand side ([1903*a*], section 105).

Yet in the first volume of the same work Frege had said

> '$\Delta = \Gamma$' shall denote the true if Δ is the same as Γ; in all other cases it shall denote the false ([1893], section 7).

And this seems to be an explanation of identity as a relation between the things themselves rather than the names for the things.

One further comment on the opening passage from 'On Sense and Reference' is called for. Why should it be that a statement which reports an arbitrary stipulation must have no cognitive content? It is, after all, an arbitrary stipulation that we are to drive on the left hand side of the road rather than on the right, but to be informed of this stipulation is surely to be told something which can make considerable difference to our behaviour. In a sense it does not matter which convention is adopted, but one could not work out *a priori* what choice had been made. Once again, I think that Frege is confused about the true grounds of objection to the theory. Against the theory which says that identity is a relation between names he ought to argue that statements of identity do not (or do not normally) report linguistic conventions, but rather extra-linguistic facts, many of which are true quite independently of our decisions. That the morning star is the evening star is such a fact, yet the theory under consideration seems to make all identity statements reports of human conventions, and this is unacceptable, even though a statement which reported the convention would not be trivial.

With this I conclude the discussion of Frege's text, and of the details of his theory. In the final chapter we shall return to the idea of sense and see how it fits into Frege's general philosophical programme.

(d) Judgement and Truth

Frege distinguishes between:

(1) The grasping of a Thought
(2) The judgement that the Thought is true (or false)
(3) The assertion of the Thought (or its rejection) ([1918*a*], p. 346 (7)).

(1) and (2) are different kinds of mental acts. (1) will be discussed in some detail later on. (3) is the external act which counts as a manifestation of (2).

(i) *The judgment stroke*

In the *Begriffsschrift* Frege used the sign '⊢' to indicate an assertion. What follows the sign is the *content* of the assertion. The sign for a judgement consists of two parts; the vertical or 'judgement' stroke, and the horizontal or 'content' stroke. A sentence preceded by the content stroke alone is to be taken in such a way that we consider the content of the sentence, without it being asserted as true. '—*A*' is to be read 'the circumstance that *A*' or 'the proposition that *A*', while '⊢*A*' indicates the assertion that *A*. Frege's exposition of this point is not very clear, and he says at one point that the judgement stroke can be read as a predicate; '⊢*A*' means '*A* is a fact' ([1879*a*], section 3). But 'A is a fact' is just a sentence which can be asserted or not. This explanation of the judgement stroke does not present it as a means of going from an unasserted sentence to an asserted one, but from the descriptive phrase 'The circumstance that *A*' to the sentence '*A* is a fact' (see Dudman [1970]). Things become clearer in the *Basic Laws*. There the horizontal stroke is explained as a function-name. It is the name of the function which takes its argument to the value true if the argument is the true, and to the false otherwise. So to write

—*A*

is to write the name of a truth value. If '*A*' is a sentence, then, as we have already learnt, '*A*' is the name of a truth value. If '*A*' is the name of a truth value, then '— A' names the true if '*A*' names the true, and names the false if '*A*' names the false. If '*A*' is not the name of a truth value then '—*A*' names the false. Thus, like all the functions in Frege's system, — (the 'horizontal function', as we shall call it) is defined for all objects as arguments. In the earlier *Begriffsschrift*, however, the horizontal could stand in front of an expression only if that expression had a 'judgement content', or was in other words a sentence. One could write '— Priam's house was made of wood', but not '— Priam's house', for 'Priam's house' does not have an assertable content. Frege's later theory of functions and objects caused him to revise this account and to say that '—' is the name of a function and must accordingly take all objects as arguments. Now the judgement stroke can be added to any expression of the form '— *A*' (and to no other expression) and an assertion is thereby indicated. It follows from this that we can assert not only sentences, but names as well. Of course on Frege's view sentences *are* names, so, for him, to assert a sentence is already to assert a name.

In his later work, Frege abandoned the view that the judgement stroke is a predicate. Instead, it is a device to indicate that the sentence following it (or, more generally, the name following it) is asserted. The judgement stroke is the only sign (apart from the variables and brackets) which is not the name either of a function or of an object. Clearly it is not the name of an object, because it has to be supplemented with an object name of the form '$—A$' in order to be a complete expression. But it is not the name of a function either, since a function takes objects as values, and in that case '$\vdash A$' would be just another name of an object, and not an assertion. Frege says

> The assertion sign cannot be used to construct a functional expression; for it does not serve, in conjunction with other signs, to designate an object. '$\vdash 2+3=5$' does not designate anything; it asserts something ([1891*b*], p. 137 (34)).

(ii) Judgement and denial

Frege's use of the judgement stroke within his formal system has often been criticised. Wittgenstein says that it merely records a psychological fact; that the writer is committed to the truth of the sentence that follows it ([1921], 4.442). Modern logic has taken over Frege's sign, but gives it a different meaning. '$\vdash A$' means that A is a theorem of the system in which deductions are being carried out. And A's being a theorem in some formal system is not the same as A's being put forward as true.

Yet there can be no doubt that for certain purposes we want to distinguish between the Thought itself and the assertion of the Thought. Frege was right that sentences may nor may not be used assertively, and that considering a sentence is a different mental act from judging that it is true. In what ways was Frege's theory an advance on previous ones? In various places, and particularly in the later article 'Negation' Frege criticises a certain theory of judgement ([1918*b*], and [1906*f*], p. 214 (198)). The fact that he does not attribute the view to anyone in particular may suggest to the reader that he was actually attacking a 'straw man' position. In fact, however, he was describing with admirable conciseness a theory which had been very influential, but which would be hard to associate in all its detail with any particular author (but see Arnauld and Nicole [1724], part 2, section 3). The theory in question failed to distinguish between a Thought and a judgement for reasons associated with the sort of views which prevailed before Frege concerning the logical structure of sentences and the nature of predication. According to the subject-predicate logic, a sentence is constructed by predicating something of a subject by means of the copula. In 'Socrates is mortal' mortality is predicated or asserted of the subject Socrates. The sentence consists of a subject, the copula and a predicate. To construct a sentence in this way is at the same time to assert something: the logical construction of the sentence gives rise to assertion.

This theory involves a number of difficulties noticed by Frege. Negation, for example, becomes something problematic. Negative statements like 'Socrates is not mortal' were said to constitute denials, and denial was thought of as an act the opposite of assertion. Thus statements of different logical structure give rise to different acts of judgement: assertion and denial. But as Frege pointed out, there is really but one act here: assertion. In one case we assert a positive sentence, in the other a negative one. The sentences are different but the act is the same. To assert that Socrates is mortal is not to engage in a different kind of act from asserting that Socrates is not mortal. Further, the distinction between positive and negative judgements is an arbitrary one. 'Socrates is not married' is negative, but is equivalent to the positive 'Socrates is single'. Thus the presence or absence of negation cannot give a firm foundation to any distinction between kinds of judgement. The heart of Frege's theory of judgement is the separation of sentences and sentence construction from judgement and its external manifestation in assertion, the denial that differences in kind between sentences induce differences in the acts of judgement, and the denial that the copula has any judgement forming role.[35] Rather, on Frege's theory, the copula is assimilated to the predicate. Thus in 'Socrates is mortal', the predicate is not, properly speaking, 'mortal' but rather 'is mortal'. The grammatical particle 'is' has no separate logical role to play.[36]

(iii) *The laws of truth*

In this section we shall note three important theses of Frege's concerning truth: first, that the laws of logic are the laws of truth; secondly, that '*P* is true' is equivalent to '*P*'; thirdly, that truth cannot be defined.

In 'The Thought' Frege says that the laws of logic are the laws of truth:

The word 'true' indicates the aim of logic as does 'beautiful' that of aesthetics or 'good' that of ethics. All sciences have truth as their goal; but logic is also concerned with it in a quite different way from this. It has much the same relation to truth as physics has to weight or heat. To discover truths is the task of all sciences; it falls to logic to discern the laws of truth ([1918*a*], p. 342 (1)).

In a paper written in 1897 he said that 'logic is the science of the most general laws of truth' ([1897], p. 139 (128)). But much earlier he had written something which sounds rather different.

Logic is concerned only with those grounds of judgement which are truths. To make a judgement because we are cognisant of other truths as providing a justification for it is known as inferring. There are laws governing this kind of justification, and to set up these laws of valid inference is the goal of logic.[37]

Does Frege think of the laws of valid inference as something different from the laws of truth? It seems not, for he goes on immediately to say that 'the laws of logic are nothing other than the unfolding of the content of the word "true"'. I suggest that when Frege speaks of the laws of truth, he means the laws of *truth transmission*, or of truth preserving inference. For a valid inference is one in which, if the premises are true, then the conclusion *must* be true.

In another sense we think of validity as no more connected with truth than with falsity. For the validity of an inference is quite independent of the truth or falsity of its premises. A conclusion (true or false) can follow validly from premises which are false. Validity simply guarantees that *if* the premises are true, then the conclusion will be true. And this can be expressed equally well in terms of falsity; the inference is valid if and only if the falsity of the conclusion guarantees the falsity of the conjunction of the premises.

But, for Frege, there was a closer connection between validity and truth, because according to him the premises of an inference must be statements which are recognised to be true.[38]

This view is closely connected with Frege's general epistemological standpoint. There are, according to Frege, two ways in which a statement can be established as true. First, it can be seen to be true on the basis of some non-inferential source of knowledge. It is the task of epistemology proper to discover and clarify these sources ([1879-91], p. 3 (3)). Secondly, a statement can be shown to be true by being deduced according to logical laws from truths already established as such. Now if logic is applied, not to the deduction of truths from known truths, but to the deduction of statements from arbitrary premises, then it is being misused, and what is involved is not inference proper but 'pseudo-inference' (letter to Dingler, p. 30 (17)).

Thus Frege's conception of the role of logic is somewhat different from our own. For him logic is inextricably bound up with the programme of justifying our knowledge. This leads to certain difficulties. If an inference is properly an inference only if it starts from premises which are recognised as true, how can we ever be sure that an inference *is* valid? We would have to have some guarantee that our recognitional abilities are infallible, or validity will cease to be a recognisable property of an inference. I shall say more about this problem when I deal with Frege's views on the justification of logical axioms (see below, chapter 6, section (e) (vii)). It is also true that Frege on occasion draws back from this view of inference as involving premises which are known to be true.

The task of logic is to set up laws according to which a judgement is justified by others, irrespective of whether they themselves are true ([-1906], p. 190 (175)).

And it is also worth remembering that, although Frege insists that the premises of an inference must be asserted (i.e. prefixed with the judgement stroke), he carries out a number of deductions in the appendix to the *Basic Laws* which involve Axiom (V), leaving off the judgement stroke 'in view of the doubtful truth of it all'. Yet he does not admit that the resulting inferences are only 'pseudo-inferences'.

Let us leave this difficult interpretative point here, and continue our discussion of truth.

In a number of places Frege says that any declarative sentence '*P*' has the same sense as the sentence 'It is true that *P*'.

It is . . . worth noticing that the sentence 'I smell the scent of violets' has just the same content as the sentence 'It is true that I smell the scent of violets'. So it seems that nothing is added to the Thought by my ascribing to it the property of truth ([1918*a*], p. 345 (6)).

This view connects with another of Frege's principles which we have already discussed: the thesis that functions are to be everywhere defined and that every proper name is to have a bearer. If this principle were not enforced, then Frege would not have been able to maintain the equivalence of '*P*' and 'It is true that *P*'. For suppose that the name 'Odysseus' has no bearer. Then, on Frege's theory, the sentence 'Odysseus landed asleep at Ithaca' would be neither true nor false, and the equivalence between '*P*' and 'It is true that *P*' would be violated. For while 'Odysseus landed asleep at Ithaca' would be neither true nor false, 'It is true that Odysseus landed asleep at Ithaca' would just be false.[39]

Another feature of Frege's logical theory would have pushed him towards the view that '*P*' says the same as 'It is true that *P*'. As we have seen, in Frege's later theory of judgement one can assert any proper name, in the sense that '$\vdash a$' is well formed for any proper name '*a*'. Now '—' is a name of the function which takes the true to the true and all other objects to the false. Thus '—' is a name of the concept *being the truth value true*. We can then read '⊢Gottlob Frege' as representing the assertion, not of the expression 'Gottlob Frege' but of the slightly more plausible sounding 'Gottlob Frege is the true'. So '$\vdash a$' should perhaps always be read '*a* is the true'. But now suppose that '*a*' is a sentence. Since '*a* is the true' is in this case presumably equivalent to '*a* is true', in trying to assert '*a*' we always end up with asserting '*a* is true'.[40] And if '*a* is true' had a content other than '*a*' this would be proof that we could never assert '*a*'. So it is important here for Frege to be able to enforce their identity of content.

Frege held that truth is indefinable. In 'The Thought' he considers the view that truth is a relation of correspondence.

It might be supposed from this that truth consists in the correspondence of a picture with what it depicts. Correspondence is a relation. This is contradicted, however, by the use of the word 'true', which is not a relation-word and contains no reference to anything else to which something must correspond. If I do not know that a picture is meant to represent Cologne Cathedral then I do not know with what to compare the picture to decide on its truth. A correspondence, moreover, can only be perfect if the corresponding things coincide and are, therefore, not distinct things at all. It is said to be•possible to establish the authenticity of a banknote by comparing it stereoscopically with an authentic one. But it would be ridiculous to try to compare a gold piece with a twenty mark note stereoscopically. It would only be possible to compare an idea with a thing if the thing were an idea too. And then, if the first did correspond perfectly with the second, they would coincide. But this is not at all what is wanted when truth is defined as the corespondence of an idea with something real. For it is absolutely essential that the reality be distinct from the idea. But then there can be no complete correspondence, no complete truth. So nothing at all would be true; for what is only half true is untrue. Truth cannot tolerate a more or less. But yet! Can it not be laid down that truth exists when there is correspondence in a certain respect? But in which? For what would we then have to do to decide whether something were true? We should have to inquire whether it were true that an idea and a reality, perhaps, corresponded in the laid down respect. And then we should be confronted by a question of the same kind and the game could begin again. So the attempt to explain truth as correspondence collapses. And every other attempt to define truth collapses too. For in a definition certain characteristics would have to be stated. And in application to any particular case the question would always arise whether it were true that the characteristics were present. So one goes round in a circle. Consequently, it is probable that the content of the word 'true' is unique and indefinable ([1918*a*], pp. 343-4 (3-4)).

We cannot deal here with the general question of whether truth can be defined in some philosophically adequate way. I shall confine myself to one or two brief observations about the character of Frege's argument. Frege claims that truth cannot be a relation of correspondence because 'true' is not a relation word. Yet he was, in other circumstances, quite willing to suppose — and even to insist — that ordinary language is philosophically misleading. His real reason for rejecting the idea of truth as correspondence can hardly have been this. He also argues that truth cannot be any kind of correspondence, because any correspondence short of identity will be partial, and any partial correspondence will represent only partial truth. But we need not take this argument very seriously because he then goes on to point out that a correspondence can be absolute in the sense that the two entities involved correspond perfectly *in certain respects*. Thus we might be able to explicate the notion of absolute truth in terms of a correspondence between some limited and well defined number of characteristics of the entities involved. At this point Frege's main objection becomes clear: any definition of truth in terms of correspondence will be circular. If being true consists in a correspondence between two entities, then when we ask whether something is true we shall have to ask whether it is true that the correspondence holds.

Frege immediately generalises his argument: any definition of truth will involve the stating of certain characteristics in terms of which truth is to be defined, and any application of the definition will raise the question of whether it is true that the characteristics hold. And this, it is claimed, involves a circularity.

As Dummett has pointed out, the argument is not very convincing as it stands. Suppose that some definition of truth is proposed in the following form:

P is true if and only if P has the property A

Then in asking whether P is true I will be asking whether P has property A. Frege thinks that 'P has property A' is equivalent to 'It is true that P has the property A'. And so, for him, asking whether P

has the property *A* is equivalent to asking whether '*P* has the property *A*' is true. So in asking whether *P* is true, we are also asking whether '*P* has the property *A*' is true, whether, '"*P* has the property *A*" is true' is true, and so on in an infinite regress. But is the regress a vicious one? Dummett argues that it is not, as long as the verification of any one of these statements does not presuppose the verification of those further down the hierarchy. He then claims that the correspondence theory cannot meet this constraint because it makes the verification of '*P*' depend upon the investigation of a state of affairs different from the state of affairs which determines the truth value of 'It is true that *P*'. Thus in verifying '*P*' we are not thereby verifying 'It is true that *P*'. So the conclusion is that Frege's argument, though not valid generally, is valid as a refutation of the correspondence theory. This might be replied to by arguing that, although '*P*' and 'It is true that *P*' are made true or false by different states of affairs, the verification of '*P*' will constitute a verification of 'It is true that *P*' since the first entails the second and the verification of a statement which entails a second counts thereby as an (indirect) verification of the second.

Frege might have had another source of worry about the correspondence theory, a worry suggested by his remarks about perfect correspondence having to be identity. If truth were a correspondence it would have to be, on Frege's view, a correspondence between a Thought and that which makes the Thought true, (presumably a fact). He would not have allowed the correspondence to be one between a sentence and a fact, because he held that it is Thoughts rather than sentences which are true. 'When we say a sentence is true, we really mean that its sense [the Thought] is' ([1918*a*], p. 344 (4)). But Frege also identifies Thoughts and facts. 'A fact is a Thought that is true' (*ibid*, p. 359 (25)). And since Thoughts and facts are identical, there can be no question of any correspondence between them short of identity.

If truth cannot, as Frege insists, be defined, how can we know what the laws of truth are? Frege would not, I think, have seen any difficulty here. Recall that, in the *Basic Laws*, Frege pointed out that his Axiom (V) does not determine what courses of values are. We know this law as a logical truth (so he thought at the time) without knowing exactly what the objects are which the law is intended to apply to. Frege's propositional approach to knowledge makes it, I think, seem unproblematic that we can know things about something without knowing exactly *what* that thing is: similarly with truth. Logic cannot tell us what truth is (that is, it cannot tell us what it is that makes a sentence a name of the true), but it can tell us about the conditions under which truth is preserved, and that is as much as we can hope for by way of analysis of this fundamental concept.

(e) Conclusions

In this chapter we have examined a number of theories and distinctions which bear upon the interpretation of Frege's logic. It is for that reason that I have grouped them under the general heading of 'philosophical logic'. Yet they have implications of a much wider kind. The distinction between concept and object counts as a broadly metaphysical one, while the theory of sense and reference has profound implications for the nature of language in general. The theories of judgement and truth also have clear application to a number of philosophical problems. I shall, for the moment, reserve judgement on the questions of how our understanding of these theories should affect our characterisation of Frege's philosophical programme. I shall try to answer this question in a later chapter. The material presented here will then constitute part of the evidential basis for such a characterisation.

Notes

1 Frege [1891*b*], [1892*a*], and [1892*b*]; Frege [1918*a*], [1918*b*], and [1923].
2 See e.g. Frege [1892-5], [1897] and [1906*e*].
3 This idea is associated with the work of Dirichlet (see particularly his [1837], but see also Lakatos [1976], p. 151).
4 See below, chapter 5, section (b).
5 In general I shall italicise an expression like 'being a square root of' to indicate that it is being used as the name of a concept or relation.
6 See below, chapter 5, section (a) (ii).
7 In his interesting [1979] Tichý reconstructs a version of the ontological argument due to St. Anselm and which is not susceptible to Frege's objection.
8 This is a much simplified version of Euclid's actual postulate, for which see Kline [1972], p. 59.
9 Euclid drew a distinction between axioms and postulates, but from our point of view we can treat them as the same. See Frege [1914], p. 223 (206) for a discussion of this point.
10 See Frege [1903*b*], Korselt [1903] and Frege [1906*a*].

11 That is, Hilbert's revised set of axioms, when they are interpreted as axioms in the traditional sense with all their terms having a determinate meaning. Frege did not deny that Euclid's own choice of axioms was defective.

12 See below, chapter 4, section (b) (ii). Frege's difficulty is discussed in Furth [1965].

13 See below, chapter 4, section (b) (iii). The reader should ignore the fact that expressions like 'a predicate refers to a concept' are susceptible to the very difficulty that we are here trying to avoid. I use these expressions simply to introduce the reader to the notion of referring.

14 Dummett's elaboration of Frege's solution to this problem depends crucially on the idea (which he takes to be a Fregean one) that 'the copula is a mere grammatical device, with no content, which serves the purpose of converting a phrase into a verbal phrase where grammar demands a verb . . . just as . . . the pronoun 'it' supplies a subject where the sense requires none' (Dummett [1973], p. 214. Cp. Frege [-1884], p. 69 (62)). This allows Dummett to make the move from an expression like 'ξ is a horse' to 'a horse'.

It is true that Frege sometimes refers to the copula as a 'mere verbal sign of predication' ([1892*a*], p. 168 (43)). But here Frege is contrasting the 'is' of prediction with the 'is' of identity. Its 'mereness' in the former case consists in the fact that it does not represent in itself any distinct denoting expression. In 'The morning star is the evening star' the copula may be taken as representing the identity relation, while in 'The morning star is a planet' the role of the copula is to make a contribution to the predicate. Its status here is similar to that of the word 'a'. Indeed, Frege says in one place that 'the content of the predicate is not comprised in the word "Saturn" alone; an essential part of it is contained in the word "is" . . .' ([1891-2*b*], p. 101 (92)). Later he wrote that '. . . the word "is" is the copula and belongs with the predicate' ([1914], p. 259 (240)). Thus Frege seems to have thought that the copula is an essential part of a predicate expression.

15 Traditional logic endorses the idea that there is a relation between the particular and the universal, by taking the copula 'is' in a sentence like 'Socrates is mortal' as a distinct part of the sentence, representing the binding together into a judgement of the subject and predicate. Frege insisted that the 'is' be treated as part of the predicate itself. In this way the mode of connection between the subject and the predicate becomes a feature of the predicate rather than of some third, additional item in the structure of the proposition itself.

16 See Long and White (*eds*) [1979], and McGuiness (*ed*) 1980.

17 Most recently the theory has come under attack from those who advocate a causal theory of naming (see, e.g., Kripke [1972]).

18 I use 'Thought' with an initial capital as a translation of Frege's term *Gedanke*.

19 In a letter to Peano of 1896 (p. 183 (115)) Frege said that in ordinary language it is possible for a sentence to have both a sense and a reference even where some of its parts lack both. He does not explain how this could be so.

20 By the principle according to which the sense of a sentence is a function of the senses of its parts it ought at least to be possible that the substitution within a sentence of expressions with different senses leaves the sense of the whole unchanged, because a function can take the same value for different arguments. Frege does not tell us whether this ever happens for senses, though one

passage may indicate that he did envisage this possibility. (See Frege [1896*a*], p. 226 (7), and Dudman [1969].)

21 See Dummett [1973], chapter 9, for a modification and defence of the theory.

22 In a letter to Russell, Frege says 'The analysis of the sentence corresponds to an analysis of the Thought, and this in turn to something in the domain of reference, and I should like to call this a primitive logical fact' (p. 224 (142)).

23 The recognition of this difficulty led Frege to abandon the view that the reference of a sentence is structured in the way that a Thought is (see [1919], p. 275 (255)).

24 'I call the concepts under which an object falls its properties' ([1892*a*], p. 175 (51)).

25 '. . . all aspects of language which result only from the interaction of speaker and listener . . . have nothing corresponding to them in my formula language, because here the only thing considered in a judgement is that which influences its possible consequences' (section 3).

26 This picture is somewhat complicated by the fact that Frege used the word 'concept' in a different way from Kant. The sense/reference distinction cuts across the concept/object distinction for Frege. On Frege's view, only some concepts are senses and only they have the epistemic aspect which is an aspect of all Kantian concepts.

27 Later, Frege recognises that he had used the word 'content' to cover both sense and reference. (See his [1892*a*], p. 172 (47); also letter to Dingler, p. 41 (28) and letter to Husserl p. 96 (63). In this passage Frege refers to the use of 'content' in the *Foundations*. But what he says there presumably applies also to the *Begriffsschrift*.)

28 See his [1884*b*], section 13. The real numbers are not to be constructed by some process of generalisation from the natural numbers (see above, chapter 3, section (b) (iii).

29 It also leaves us with a problem about the epistemological status of the logical axioms. See below, chapter 6, section (e) (vii).

30 Geach actually suggested once that sense was introduced to overcome the difficulty about oblique contexts (Geach [1961], p. 162). Frege's first, parenthetical, discussion of sense ([1891*b*], p. 29) is mostly concerned with mathematical examples, but turns briefly to the example of the morning star and the evening star.

31 The 'constructive definitions' referred to in this quotation are the ordinary explicit, eliminable definitions which occur in formal theories.

32 It might be objected here that we cannot establish that '$a = a$' is true unless we know that 'a' denotes. But in Frege's system this requirement will automatically be met.

33 Nusenoff ([1978] and [1979]) and Ray ([1977]) both differ from my account in interpreting lines 13-23 as saying that '$a = a$' would have as *much* content as '$a = b$', rather than as saying that '$a = b$' would express just as little proper knowledge as '$a = a$'. This seems to me to be unjustified by the text and to lead to subsequent difficulties of interpretation. But I shall not argue this here.

34 See letter to Russell, pp. 234-5 (152). 'Wherever the coincidence of reference is not self-evident, we have a difference in sense.'

35 '. . . assertoric force, which is often connected with the copula . . . does not belong to the expression of the Thought' ([1906*c*], p. 192 (177)).

36 'The content of the predicate is not comprised in the word "Saturn" alone; an essential part of it is contained in the word "is" or at least has to be added in thought' ([1891-2*b*], p. 101 (92)).

37 Frege [1879-91], p. 3 (3). Elsewhere Frege advocates a subjectivist view of aesthetics (see his [1897], pp. 143-4 (132)). Also, in an unpublished paper of 1915 Frege actually denies that truth plays a role in logic analagous to that of goodness in ethics and beauty in aesthetics. He says that the 'essence' of logic is 'the assertoric force with which a sentence is uttered'. And the nature of assertoric force is not to be explained with reference to truth; the sentence 'sea water is salty' has the same sense as the sentence 'It is true that sea water is salty'. The latter can be uttered without assertoric force just as easily as the former (Frege [1915]). It is not entirely clear what Frege is trying to get at here. He does not say why assertoric force rather than truth is the essence of logic. Perhaps he was trying to deal with the problem that we do indeed assert false sentences and use them in deduction. At any event, there is no trace of what he says here in the later 'The Thought'.

38 See Frege [1906*a*], p. 319 (105); [1912], p. 337, and letter to Dingler, p. 30 (16). See also Stoothoff [1963].

39 In 'It is true that *P*', '*P*' is here assumed to have indirect reference; that is, the Thought that *P* is said to be true, not the truth value named by '*P*'. Otherwise 'It is true that *P*' would have no reference since *P* has, by hypothesis, no reference. (See footnote 40.)

40 In '*a* is identical with the true' the expression '*a*' has its usual reference, i.e. a truth value. In '*a* is true' it has indirect reference, i.e. it refers to the Thought that *a*. To say that *a* is true is to say something of the Thought, not of the truth value. If '*a*' is a name of a truth value but not a sentence, the equivalence of '*a* is the true' and '*a* is true' breaks down. Let 't' be a non-sentential name of the truth-value true (it could be just an ordinary proper name); then '*t* is the true' is true while '*t* is true' is false, since the sense of '*t*' is not a Thought, and only Thoughts are true or false.

5 *The Logical System of the 'Basic Laws' and the Paradox*

FREGE'S deduction of arithmetic from logic, together with the introduction of magnitudes in the *Basic Laws* is carried out in the context of a system of formal logic, a set of axioms, rules of inference, and rules for the construction of formulae. The system which Frege employs is similar to that of the *Begriffsschrift*. There are, however, a number of differences between the two systems: certain new axioms have been introduced, along with courses of values and a proper notation for generality with respect to functions. The symbolic language has been augmented with certain devices, and is now explained with the help of the new distinctions between concept and object and between sense and reference. The formation rules and the rules of inference are more precisely specified.

Now that we understand some of the philosophical theses relating to Frege's logic, we are in a position to explain some of his technical devices. This will be our first concern. But perhaps the most significant fact about the *Basic Laws* is that its system of logic is flawed by a contradiction which can be derived in it, and which Frege learned of just as his second volume was to be published. We will see how this contradiction can be generated, and what Frege's reaction to it was.

(a) The System

(i) The formal language

Frege's symbolic language underwent certain changes between the *Begriffsschrift* and the *Basic Laws*. Some of the changes have to do with his sharpening of the distinction between functions and objects. In the later system, all symbols other than variables and the judgement stroke appear as names either of functions or of objects. In the *Begriffsschrift* Frege had explained the meanings of the symbols which represent connections between sentences by explaining the conditions under which sentences in which they appear are true. Thus the sign

$$—\!\!\top\!\!—$$
$$\quad\llcorner—$$

is explained by saying that the sentence

$$\begin{array}{l} —\!\!\top\!\!— B \\ \quad\llcorner— A \end{array}$$

is true in every case except that in which *A* is true and *B* false (see [1879*a*], section 5). In the *Basic Laws*

$$\begin{array}{l} —\!\!\top\!\!— \xi \\ \quad\llcorner— \zeta \end{array}$$

appears as the name of a function; the function which takes the value false just in case the ζ-argument is the true and the ξ-argument anything other than the true. Otherwise it takes the value true (see [1893], section 12). Like all functions in Frege's system, this function is defined for all arguments, not just for truth-values. We can write

$$\begin{array}{l} —\!\!\top\!\!— \sqrt{81} \\ \quad\llcorner— \text{Gottlob Frege} \end{array}$$

without offending the formation rules of the system. But whenever, as in this case, the arguments are something other than truth-values, the function takes the value true. Negation is defined similarly. It is a function which takes the true to the false, the false to the true, and everything else to the true.

In his earlier work Frege had thus been content to explain the roles of certain expressions by pointing to their uses in sentences. In his later work he wants to explain them independently of such contexts. We have seen that in his later work Frege explains a symbol for generality as representing a (higher order) function. His earlier explanation had simply been to state the conditions under which a sentence like

$$—\!\!\smile^{\mathfrak{a}}\!\!— f(\mathfrak{a})$$

is true (see [1879*a*], section 11), pointing out that in a sentence like 'Every positive integer can be represented as the sum of four squares' the expression 'Every positive integer' cannot be treated as representing an entity which is the subject of the sentence, for there is no such entity (see *ibid*, section 9). In terms of his later distinction between function and object, Frege would have said that, although 'Every positive integer' does not represent a separable part of the sentence, 'every' does correspond to a distinct functional part; a function from first level functions to truth-values.

Although Frege's explanation of the judgement stroke had changed between the *Begriffsschrift* and the *Basic Laws* his use of it was basically the same. It is prefixed to every sentence which belongs to the chain of deductions carried out in the system.

(ii) The axioms

Now that we understand something of Frege's symbolic language, together with the assimilation of concepts to functions and the use of courses of values, we are in a position to understand the axioms on which the system of logic in the *Basic Laws* is based.

First let us consider the changes that have taken place since the *Begriffsschrift*. Frege has managed some economy in the axioms which involve only propositional letters. Axiom (1) remains unchanged,[1] and there is just one other axiom of this kind:[2]

$$\begin{array}{l} \vdash\!\!\top\; (-a)=(-b) \\ \quad\llcorner\!\top\; (-a)=(\top b) \end{array}$$

(Either the truth-value of *a* is the same as that of not-*b* or it is the same as that of *b*.)

Axiom (9) of the *Begriffsschrift* appears now as Axiom (II*a*), but there is also a corresponding axiom for quantification over functions:

$$\begin{array}{l} \vdash\!\!\top\; M_\beta(f(\beta)) \\ \quad\llcorner\!\overset{\mathfrak{f}}{\smile}\; M_\beta(\mathfrak{f}(\beta)) \end{array}$$

which says that what holds of all first level functions of one argument holds of any such function.

Axiom (VI) involves a device which Frege did not use in his earlier work. He introduces a function written

$$\backslash\,\xi$$

which is to serve the purpose of the definite article. Thus if the argument of the function is the extension of a concept under which exactly one thing falls, then the value of the function is that one thing. So we have $\backslash\,\acute{\varepsilon}(\Delta = \varepsilon) = \Delta$. If, on the other hand, the argument is not such an extension, the function takes as value the argument itself. The second stipulation is simply a convenient way of making sure that the function is defined for *all* possible arguments. It is for the first class of cases that the function serves its intended purpose.

Axiom (VI) governs this function, and is written

$$\vdash a = \backslash\, \grave{\varepsilon}(a = \varepsilon)$$

It says that the value of the function for an argument which is the extension of a concept under which exactly one thing falls is that thing itself.

Axiom (III) is written as

$$\vdash\!\begin{array}{l} g\left(\neg\overset{\mathfrak{f}}{\smile}\begin{array}{l}\mathfrak{f}(a)\\ \mathfrak{f}(b)\end{array}\right) \\ g\,(a = b) \end{array}$$

the interpretation of which requires some preliminary comment. In the *Basic Laws*, Frege treats sentences as names of truth-values; a true sentence names the truth-value true ('the true') while a false sentence is a name of the truth-value false ('the false'). Thus '$(a=b)$' and '$\overset{\mathfrak{f}}{\smile}\begin{array}{l}\mathfrak{f}(a)\\ \mathfrak{f}(b)\end{array}$' are both names of truth-values. Axiom (III) is intended to say that anything which holds of the truth value named by '$(a=b)$' holds of the truth value named by '$\overset{\mathfrak{f}}{\smile}\begin{array}{l}\mathfrak{f}(a)\\ \mathfrak{f}(b)\end{array}$'. From this axiom we can deduce that if $a=b$, then anything which holds of a holds of b, and that everything is identical to itself (Axioms (7) and (8) of the *Begriffsschrift*).

The most important axiom in the new system is Axiom (V) which governs courses of values, and which we have already discussed. This axiom is vital to Frege's programme for deducing arithmetic from logic, since it allows us to assume that to every concept (or more generally to every function) there is a corresponding course of values. And Frege will try to show in the *Basic Laws* that the numbers can be defined as the courses of values of certain functions. The axiom is written

$$\text{(V)} \qquad \vdash (\grave{\varepsilon} f(\varepsilon) = \grave{\alpha}\, g(\alpha)) = (\overset{\mathfrak{a}}{\smile} f(\mathfrak{a}) = g(\mathfrak{a}))$$

and says that two courses of values are identical if and only if the corresponding functions are such that they take the same values for the same arguments.[3]

(b) The Paradox

(i) Russell's discovery

In an appendix to the second volume of the *Basic Laws* Frege had this to say:

> Hardly anything more unwelcome can befall a scientific writer than that one of the foundations of his edifice be shaken after the work is finished.

I have been placed in this position by a letter of Mr Bertrand Russell just as the printing of this [second] volume was nearing completion. It is a matter of my *Basic Law* (V). I have never concealed from myself its lack of the self-evidence which the others possess, and which must properly be demanded of a law of logic, and in fact I pointed out this weakness in the Introduction to the first volume. I should gladly have relinquished this foundation if I had known of any substitute for it. And even now I do not see how arithmetic can be scientifically founded, how numbers can be conceived as logical objects and brought under study, unless we are allowed — at least conditionally — the transition from a concept to its extension. Is it always permissible to speak of the extension of a concept, of a class? And if not, how do we recognise the exceptional cases? Can we always infer from the extension of one concept's coinciding with that of a second, that every object which falls under the first concept also falls under the second? These are the questions raised by Mr Russell's communication ([1903*a*], p. 253 (127). See also letter to Russell, p. 213 (132)).

What Russell had communicated to Frege was his discovery of a paradox which can be derived in two different ways, either for classes or for concepts (though Russell himself speaks in terms of predicates). Consider first the concept (property) *not holding of itself.* Under this concept fall all concepts which do not fall under themselves. Call this the concept *P*. Now either *P* holds of itself or it does not. Suppose that it does. Thus *P* holds of *P*, in which case *P* is a concept which does not fall under itself, and so *P* does not hold of *P*. Then *P* is a concept which does not fall under itself, and so *P* does hold of *P*. On either assumption there is a contradiction involved. Now this, it appears, is not a difficulty for Frege, because in his system there can anyway be no property which holds of itself. Properties (concepts) are always such that they hold of entities of a kind other than the kind to which they themselves belong (see above, chapter 4, section (a)(v)). In Frege's system we can write neither '*P* (*P*)' nor 'not-*P* (*P*)'. Both expressions are forbidden by the formation rules. But now consider another version of the same paradox. Consider the concept *being an extension of a concept but not falling under that concept.* An extension which falls under this concept we shall call a 'normal extension', and we shall say that it falls under the concept *normal extension.* This concept, call it *F*, seems then to be a legitimate one, and under it fall all normal extensions. Call the extension of this concept *a*. Now the extension of a concept must be determinate in the sense that every object does or does not fall under that concept. In particular *a* itself does or does not fall under *F*. Suppose that it does. Then *a* falls under the concept *normal extension*, and so *a* does not fall under *F*. Suppose on the other hand that *a* does not fall under *F*. Then *a* does not fall under the concept *normal extension* in which case a does fall under F. In either case a contradiction is involved.

(ii) The damage to Frege's system

What is the exact source of the difficulty in Frege's formal system? First let us introduce some notation. If b is the extension of the concept $f(\xi)$, that is, if $b = \acute{\varepsilon}f(\varepsilon)$, then we write '$a \cap b$' for '$a$ falls under f', and '$a \pitchfork b$' for its negation. The first theorem of the *Grundgesetze* says that for all a, $f(a)$ if and only if $a \cap \acute{\varepsilon} f(\varepsilon)$.[4] Another way of putting the same point is this: to every concept f there corresponds an object which is the extension of that concept. But suppose that in place of f we consider the concept *normal extension* (F), and take a to be the extension of the concept F, written $\acute{\varepsilon}(\varepsilon \pitchfork \varepsilon)$. Ask now whether a is a normal extension. Suppose it is. Then a falls under F, and by Theorem 1, $a \cap \acute{\varepsilon}F(\varepsilon)$ or $a \cap \acute{\varepsilon}(\varepsilon \pitchfork \varepsilon)$, and since $a = \acute{\varepsilon}(\varepsilon \pitchfork \varepsilon)$, we have $a \cap a$; a is thus not a normal extension. Suppose instead that a is not a normal extension. Then a does not fall under F, and so $a \pitchfork \acute{\varepsilon}(\varepsilon \pitchfork \varepsilon)$ or $a \pitchfork a$; a is a normal extension. Each alternative leads to its own negation. Theorem 1 must then be false, and so must be at least one of the axioms from which it is derived. In fact several of the axioms go into the derivation of Theorem 1, but the only one about which it seems there could be serious doubt is Axiom (V) according to which the extensions of two concepts are the same if every object which falls under the one falls under the other. At the very beginning of the *Grundgesetze* Frege had remarked that

> A dispute can arise, so far as I can see, only with regard to my Basic Law concerning courses of values (V) which logicians have perhaps not yet expressly enunciated, and yet is what people have in mind when they speak of the extensions of concepts. I hold that it is a law of pure logic ([1893], p. vii (3). See also letter to Hönigswald, p. 87 (55)).

His initial doubts having been so strongly confirmed, Frege goes on now to derive the falsity of Axiom (V) in his system from the other axioms. Axiom (V) is a bi-conditional statement: it says that two extensions are identical if and only if the corresponding concepts have the same values for the same arguments.[5] But what is really in doubt is only half of the bi-conditional. It is only the assumption that *if* two extensions are the same *then* the corresponding concepts have the same values for the same arguments that is implicated in the proof of Theorem 1. It is this (V*b*) which we are now going to prove false. In order to do this we must find concepts f

and g which have the same extensions but are such that for some a, $f(a) \neq g(a)$. Here I shall greatly simplify Frege's own exposition.

In the argument which follows we shall use a logical principle: If the falsity of A follows from the joint assumption of A and B, then the falsity of B follows from the assumption of A alone. Now let A be the assumption that, if a is the extension of a concept f, then a falls under f. Let B be the assumption that a is the extension of the concept *normal extension.* From these two we shall deduce not-A, that is, a is the extension of f and a does not fall under f.

By B, a is the extension of the concept *normal extension*. Call that concept 'F'. Then by assumption A, a falls under that concept. But that means that a does not fall under the concept *normal extension.* So, a does not fall under the concept F. Hence a is the extension of F and a does not fall under F: this is not-A. By the principle just stated it follows that A implies not-B, or

(1) If a is such that, if it is the extension of a concept f then it falls under f, then a is not the extension of the concept *normal extension*.

Equivalently (by the principle that if A implies not-B then B implies not-A) we have that

(2) If a is the *extension* of the concept *normal extension* then there is a concept such that a is the extension of that concept and a does not fall under it.

Let us now assume that a is the extension of the concept *normal extension*. So by (2) there is a concept f such that a is the extension of that concept and a does not fall under f. Since we are assuming that a is the extension of the concept *normal extension*, which we call the concept F, we can write a as '$\grave{\varepsilon}F(\varepsilon)$'. Now we can rewrite (2) as

(3) If $\grave{\varepsilon}F(\varepsilon)$ is the extension of the concept *normal extension*, then $F(\grave{\varepsilon}F(\varepsilon))$.

But $\grave{\varepsilon}F(\varepsilon)$ *is* the extension of the concept *normal extension*, and so we have

(4) $F(\grave{\varepsilon}F(\varepsilon))$.

We have shown that F holds of its own extension a. But a is also the extension of the concept f. Does f hold of a? No. By (2) a does not fall under f. So we now know that the concepts F and f have the same extension, but that there is an object,namely a, such that $F(a)$ but not $f(a)$. And this contradicts Axiom (V).

(iii) The proof that all the names in the Basic Laws *refer*

Russell's paradox shows us that there are first level functions which have no corresponding course of values. The concept *normal extension* is such a function. The course of values name 'ἐ$F(\varepsilon)$' does not refer to any course of values. But in section 31 of the *Basic Laws* Frege caried out a proof which, if successful, would have shown that all the syntactically well-formed names in his system refer to entities. Something must have gone wrong with this proof.

Frege gives a somewhat informal exposition of the proof. If we were to formulate it more precisely it would take the form of what we now call an inductive argument. First it is argued that the primitive undefined names in the system refer. Then Frege shows that names formed from these by any of the means allowed in his system must also refer. Frege's main error occurs in the first part, and the error is contained in that part of the proof which shows that names of courses of values refer. In his system 'ἐ$\Phi(\varepsilon)$' is a primitive name; it is supposed to refer to a certain second level function ('Φ' is a variable ranging over first level functions) which takes every first level function of one argument to its course of values. Frege reasons as follows. This function refers if it takes a definite value for every argument. Thus all he needs to show is that if '$f(\xi)$' refers then 'ἐ$f(\varepsilon)$' refers. How can we show that 'ἐ$f(\varepsilon)$' refers? Frege's answer is to appeal to the principle that an object name 'a' refers if and only if, given that '$g(\xi)$' refers then '$g(a)$' refers. So Frege must show that whenever '$g(\xi)$' is a referring name of a first level function, '$g($ἐ$f(\varepsilon))$' refers. Having satisfied himself that all names refer if the primitive ones do, Frege need only concentrate on the case where '$g(\xi)$' is a primitive name in his system. Frege thinks that these in turn can be reduced to the case of the identity function since '—' and the truth functional connectives can be defined in terms of identity. At this stage the only objects introduced into Frege's system are the courses of values and the truth-values and the latter have been defined as courses of values themselves.[6] So the only case we need to consider is the value taken by an expression of the form 'ἐ$f(\varepsilon)=$ ἀ$g(\alpha)$'. Truth conditions for statements of this kind are given by Frege's Axiom V; we know that 'ἐ$f(\varepsilon)=$ ἀ$g(\alpha)$' refers (has a truth-value) if and only if '$-\!\!\smile^{\mathfrak{a}}\!\!- f(\mathfrak{a})=g(\mathfrak{a})$' refers. And the latter refers if $f(\xi)$ and $g(\xi)$ refer. In this way Frege satisfies himself that '$\grave{\varepsilon}\Phi(\varepsilon)$' refers.

But the proof is invalid. The main difficulty concerns the proviso that $f(\xi)$ and $g(\xi)$ refer. In fact this cannot be established generally unless we *already* assume that '$\grave{\varepsilon}\Phi(\varepsilon)$' refers. There are, in other words, first level functions, the definitions of which presuppose the existence of all courses of values. An example of this is the course of values name built up from the first level function name '$\neg\smile^{\mathfrak{f}}\!-\xi = \grave{\varepsilon}\mathfrak{f}(\varepsilon)$'. It is not possible to construct this function name in such a way as to give it reference without previously having given reference to '$\grave{\varepsilon}\Phi(\varepsilon)$'.

(iv) The repair

As Frege noted, what is interesting about the construction of his counter-example to Axiom (V*b*) is that the object that falls under the one concept and not under the other is the object which is the extension of both concepts. This suggests amending (V*b*) so as to say that if two functions have the same extension, then everything which falls under the first, except the extension of the first concept, falls under the second, and every object which falls under the second, except the extension of the second, falls under the first.[7]

As Frege shows, this modified Axiom (V′) easily blocks the derivation of the contradiction. Is it acceptable as a substitute for (V)? Frege initially thought that it was. There are, however, three objections that can be brought against it.

The first is a methodological one, perhaps less decisive than the other two. Frege's replacement of (V) by (V′) is, in a sense immediately to be described, an *ad hoc* solution to the problem raised by the paradox. I call a solution *ad hoc* if it involves making an adjustment to a theory in order to overcome a known difficulty, without at the same time introducing any new, deeper theoretical concepts, or providing a guarantee that other difficulties, as yet unknown, will not emerge in the future.

Consider the case of a physical theory, say Newtonian mechanics and gravitation theory, which is faced with an anomaly, say the anamolous behaviour of a planet's orbit. It would clearly not be acceptable from a methodological point of view to attempt to avoid the difficulty of reformulating the theory by simply side-stepping this one anomaly. It would not be acceptable, in other words, to replace Newton's theory by a new theory which says that Newton's laws are valid in all cases except the case of the orbit of planet *X*.

But Frege's axiom (V′) is in essentially the same situation as this; it replaces the refuted statement that having the same extension is sufficient to guarantee that two functions take the same value for the same argument by the weaker statement that having the same extensions is sufficient to guarantee that the functions will have the same values for the same arguments, except where the argument is the extension itself. Theorem 1, which originally read (if we restrict its application to concepts) 'concept *f* holds of the object *a* if and only if *a* belongs to the extension of *f*', will now read '*f* holds of *a* if and only if *a* belongs to the extension of *f*, except in the case where *a* is the extension.'

I do not know whether this objection ever occurred to Frege. Perhaps, if the resulting system were free from contradiction, and the same mathematical results could be proved in it, the move from (V) to (V′) could still be regarded as an acceptable one. Unfortunately neither of these two other conditions holds.

At the end of the 'Appendix' in which he discussed the paradox and its solution Frege remarked

> To pursue further here the consequences of replacing (V) by (V′) would be too great an undertaking. We cannot but acknowledge that subcomponents must be added to many of the propositions; but certainly we need not fear that this will raise obstacles that actually block the course of the proofs. Nevertheless it will be necessary to check thoroughly all propositions discovered up to this point ([1903*a*], p. 265 (143)).

It is evidence of the hurry in which this 'Appendix' was written that Frege had not had time to give even superficial thought to the question of whether the proofs go through as before. For it can easily be seen that one of the most important theorems about the natural numbers — that every natural number has a successor — cannot be proved if (V) is weakened to (V′)[8]. As Dummett remarks, Frege would naturally have spotted this very quickly once he turned his attention to the reconstruction of proofs, and his discovery of the inadequacy of the revised axiom system is the probable explanation for his silence on the issue of the relation between logic and mathematics over the next twenty years.[9]

The third difficulty, and the most decisive from a logical point of view, is that Axiom (V′) leads to a new contradiction. Care must be taken in the formulation of this point. It can be shown (though there is no reason to think that Frege was ever aware of it himself) that (V′) has the consequence that there is at most one object (see Quine [1955]). This is not in itself a contradiction (though it is also not a very encouraging result if our aim is to use our logic for mathematical or other purposes). But a contradiction does result when (V′) is combined with the other axioms of the system. Remember that '—*a*' is the name of a truth value whatever *a* is. It is a theorem of *Grundgesetze* that for all *a*, —*a* does not equal ┬*a* or in other words that the two truth-values, the true and the false, are distinct. Hence it follows from the axioms that there are at least two objects, and this generates a contradiction with (V′).

(c) After the Paradox

(i) Abandoning the programme

It is clear that the discovery of Russell's paradox had a profound effect on Frege's thought. He seems not to have done any further work in the project of the *Grundgesetze* after 1902; he put out some polemical work on the foundation of geometry occasioned by Hilbert's *Foundations of Geometry*, and later he wrote some important papers on the philosophy of logic. He continued to do a certain amount of writing in the philosophy of arithmetic, but what he has to say now mostly concerns what we might call 'mathematical hygiene'. The demand for clarity of concepts, unambiguous notation, a proper distinction between axioms and definitions are still there (see Frege [1914]). What is missing now is the original impetus behind these demands; the belief that arithmetic can be shown to be derivable from pure logic.[10]

Others pursued the goal which Frege had abandoned. Russell tried out a number of possible solutions to the paradoxes and eventually opted for what is called the theory of logical types (see Russell [1908]). Zermelo and others began investigating systems of postulates which would be strong enough to build mathematics on, but weak enough to avoid contradiction.[11] It is not hard to see why Frege, even if he took any interest in these developments, did not want to pursue either of them himself. Russell's theory, though massively complicated in its details, can most easily be described as the application to classes of Frege's theory of levels of concepts. In Frege's theory the paradox cannot arise for concepts because a concept can never apply to itself. First level concepts have objects as their arguments, while second level concepts have first level concepts for their arguments, and so on (with additional stipulations for concepts with several argument places). Russell proposed that classes also should form a hierarchy and that a class at one level in the hierarchy can have as its members only objects of one level lower. This avoids the possibility of there being classes which are members of themselves. The syntactic rules of the system prevent assertion or denial of the relation of class membership between objects of the same level. What might Frege have objected to about such a solution? He was, as we have seen, very insistent that we recognise distinctions which he took to be grounded in the nature of things, such as that between concept and object. The same outlook would, I think, have set him against the introduction of distinctions which are *not* so grounded. Concepts and functions in general divide naturally into levels because the argument places they carry with them are naturally suited for certain types of arguments and not for others. But objects are complete entities which have no argument places, and so there is no basis in their natures for the same kind of distinctions which apply to functions. For this reason Frege would probably have regarded Russell's type theory as an arbitrary solution to the problem of the paradox.

Even less would the set theoretic approach of Zermelo have appealed to him. In 1908 Zermelo argued that mathematics could not wait for a definitive solution to the paradoxes (Zermelo [1908]), and that the most reasonable course to take in the mean time from the point of view of the working mathematician would be to look for a set of postulates which would provide us with enough sets to build up the mathematical structures that we need, at the same time avoiding the known contradictions. This would have been anathema to Frege. First of all he never tires of telling us that sets cannot coherently be introduced *qua* sets. They must be given as the extensions of concepts. Only in this way can we, for example, justify the introduction of an empty set. Zermelo's set theory, on the other hand, contains, in addition to a postulate which says that, under certain circumstances, sets correspond to properties, also axioms which simply state that certain sets exist, for example a set with infinitely many members (see Fraenkel, Bar Hillel and Levy *ibid*, p. 44). Secondly, Frege held resolutely to the view that any acceptable system of axioms must meet the epistemological demand of self-evidence. Propositions which simply assert the existence of certain sets can hardly be said to have this property. Frege's original Axiom (V) had seemed to him to be attractive because it guaranteed the existence of all the mathematical objects that he wanted, without actually being an assertion of existence itself. Courses of values appeared, as it were, out of nowhere.

Given Frege's epistemological demands, this was just about the only solution to the problem of founding mathematics which he could have accepted. This was why his work was so completely shattered by the discovery of the paradoxes, and why he could not generate any enthusiasm for alternative solutions.

(ii) The geometrical foundation

During the last two years of his life Frege wrote some brief reflections on his theses of the identity of logic and mathematics. He now regarded it, apparently, as utterly mistaken (see letter to Zsigismondy, p. 272 (176)). Certain forms of language seduce us into believing that there are logical objects. We talk about concepts under which the same objects fall, and language allows us to introduce terms like 'the extension of a concept', the definite article indicating that here we have a self-subsistent object. But this is not at all the case. All there is really is a relation between concepts of having the same objects fall under each. Numbers, however, must be treated as objects. It follows therefore, that since there are no logical objects, that logic cannot provide the foundation for arithmetic. We must look elsewhere for a foundation (see [1924-5*b*] and letter to Hönigswald, p. 85 (55)). Though he did not have time seriously to develop the suggestion, Frege thought that geometry, with its basis in the Kantian synthetic *a priori*, could provide what he was looking for. (In particular, Frege never said how his own earlier arguments *against* the possibility of uniting geometry and arithmetic could be answered (see [1884*b*], sections 13, 14, 19 and 41)).

Frege begins by reiterating his demand that the numbers are not to be constructed by successive generalisations from the whole numbers. But he now rejects the distinction, so basic to the *Basic Laws*, between the natural numbers, which are used for counting, and the real numbers which serve for measurement. He now says that the fact of the numbers having different uses is something merely of psychological interest which is imposed on us by the needs of practical life, and which tells us nothing about the nature of the numbers themselves. Thus all the numbers are to be treated as belonging to a homogeneous class. Instead of aiming, as before, for a direct construction of the real numbers, he attempts a definition of the full system of complex numbers. These include the real numbers, together with other numbers required for the solution of certain equations; $\sqrt{-1}$ is such a number. It had been known since the early 1800s that complex numbers could be geometrically interpreted as points on a Euclidean plane, relative to a given set of co-ordinates. In the *Basic Laws* Frege had proposed that the real numbers be interpreted as ratios between magnitudes. Now the complex numbers are to be defined as ratios between intervals in the plane.

Frege's suggestions are too briefly outlined by him to make a proper assessment easy or even worthwhile. Certainly a number of questions can be asked about the justification for his procedure. Even forgetting the difficulties involved in claiming that in Euclidean geometry we have an epistemologically sound basis for mathematics, it is unclear whether Frege's programme is an attractive one. For one thing, the notion of a ratio with which he is here working is not the intuitive one which simply involves the comparison of magnitudes. For when two intervals are compared by Frege's method and a point in the plane made to correspond to their ratio, the point chosen will depend also on the angle at which the intervals are orientated to one another. Thus two pairs of intervals which intuitively have the same ratio will not have the same ratio in Frege's technical sense. But then it is no longer clear that anything is to be gained by treating the complex numbers as ratios of intervals. Clearly Frege could not achieve a construction of the complex numbers by regarding them as ratios of intervals in the ordinary sense, because taking such ratios will not lead us out of the class of real numbers. But the attempt to treat the complex numbers as ratios in the extended sense seems an artificial one.

Notes

1 See above, chapter 2, section (b) (iii). In achieving a more economical set of axioms Frege is obliged to add several rules of inference.

2 Strictly speaking this axiom belongs partly to propositional logic and partly to the theory of identity.

3 I omit here a detailed discussion of the rules of inference of Frege's system (see his [1893], section 48). There are three kinds of rules; rules for simplifying formulae by amalgamating horizontal strokes and omitting parentheses; rules of propositional inference; and rules of quantificational inference. Rules of the last kind are very difficult to get quite right, and Frege did not get them all quite right. But the set of rules represents considerable progress over his work in the *Begriffsschrift* (see above, chapter 2, section (b) (ii)).

4 See Frege [1893], p. 75 (125). What I give here is a special case of Frege's Theorem 1, which holds for functions generally and not only for concepts.

5 Once again, what I give here is a special case of the axiom which is to hold for functions generally.

6 The true is defined as the extension of the concept under which falls only the true (see Frege [1893], section 10).

7 See *ibid*, p. 262 (139); and letter to Russell, p. 232 (150). Frege writes (V*b*) as

$$\vdash\!\!\begin{array}{l} f(a) = g(a) \\ a = \grave{\varepsilon}f(\varepsilon) \\ \grave{\varepsilon}f(\varepsilon) = \grave{\alpha}g(\alpha) \end{array}$$

8 This point needs careful formulation. Since the revised set of axioms containing (V′) is inconsistent (see below) *everything* follows from the axioms. The theorem concerned cannot be proved in the revised system *except* by exploiting this inconsistency.

9 See Dummett [1973], p. xxiii. In 1906 Frege referred again to the difficulties over Axiom (V), without mentioning his modification of it (see his [1906*c*], p. 198 (182)).

10 A letter from Jourdain (p. 124(76)) indicates that Frege may have been working on the theory of irrational numbers as late as 1913. But what form that work took we do not know.

11 See Fraenkel, Bar-Hillel and Levy [1973], chapter 2 for an account.

6 *Frege's Philosophical Method*

THE PRECEDING chapters have provided an outline of Frege's philosophical and logical doctrines. In the present chapter I want to bring this material to bear upon the problem of how best to characterise Frege's philosophical programme. Some of Frege's views will appear here for the first time, but much else will simply be assumed on the basis of what has gone before. What will emerge will, I hope, substantiate the conviction that the various aspects of Frege's work are best understood as contributions to an epistemological enterprise. First, I shall examine Frege's arguments against rival philosophies of mathematics — views which Frege saw as defective exactly because of their inability to justify mathematical knowledge. Secondly, I shall describe some of the problems raised for Frege about the nature of human cognition by his insistence on the objectivity of knowledge, and examine his attempts to solve these problems. Thirdly, I shall discuss the distinction between sense and reference, its emergence from Frege's logical and mathematical problems, and in particular the issue of whether the theory of sense is intended by Frege as a contribution to the theory of meaning. Finally, and in the light of this material, I shall examine the question of Frege's ontology and the extent of his commitment to the existence of abstract objects. A central theme of these discussions will be the role in Frege's philosophy of what has come to be known as his 'Context Principle'.

(a) The Refutation of Naturalism

(i) Introduction

We have seen that there were strong psychologistic and other naturalistic elements in German philosophy during the nineteenth century. Naturalism had, in fact, a considerable influence upon the interpretation of mathematics and logic. Thus it was that when Frege came to consider views in opposition to his own, he was not confronted by extravagant metaphysical theories (to which he would no doubt have been opposed) but rather by somewhat naive attempts to make the subject matter of these sciences part of the natural world.

There were several versions of the naturalistic approach to logic and mathematics, but their common aim was to avoid any 'transcendental' element in these subjects — by which I mean any invocation of entities not sanctioned by the natural sciences — psychology being considered a natural science for present purposes.[1] Kant and others had argued for the view that logic is a normative discipline which can answer questions about the correctness or incorrectness of thinking, but which does not seek to describe the ways in which, or the laws according to which, actual thinking takes place. For those, on the other hand, who inclined towards naturalism, it was tempting to suppose that the laws of logic are just the descriptive laws of thinking.

(ii) Naturalism and scepticism

What was it that Frege found so objectionable about this naturalistic approach? He advances a number of specific objections to the various forms that naturalism in logic and mathematics took, and we shall examine some of them as we proceed. Yet I think that there is something deeper involved in Frege's rejection of these doctrines, and that is their association with relativism, subjectivism and, ultimately, with scepticism. The aim of Frege's programme for the reduction of mathematics to logic was to refute doubts about the validity of our mathematical knowledge. He wanted to show that, according to certain objective standards, mathematics can count as a successful product of our intellectual activity. But relativism denies that there can be objective, interpersonal standards, and subjectivism, the view that all knowledge is private, personal knowledge, leads to relativism. Thus for Frege the main philosophical question about arithmetic was one concerning objective validation. Naturalistic theories of arithmetic, however, are inclined to give support to relativism. This may come about through an overtly psychologistic interpretation of arithmetic, which leads, Frege argued, to the impossibility of interpersonal standards in mathematics. Or it may come about because other forms of naturalism in mathematics — formalism and empiricism — make it impossible for us to have genuinely *a priori* knowledge of mathematics, and the *a priori* nature of mathematical knowledge was one of the primary assumptions of Frege's epistemology.

Now those who advocated naturalism in logic and mathematics

did not embrace the negative epistemological conclusions that Frege drew from their assumptions. On the contrary, their positions seemed attractive to them at least partly because they were thought to have a sound cognitive basis. For all their ubiquity in philosophical discussions, abstract entities of various kinds have rarely been popular amongst philosophers. Certainly they were not popular in the latter part of the nineteenth century. Any theory according to which our knowledge of mathematics and logic is knowledge about essentially non-empirical objects which stand outside of us and which must be grasped by specially postulated cognitive faculties, would not have been favourably looked upon. To such implausible views naturalism seemed to be a refreshingly scientific and commonsensical alternative. (To anticipate some of my later remarks: while Frege showed convincingly that the forms of naturalism then available were too crude to have any plausibility themselves, his own attempt to grapple with the faculty by which we obtain knowledge, and in particular knowledge of mathematics and logic, was itself a failure.)

There is another sense in which naturalism can lead to conclusions of a sceptical nature. Sceptical arguments, particularly after the work of Hume, have been raised most often against the possibility of the natural sciences. Sciences which are based upon a limited number of observations and yet trade in hypotheses of unrestricted generality seem particularly susceptible to scepticism. Now if the laws of logic have a genuinely descriptive content then they must be, epistemologically speaking, on a par with the other hypotheses of natural science. They can be given, at best, strong inductive support from empirical evidence about thought processes, but this can render them merely probable. In that case the attempt to base mathematics on logic could never justify mathematics in the desired sense, because the grounds for our mathematical knowledge would have been shown to be an empirical theory, to which all the well known sceptical arguments about the precariousness of inductively-based hypotheses would apply. Mathematics cannot be rendered more certain than it already is by appeal to contingent facts, however well established those facts may seem to be.

(iii) Naturalism in logic

Frege's most concerted attack on psychologism in logic is contained in his introduction to the *Basic Laws*. 'Law', he notes, has a double sense; it can refer to a description of how things are in the natural and social worlds, or to how they ought to be. It is really in the latter sense that we are entitled to speak of laws of logic. For if the laws of logic were taken to be descriptive laws of thought — that is, laws which govern how thinking actually occurs — we would have no right to use logic as a standard for judging between good and bad arguments. When we come upon an example of illogical thinking we do not want to pronounce it as contrary to an empirical regularity, but rather as an example of bad judgement or irrationality.

Although Frege's general intention in these passages is clear enough, there is a difficulty with some of his formulations. For he presents his anti-psychologistic case sometimes in such a way as to give the impression that it is built upon a misconception of the nature of natural law. Thus he says that if we think of laws of logic as empirical generalisations we would have to concede that these laws might change with the passage of time, or that there might be thinking beings in the universe to whom these laws did not apply.

> And if logic were concerned with these psychological laws it would be a part of psychology; it is in fact viewed in just this way. These laws of thought can in that case be regarded as guiding principles in the sense that they give an average, like statements about 'how it is that good digestion occurs in man', or 'how one speaks grammatically', or 'how one dresses fashionably'. Then one can only say: men's taking something to be true conforms on the average to these laws, at present and relative to our knowledge of men; thus if one wishes to correspond with the average one will conform to these. But just as what is fashionable in dress at the moment will shortly be fashionable no longer and among the Chinese is not fashionable now, so these psychological laws of thought can be laid down only with restrictions on their authority ([1893], p. xv (13)).

Frege is arguing against a specific opponent here — Benno Erdmann, whose *Logik* appeared in 1892. According to Frege, it is Erdmann's opinion that the laws of thought must have this restricted character: '[Herr Erdmann] doubts [the] unconditional and eternal validity [of laws] and would restrict them to our thought as it is now' (*ibid*, p. xvi (13–4)). So perhaps Frege is not operating with his own conception of natural law, but rather that of his opponent. But if Frege's arguments against psychologism in logic depend upon exploiting a weakness in his opponent's view which could easily be remedied they would have little interest. The difficulty is, of course, that our normal conception of natural law — and certainly this was the dominant paradigm in the mid-nineteenth century — is one according to which a genuinely law-like statement is true at all times and in all parts of the universe. Thus to point out the possibility that there are beings in the universe who do not think in accordance with the laws of thought as we see them means only that in that case the putative law would be false, and would have to be replaced by some more embracing formulation. If there were genuine empirical laws of thought they would be universally true, and so Frege's comparison of psychological laws with fashion and with low level statistical regularities is inappropriate.

Not all of Frege's objections, even as stated by him, depend upon this questionable assumption about natural law. Thus, for instance, it is with perfect right that he points out that we can imagine kinds of thinking so contrary to reason that we would have to regard them as simply illogical, whereas the psychological logician would have to find a place for them in his descriptive scheme of things. And the claim that logic is normative rather than descriptive does not depend upon any particular conception of natural law. Did Frege really think that laws of nature have a restricted generality? A much earlier paper in which he attempted a philosophical discussion of the nature of logic indicates that he did not. There he deals more carefully with the question, what assumptions are involved in the proposition that the laws of logic are natural laws?

> If man, like all other living creatures, has undergone a continuous process of evolution, have the laws of his thinking always been valid, and will they always retain their validity? Will an inference that is valid now still be valid after thousands of years and was it already valid thousands of years ago? Clearly, the laws of how men do in fact think are being confounded here with the laws of valid inference. Let us take a somewhat closer look at this question. In the sense in which we speak of natural laws, psychological, mathematical or logical laws, it is, strictly speaking, impossible for laws to change at all. For such a law, expressed in full, must include mention of all relevant conditions, in which case it will hold independently of time and place. The law of inertia, for instance, claims to be valid for all times and regions of space. If it appeared not to be valid in, say, the neighbourhood of Sirius, we should assume that it had not been fully expressed, a condition having been overlooked which is satisfied here but not in the neighbourhood of Sirius. A genuine condition always contains something indefinite, and so, according to how this something is determined, it can assume the form of a true or false proposition. Thus if after some time the law of inertia no longer seemed to hold, this would be an indication that a further condition needed adding, a condition which had been satisfied up to a certain date but not subsequently. The supposed change in the laws of thought would have to be interpreted in this way too; this could be no more than an apparent change and would be an indication that our knowledge of these laws was incomplete ([1879-91], pp. 4-5 (4-5)).

But if this is Frege's view of natural law, what is his objection to the construal of the laws of logic as natural laws? He falls back on the objection that logic is normative rather than descriptive, and that the association of logic with any empirical assertions about thinking falsifies the content of logic.

This is utterly contrary to the nature of a law of logic since it is contrary to the sense of the word 'true', which excludes any reference to a knowing subject (*ibid*).

(iv) Naturalism in arithmetic

Frege discussed psychologism in arithmetic in his *Foundations* where he attempts an informal analysis of the concept of number. In addition to the psychologistic theory which tries to interpret numbers as ideas there were two other prominent naturalistic approaches: empiricism, which tries to treat numbers as properties of empirical collections and number statements as empirical laws; and formalism, according to which numbers are to be identified with numerals, construed as physical marks on paper.[2]

As with Frege's objections to psychologism in logic, his criticisms of psychologistic theories of arithmetic are best understood against the background of his concerns about knowledge. Many of his objections boil down to the assertion that psychological considerations can do nothing to improve the status of our mathematical knowledge and that indeed they tend to make matters worse by preparing the ground for scepticism.[3]

The psychological theory of number would, if taken seriously undermine the certainty which we are trying to attain in mathematics: 'It would be strange if the most exact of all the sciences had to seek support from psychology, which is still feeling its way none too surely' (*ibid*, p. 38).

In addition to these general considerations, Frege adds one specific argument: that the nature of ideas is fundamentally at odds with the nature of mathematical objects. Ideas are subjective. For Frege this means two things. First, each person has his own ideas which are the content of his own consciousness. Thus if the number two is an idea there would not be one such number but many — my number two would be different from everyone else's. Secondly, ideas are private to those whose ideas they are. I cannot compare my idea with those of another person to see how close is the similarity between them: 'If the number two were an idea, it would have straight away to be private to me only' (*ibid*, p. 37). It is this notion of privacy which Frege uses as the basis for distinguishing between subjective and objective. Something is subjective if there is no basis for intersubjective comparisons. Ideas are subjective, according to Frege, in this sense. Yet arithmetic is palpably not subjective. There are intersubjective comparisons which we can make, and which enables us to decide who is right and who wrong in a dispute about arithmetic.

Here again it is possible to see the epistemological basis of Frege's critique. It is epistemological in a double sense. In the first place the critique of psychologism is clearly motivated by the feeling that if psychologism were accepted it would make the serious justification of mathematics impossible. If numbers are ideas, then each person would have his own arithmetical system which he would be unable to compare with that of anyone else. Thus any justification of mathematics could only be a justification of the system known to that person and could not constitute a generally acceptable argument. This is one respect in which Frege differed quite radically from philosophers like Locke and Berkeley who were attracted by subjective ideas as a possible source of certain knowledge. For Frege, inner certainty was not enough; an anti-sceptical argument was effective only if it would be seen to have weight with all rational beings equally, and not be dependent upon private features of the individual's consciousness.

Frege's argument is epistemological in a second, quite different sense. It depends for its effectiveness upon certain premises about the nature of ideas and of our knowledge of subjective experience — our own and that of others. Frege is assuming that we have, as it were, private access to our own inner experiences, and no access at all to the experiences of others. As I shall try to show later, this theory had important consequences for Frege's theory of cognition and of language (see below, chapter 6, section (b)).

Mathematical empiricism was a theory which had been taken very seriously by the English philosopher John Stuart Mill in his book *A System of Logic*. According to Mill, numerical formulae like 1+2=3 serve not only as definitions of numbers (in this case a definition of the number three), but also to assert empirical facts; that, for instance, there are empirically given collections of objects which can be split up into two distinct collections which appear to us as two units and as one unit. Arithmetical propositions strike us as necessarily true because they are so often exemplified by our experience, and are never found refuted.

What renders arithmetic the type of a deductive science is the fortunate applicability to it of a law so comprehensive as 'The sums of equals are equals': or (to express the same principle in less familiar but more characteristic language),

'Whatever is made up of parts, is made up of the parts of those parts.' This truth, obvious to the senses in all cases which can be fairly referred to their decision, and so general as to be co-extensive with nature itself, being true of all sorts of phenomena (for all admit to being numbered), must be considered an inductive truth, or law of nature, of the highest order. And every arithmetical operation is an application of this law, or of other laws capable of being deduced from it. This is our warrant for all calculations. We believe that five and two are equal to seven, on the evidence of this inductive law, combined with the definitions of those numbers ([1879], Book III, chapter 24, section 5).

To this view Frege has a number of objections: that it makes arithmetic dependent upon contingent empirical facts about the nature of objects in the world; that it fails to explain how numbers could have application to non-empirical situations, as when we say that there are three roots to a certain equation; that it would jeopardise the existence of very large numbers, to which there might be no corresponding empirical collection; that there is no observable collection corresponding to the number zero (see [1884*b*], pp. 9-11). Following Kant, he admits that without empirical facts we would never be brought to an awareness of mathematical truths, but this does not mean that arithmetic depends for its justification on empirical truths (see *ibid*, p. 12). In general, mathematical empiricism arises from a confusion between mathematical propositions themselves and the application of those propositions to empirical circumstances. Addition itself is not a physical operation, but one which can be used to mirror certain physical operations (see *ibid*, p. 13).

Another difference between empirical and mathematical facts emerges when we consider the way in which the numbers are determined as a sequence given in a definite way. If we engage in an empirical search through a collection of objects, what arises at each stage is something that cannot with certainty be predicted in advance; picking out each new element constitutes a genuine discovery. But this is not the way in which the numbers are given to us, they are generated as members of a series the nature of which is determined wholly in advance by the principle that we add one to each number in the series to obtain the next one. The structure which the numbers form together is determined in a way quite different from that which determines the nature of structures in the empirical world, which do not of necessity conform to any such stateable pattern (*ibid*, p. 15).

There is, says Frege, a relation between mathematical and empirical truths, but it is rather the reverse of that supposed by the mathematical empiricists; reasoning in the empirical sciences is actually dependent upon the prior establishment of mathematical truths. Empirical science proceeds by induction; hypotheses are rendered more or less probable by pieces of empirical evidence. But the relation of evidential support has to be explicated by a mathematical theory of probability, if induction is to be accorded any status higher than that of a psychological fact about our expectations. But we cannot have a theory of probability without having established certain basic arithmetical truths (*ibid*, pp. 16-7).

Frege subjects formalism to criticism similar to some of those he brought against psychologism. He shows that the crude formalism which identifies numbers with physical marks such as '1', '$\sqrt{2}$', etc. is also susceptible to consequences which the advocates of the theory never squarely face (see e.g. [1885*c*], p. 105 (145) and [1891*b*], p. 126 (22)). For if a number is a physical sign, then there will not be a single number 2, but many, since there are many signs which we normally take to be designations of that number — '2', '1+1', '5-3', etc. And, as in the case of the identification of numbers with ideas, there is no way in which the arithmetical properties of numbers can be deduced from a definition couched in terms of physical marks. For if the number one is a stroke of ink, then the fact of it being such as to leave every number the same when multiplied by itself should be deducible from the properties of ink marks, and this is clearly not the case.[4]

(b) The Context Principle

(i) Introduction

We have examined Frege's objections to the rival philosophical theories of number which were available when he was writing. I want now to examine the general methodological principles behind his critique. This will help to motivate an interpretation of Frege's famous principle that 'Only in the context of a sentence does a word have significance'. Exactly what role does the Context Principle, as it will be called here, play in determining the polemical and constructive strategy of the book? It is often assumed, I think, that it provides a kind of semantic background against which the discussion of numbers and number designators proceeds; a semantic background which is radically shifted in later works by the introduction of a theory of sense and reference and by the assimilation of sentences to names. Even those who hold that Frege did not abandon the principle in later works usually interpret it as a semantical thesis.

By examining the connections between the principle and Frege's methodology in the *Foundations* and in later works I hope to show that it can be more fruitfully understood as advocating a certain strategy for conceptual analysis. Understood in this way, the principle will be seen to be methodological rather than semantic in orientation.

(ii) The role of the Principle in the Foundations of Arithmetic

Central to the *Foundations* is a choice between rival theories of arithmetic. Frege begins that work by rebutting accounts which others have offered of the concept of number. We have already examined some of the arguments which he gave there. He then offers a theory of his own. Perhaps the role of the Context Principle will be to provide a means of selecting between rival theories of arithmetic' revealing the essential superiority of Frege's theory over these others. This idea gains strength from the fact that Frege explicitly announces the principle as a means of avoiding psychologistic and empirical theories of number, the two theories of arithmetic to which he devotes most critical attention in the book. We can now formulate a constraint on interpretations of the principle:

An interpretation must show how the principle functions in the *Grundlagen* as a defence of Frege's own theory, and as a means of analysing the defects in rival views about the foundations of arithmetic.

There are interpretations of the principle which violate the constraint in various ways. It is tempting, for example, to understand the principle as an endorsement of contextual definitions. But Frege eventually rejects the idea of a contextual definition of the numbers and provides instead an explicit one (see [1884*b*], section 66). Why then insist upon the Context Principle on so many occasions when the method of the book does not employ it? It is true, as Michael Dummett remarks, that Frege's failure to give a contextual definition of the numbers does not show that he altogether rejected such definitions (see his [1973], pp. 495–6). But a puzzle still remains; why introduce the principle in a place where it is not shown to its best advantage?

Dummett's subtle and complex interpretation of the principle gives it considerably more content than simply a defence of contextual definitions. His central contention seems to be this: the

Context Principle was intended by Frege as a means of showing that there is nothing philosophically problematic about the assertion that abstract objects like numbers exist.

> ... it is ... part of Frege's thesis that the nominalist is the victim of a superstition about what has to be done in order to confer a reference on a name ([1973] p. 497).

If the name '*a*' belongs to a language for which we have provided a semantics, and if a sentence which says that *a* exists is true under that semantics, then '*a*' has reference. Once we have established that an expression is a name and that there are well defined truth conditions for all the sentences in which it occours

> Any further question about whether any such name has reference or not can be, at most, a question about the truth of an existential statement: just as the question whether the name 'Vulcan' has reference is an astronomical question, namely as to whether, say, 'ω_1' has a reference is a mathematical question, namely as to whether there is a least non-denumerable ordinal. The truth of the relevant whether there is a least non-denumerable ordinal. The truth of the relevant existential statement is to be determined by the methods proper to that realm of discourse, i.e. in accordance with the truth-conditions that we are supposing have been stipulated (*ibid*).

Our problem is not to decide whether this position is philosophically satisfactory, but whether it coincides with Frege's own understanding of the principle. If it does there should be evidence that the *Foundations* was written in conscious opposition to nominalism, since on Dummett's interpretation this is the position to which the principle is opposed. But, as Dummett himself remarks, nominalism is not the target of Frege's criticisms in that book:

> The philosophical error that Frege wishes to guard against [in the *Grundlagen*] is not nominalism — the rejection of abstract objects — but psychologism, that is, the interpretation of terms for abstract objects as standing for mental images or other results of mental operations (*ibid*, pp. 494–5).

Psychologism, along with mathematical empiricism, was indeed Frege's target in the *Foundations*; a fact explained by the interpretation I shall offer but not, I believe, so easily explained by Dummett's.

I shall now introduce my own account of the Context Principle.

The task which Frege has set himself in the *Foundations* is to provide a theory of number. Two questions arise concerning the methodology of such an investigation. First of all, what is the relation between the concept *number* and the judgements in which it typically occurs? Must we be clear about the concept before we can decide the acceptability of these judgements, or can an analysis of these judgements themselves help to clarify the concept? Secondly, what is the relation between our knowledge of the concept and our familiarity with those objects which fall under the concept? Do we grasp the concept through acquaintance with its instances? Are all concepts arrived at through abstraction? These questions are particularly difficult to answer in the case of the concept number, exactly because the objects which fall under the concept do not seem to be empirical. Our access to them is therefore problematic.

The Context Principle offers Frege a way of answering both these questions. The first question, concerning the relation of concepts to judgements, is answered by the adoption of a certain approach to conceptual analysis: *that such an analysis, and the definitions to which it gives rise, should, in conjunction with certain other principles, entail intuitively correct judgements concerning that concept.* I shall try to show how this apparently trivial principle was the key to Frege's critique of other theories of number, and how he used it to display the advantages of his own theory.

The second question, concerning the relation of concepts to objects, is answered by an extension of the approach just outlined. the problem is to justify the adoption of a view about the concept number which seems to entail that we have no direct access to the objects which fall under that concept. The problem is solved by adopting the principle that *we have an adequate grasp of a concept once our analysis is shown to deliver intuitively correct judgements, independent of any ability we may have to form an idea of the objects concerned.*

So when Frege enjoins us to ask for the significance of a word only in the context of a sentence, he is urging us to give an explanation of a word (i.e. to analyse the concept which it expresses) which will be faithful to the intuitively correct judgements in which that word occurs. If we can do this our grasp of the associated concept will be seen to be secure, even if the analysis leaves us without a mental picture of those things which fall under the concept.

I shall try to show how the principle can be seen as guiding almost the entire argument of the *Foundations*, in both its critical and its constructive aspects.

Let us see first of all how Frege applied the principle in criticising contemporary theories of number. Frege reasoned that these theories are mathematically sterile, since we cannot deduce the mathematical properties of numbers from the properties of ideas, physical collections or inscriptions. In other words, these approaches do not provide a theoretically adequate analysis. If numbers were ideas in the mind, then arithmetical operations like addition and multiplication ought to apply to ideas. But for Frege it is nonsense to say that ideas can be summed or multiplied. We discover nothing of mathematical interest by studying the properties of ideas, and so the definition does not help us discover why numbers relate to each other as they do. Frege sums this up by saying:

> ...psychology should not imagine that it can contribute anything to the foundations of arithmetic. To the mathematician as such these mental pictures, with their origins and their transformations, are immaterial ([1884*b*], p. vi).

Similar criticisms apply to the attempt to define numbers as marks on paper. No amount of chemical investigation into the properties of paper and ink will tell us what algebraic rules numbers obey. It is an intrinsic property of the number zero that its multiplication by any other number gives zero as a result. But this is certainly not an intrinsic property of a physical mark (see Frege [1885*c*], p. 106 (145)). Formalist definitions of number are, therefore, mathematically irrelevant. Later Frege wrote, concerning formalist theories of arithmetic. 'What use to us are explanations when they have no inner connection with a piece of work, but are only stuck on to the outside like a useless ornament?([1914], p. 181 (166)).

Empiricism gains plausibility from our tendency to think that certain observable situations exemplify the mathematical properties of numbers and that, by defining a number as a characteristic of an empirical collection, we enable ourselves to derive the familiar properties of addition, etc., from its observable behaviour. Frege argued that this appears to be so only because we interpret the empirical situation *in the light of* the mathematical truth which is actually given *a priori*. Experience is not being used to verify the arithmetical law, the law is being used to interpret the experience ([1884*b*], section 9).

Definitions based on ideas such as these are philosophically objectionable partly because they are mathematically useless; they give us no insight into the mathematical properties of numbers. Frege realised that a definition of number must connect with our mathematical knowledge by having as consequences all the intuitive properties of the numbers. He then offers a definition of number from which, he claims, we can obtain genuinely mathematical results.

Definitions show their worth by proving fruitful. Those which could just as well be omitted and leave no link missing in the chain of our proofs should be rejected as completely worthless.

Let us try, therefore, whether we can derive from our explanation of . . . number . . . any of the well known properties of numbers ([1884*b*], section 70).

The demand that definitions be fruitful is a puzzling one, since Frege insists elsewhere that definitions should not extend the proving power of a theory. But in the passage quoted above Frege does not have in mind any violation of this formal requirement. To understand this we need to know more about the role that definitions are intended to play in his work.

Notice first that in a number of places in the *Foundations* Frege uses the terms 'definition' and 'explanation' [*Erklärung*] interchangeably; a fact which is obscured in Austin's translation by his using 'definition' for both (*ibid*, pp. 81 and 116). Perhaps, then, Frege took his definitions not *simply* to be stipulations about the meanings of expressions like 'number', 'zero' and 'successor of' etc. These expressions have meanings already; meanings which Frege inherited along with the mathematical tradition which he was trying to place on a firm foundation. It was not his aim to give new meanings to these terms, but rather to explain, or, as he put it in a later work, 'analyse' their meanings (see above, chapter 4, section (c) (iv)). Thus his definitions have a double aspect. A statement like:

> A number is the extension of a concept of the form *Equinumerate with the concept F*, for some *F*.

when read from right to left, so to speak, offers an abbreviation of the expression on the right. In this sense Frege's definitions are conservative; we will not be able to prove anything about the extensions of concepts that we could not otherwise have proved. But read from left to right the definition offers an analysis of the term 'number'; a term which already has a meaning (perhaps an imprecise one) but which is now clarified. It is with respect to this left to right reading that the question of fruitfulness arises. The definition enables us to graft the informal concept of number on to a theory (the theory of conceptual extensions) which has, from a philosophical point of view, certain advantages over the informal arithmetical theory with which we are familiar. The definition will be fruitful if we can use the theory of extensions to prove the arithmetical results that we require concerning number.[5] Frege begins to show that this is the case in the *Foundations*, and takes the process considerably further in the *Basic Laws*.

The fruitfulness of a definition is thus something which cannot be judged in isolation. We must ask: when we substitute the term on the left for that on the right in certain of the theorems about extensions, do we get a correct sentence of informal arithmetic? In other words, do extensions obey the arithmetical laws of addition, do they form an inductive progression, etc? Psychologistic, formalistic and empirical theories treat numerical terms in isolation in so far as the terms which they substitute for numerical terms — terms from psychology, the theory of signs or from empirical discourse — are not built into a body of statements which can explicate the arithmetical concepts in a satisfactory way.

If what I have suggested here is a correct account of Frege's understanding of the principle, why does he announce it in a discussion of contexts of the form 'The number of *F*'s is identical with the number of *G*'s' (section 62), since judgements of this form do not always belong to arithmetic proper? The answer is, I think that two stages of analysis are contemplated; the heuristic stage where the definition is constructed in accordance with plausible constraints, and the deductive stage where the worth of the definition is shown by the derivation of the required arithmetical results. The Context Principle is useful at both stages. Frege announces it at the beginning of the whole process intending it to be borne in mind throughout. At the heuristic level the principle tells us that the best way to analyse the concept number is not by pure reflection on the concept itself but by a consideration of typical propositions in which the concept occurs. Now it was important to Frege that the sort of contexts which are used heuristically to motivate the definition be of a kind different from those which figure in the deductive stage; otherwise the definition will have the appearance of being 'rigged'. Frege wanted to give his definition maximum impact by it being shown that the right results flow naturally from the definition, even though the definition has not been constructed with those results explicitly in mind.

We can now see how the Context Principle enables Frege systematically to criticise extant theories of number, and to present his own theory in such a way as to reveal its explanatory power. But the same idea enables him also to deflect metaphysical criticism from his claim that numbers are objects. One of these criticisms is that we are not able to form an idea (mental image) of the objects which numbers are supposed to be.

Frege offers two replies: first, this shows merely that numbers are not sensible objects, not that they are not objects: 'We can form no idea of the number ... as a self-subsistent object ... because it is not in fact ... anything sensible' (section 58). Secondly, Frege points out that we are often unable to form an adequate idea of a concrete object such as the earth. But this does not prevent us from making judgements about it, or from making inferences from those judgements. Our words have meaning even when we cannot associate with them any mental picture. He says:

> We ought always to keep before our eyes a complete sentence. Only in a sentence have words really a significance. It may be that mental pictures float before us all the while, but these need not correspond to the logical elements in the judgement. It is enough if the sentence taken as a whole has a sense; it is this that confers on its parts also their content (*ibid*, section 60).

Frege then goes on to begin his own analysis, starting with judgements of numerical identity. He asks:

> How, then, are numbers to be given to us, if we cannot have any ideas or intuitions of them? Only in the context of a sentence do words have any significance. It comes, therefore, to this: to explain the sense of a sentence in which a number word occurs (*ibid*, section 62).

I take his argument to be this. If we can give an analysis of the concept number which adequately explains the senses of sentences which express judgements about number, then we have nothing more to show concerning the adequacy of our grasp of number. We need not, in particular, show that there is any direct epistemic relation between us and the numbers themselves. It is the desire to meet this unreasonable demand which has led to theories which make numbers part of the natural world: psychologism, empiricism and, as Frege was soon to realise, formalism. The whole motivation for providing a theory such as they offer is the desire to make numbers 'pictureable'; to show that there is some direct epistemic relation between numbers and the mind. Empiricism and formalism do this by making use of the perceptual relation, psychologism by making numbers part of the content of the mind.

Thus while the Context Principle tells Frege that a definition of number must meet constraints not recognised by the proponents of other theories, it eases his epistemological problems in other directions. It obviates the necessity that he would otherwise be under to postulate some special faculty which enables us to 'perceive' mathematical objects. It tells him, in other words that, while a theoretically adequate definition of number is necessary for a successful analysis of the concept, it is also, happily, sufficient.

(iii) The Context Principle and the theory of meaning

It is widely assumed that the Context Principle was understood by Frege as a semantical thesis. In stating the principle he used the word *Bedeutung*, a natural translation of which is 'meaning'. Later, so the story goes, Frege distinguished within the intuitive notion of meaning two separate components; sense and reference. The assumption has been, then, that the principle contains two distinct but not distinguished principles, one a principle about sense and the other about reference. A number of questions then arise: Which of the two interpretations of the principle is primary? Are both of equal importance? Taken as a dual thesis about sense and reference, does the Context Principle conflict with Frege's later way of assigning senses and references to expressions as if these senses and references were independently existing entities? Some have argued that the principle does conflict with Frege's later semantics and that he therefore abandoned the principle in his later work. (See Dummett [1973], pp. 495-500 and Resnik [1976]). Others have argued that he did not abandon it and that the Context Principle is itself one clue to the fact that Frege did not, despite appearances, regard sub-sentential expressions as having independently existing senses (see Sluga [1971] and [1977], Tugendhat [1970] and Hacker [1979]).

On the account I have offered questions such as these do not arise, since the principle is neither closely related to the notions of sense and reference, nor intended as a strictly semantical thesis. It is a methodological rule for judging between competing theories which seek to explicate the same pre-theoretic notion.

But what of Frege's use of the expression *Bedeutung* in his statement of the principle? Since this is naturally interpreted as 'meaning' is it not reasonable to suppose that the principle is in some way or other a principle about meaning? In fact, as others have pointed out, *Bedeutung* can quite naturally have the same force as 'significance'. The epistemological ideas which Frege wanted to express by means of the Context Principle would fairly naturally suit such a formulation as 'Only in the context of a sentence does a word have any significance'; in other words what is significant about a concept (such as the concept of number) is the role it plays in a body of propositions.

(iv) Did Frege abandon the Principle?

Frege never explicitly stated the Context Principle after 1884. Was this because he had abandoned the principle? I do not believe so. The reason is rather that his later use of the term *Bedeutung* precluded a straightforward restatement of the principle. He could no longer use the term *Bedeutung* in the intuitive way that he had done in the *Foundations*, since he had given it a quite specific meaning according to which the *Bedeutung* of a name is the entity named by the expression (see above, chapter 4, section (b)). Let us recall that, according to Frege's 'mature' theory, proper names, concept words and sentences all have both a reference (i.e. a *Bedeutung*) and a sense, the sense being, roughly speaking, the information conveyed by the expression about the reference. To have said that a word has either sense or reference only in the context of a proposition would have been out of step with his views of that period, for according to that theory, the reference (sense) of a sentence is determined by the references (senses) of its parts. And Frege makes it clear that the idea that an expression has a sense only in a sentential context is, for him, an undesirable feature of natural languages.

To every expression belonging to a complete totality of signs, there should certainly correspond a definite sense; but natural languages often do not satisfy this condition, and one must be content if the same word has the same sense in the same context ([1892*b*], p. 144–5 (58)).

Being thus denied the use of his old terminology — terms like *Sinn* and *Bedeutung* which he had once used in an intuitive way but which were now for him terms of art — Frege cast around for a new way of expressing his old idea. And, indeed, after the early 1890s when he introduced the theory of sense and reference, there emerged in his work a new slogan — that 'thinking is the grasping of a Thought'.[6] In this way Frege again expressed the irrelevance of ideas for cognition, and the epistemological primacy of the contents of sentences over that of their constituents.

That Frege never explicitly stated the principle in any work after the *Foundations* is therefore explicable on assumptions other than that he had abandoned it. But it is important that we find evidence of the principle's sustained influence on his methodology.

Underlying Frege's adherence to the principle is his appreciation of the fact that concepts like number are important because of the propositions that are true of the numbers. This is why he insists that the acceptability of explications of such concepts should depend upon their ability to deliver those very propositions. There are two places in Frege's later work where his method seems to be informed by this insight; the account of courses of values [*Werthverläufe*] in volume 1 of the *Basic Laws*, and the theory of magnitudes and real numbers in volume 2. I shall now consider the role of the Context Principle in these constructions.

In Frege's logical system Axiom V governs the relation between functions and their courses of values. It says:

> The course of values of the function f = the course of values of the function g if and only if $\forall x(f(x) = g(x))$.

This axiom gives us all the information about courses of values that is available within the system and Frege does not offer us an informal, extra-systematic 'elucidation' of their nature. How much, then, does the axiom tell us about courses of values? As Frege showed, it does not distinguish courses of values from other objects. Suppose we know that $a = b$ if and only if f and g have the same values for the same argument. We cannot conclude from this that a and b are the courses of values of these functions, nor even that they are courses of values at all. Frege claims to overcome the difficulty by specifying 'for every function when it is introduced, what values it takes on for courses of values as arguments' ([1893], section 10). In carrying out this procedure Frege specifies *some* of the properties of courses of values (since properties are functions on to truth values) but not all of them; there are properties other than those specified within his system. We cannot evade this limitation by saying that courses of values have only mathematical properties and that the application to them of other properties is something like a category mistake, since Frege insists that every property be globally defined. So if courses of values are not red (as they presumably are not) they must be non-red. But this is no thanks to the specification given in the *Basic Laws*, neither redness nor non-redness being properties named under the intended interpretation of that system.

It seems best, then, not to interpret Frege as trying to specify exactly what courses of values are, but rather as trying to determine what role they play in the logical system of the *Basic Laws*. That system is a functional calculus; complex expressions, including sentences, are constructed by the application of the name of a function to the name of another entity; in the case of a function of first level the other entity is always an object. In order to specify the role of courses of values within his theory Frege thought he had only to specify the value which a first level function of that system takes for a course of values as argument. To do more than this would be simply to engage in a mathematically irrelevant investigation into the metaphysical nature of courses of values. Without the Context Principle Frege might have been worried by his inability to specify exactly what courses of values are. But the principle tells him that what we need to know about courses of values is relative to those propositions in which course of values terms occur and which are important to our purpose. Since that purpose is, presently, the construction of a theory of number, the propositions which concern us are precisely those formulable in the system — presuming, as Frege must have presumed at this time, that that system is adequate to the expression of all arithmetical truths. So Frege does not ask, ' What is a course of values?' but rather, 'What do we need to know about courses of values for the purposes of our logico-arithmetical system?' I shall say more about the philosophical implication of Frege's introduction of courses of values below in section (e) (vi).

Frege published this account of extensions in 1893. Ten years later he published the second volume of the *Basic Laws*, beginning a detailed theoretical construction of the complete ordered field of real numbers. Because of the discovery of Russell's Paradox, this work was not completed. All we have is a few preliminary results together with a general account of the method which Frege intended to pursue.

What Frege found particularly deficient about current definitions of the real numbers was the fact that they offered no explanation of the application of real numbers to measurement. To such definitions an account of the applicability of the real numbers must, he says, be 'externally patched on' ([1903*a*], section 159). Since the natural numbers and the real numbers have different application, the one to counting, the other to measurement, he did not try, as others had done, to generate the real numbers by some method of set-theoretic generalisation from the natural numbers. Instead we are to start again from the beginning.

We have seen that, according to Frege, real numbers must be constructed as the extensions of relations between magnitudes. To show that the real numbers exist Frege must now show that magnitudes exist, and in doing so he may draw only upon logical assumptions. The kind of objects whose existence can be proved using just the axioms of his logical theory are exactly the courses of values of functions, of which the extensions of concepts and relations are special cases. His task, then, is to show that there are courses of values (actually extensions) which can be considered as magnitudes. How can we establish that certain extensions actually are magnitudes?

Frege solves this problem with a further and more radical application of the Context Principle. We should not ask, 'What is a magnitude?' in isolation from a theoretical context. Being a magnitude is not an *intrinsic* property of an object; whether or not something is a magnitude depends upon its standing in certain relations to other entities. Specifying what a magnitude is is not a matter of identifying certain objects in isolation, but rather in offering a structure (a 'magnitude field') which satisfies the theory of magnitudes. Frege put the point like this:

Instead of asking, what properties must an object have in order to be a magnitude? we must ask, how must a concept be constituted so as to have as its extension a magnitude field [*Grössengebiet*]? . . . what properties must a class have in order to be a magnitude field? *Something is not a magnitude in itself, but only in so far as it belongs, with other objects, to a class which is a magnitude field.* (*ibid*, section 161, my italics).

Thus the problem of deciding whether there are extensions which are magnitudes resolves itself into the problem of showing that there is a class of extensions which stand to each other in those relations which determine a magnitude field.

In the theory of magnitudes the use of the Context Principle is again evident. Frege explicitly disavows any attempt to identify magnitudes outside their theoretical context. Any object can count as a magnitude as long as it satisfies the principles which determine the structure which is a magnitude field.

I have argued that the Context Principle has important epistemological implications. It argues the replacement of the naturalistic model of epistemic relations in terms of perceptual ones, and the abandonment of criteria of knowledge drawn from the perceptual analogue. Abandoning the naturalistic model was an essential step in the construction of a viable theory of mathematical knowlege. It is as a contribution to such a theory, rather than to a theory of meaning, that the Context Principle must be understood.

(*v*) *The reality of Thoughts*

I have said that according to Frege thinking is the grasping of a Thought. He seems to have held a particularly strong version of this theory. In several places he argues that Thoughts are not only objective, they also have what he calls 'actuality' or 'reality' (*Wirklichkeit*): the ability to act (*wirken*) causally on other entities. In 'The Thought' he says

> How does a Thought act? By being grasped and being taken to be true. This is a process in the inner world of a thinker which may have further consequences in this inner world, and which may also encroach upon the sphere of the will and make itself noticeable in the outside world as well. If, for example, I grasp the Thought which we express by the Pythagorean theorem, the consequence may be that I recognise it to be true and further that I apply it, making a decision which brings about the acceleration of masses . . . *And so Thoughts can have an indirect effect on the motion of masses* . . . Could the great events of world history have come about without the communication of Thoughts? And yet we are inclined to regard Thoughts as unreal, because they appear to do nothing in relation to events . . . How very different the reality of a hammer appears, compared with that of a Thought? When a Thought is grasped it at first brings about changes in the inner world of the one who grasps it; yet it remains untouched in the core of its essence, for the changes it undergoes affect only inessential properties.
>
> There is lacking here something we observe in every physical process — reciprocal action. Thoughts are not wholly unreal, but their reality is quite different from that of things. And their action is brought about by the performance of a thinker; without this they would be inactive, at least as far as we can see. And yet the thinker does not create them, but must take them as they are ([1918*a*], pp. 361-2 (28-30). My italics).

Frege's idea seems to be this: a physical object may interact with the inner world of someone's psyche by being perceived and thereby bringing about new ideas. These new ideas may change that person's overt behaviour, thus acting back on the physical world. But, so the argument continues, the same thing can be seen to apply in the case of a Thought. A Thought may be grasped by the act of thinking, and, via its effects on the mental world, may induce us to bring about changes in the physical world. It is this which gives us the right to say that Thoughts are real.[7]

This view goes back at least to 1897.[8] In a paper of that year Frege says:

> If one talks of the reality of Thoughts, this can be meant only in the sense that the knowledge that someone has of, for instance, a law of nature, affects his decisions and has further consequences for the motion of masses. The recognition of a law would then be considered as an effect upon the knowing subject — which is perhaps possible — in the same way in which the seeing of a flower can be regarded as the indirect effect of the flower upon the viewer.

If it is perhaps possible to speak of the effects of Thoughts upon men, one cannot say that there is an effect of men upon Thoughts ([1897], p. 150 (138)).

This seems to be a tentative statement of the view more forcefully propounded in 'The Thought'.

(vi) Thoughts and intersubjectivity

Frege's view that Thoughts are real or actual faces many difficulties. It asserts the existence of a causal relation between that which has no spatio-temporal position and is unchanging, and the psychological processes of a living being. It would not be easy to adjust our notions about causal relations to fit such a case.[9] But perhaps we should not rule a theory out *simply* because it seems metaphysically questionable. After all, we often tolerate bizarreness in a scientific theory if it has explanatory power to compensate. Yet in this respect the theory fares no better. It is, I believe, an unhelpful theory in the sense that it does not shed any light on the really important issues about knowledge and human cognition.

The thesis of the objectivity of knowledge can be construed in two different ways. We can interpret it as the claim that knowledge as a *social* phenomenon is objective in the sense that people are capable of arguing in a rational way; that knowledge is preserved and perhaps accumulated over generations; that we are capable of understanding each other and of recognising the same intersubjective standards of rational debate (though it would be wrong to construe the thesis of objectivity as the descriptive claim that people always or usually *do* recognise such standards). Objectivity can, on the other hand, be construed as the claim that there *exist* objective, abstract entities called Thoughts which resist change or obliteration as a result of changes in our human world, and which impose upon our thinking and communication their own objectivity. This second sense of objectivity seems to offer no genuine insights into the nature of our knowledge. First of all, whatever the role played by Thoughts in making knowledge objective, the Thoughts themselves cannot be sufficient to *guarantee* objectivity. Thoughts can be as objective as anything possibly can be, yet subjective chaos might still reign here in our world of human communication and thought. If we had no common language intersubjective knowledge would presumably be impossible, and the same could be said if we had no capacities for judging the acceptability or otherwise of claims to knowledge. Surely then it is the institutions of language, socially enforced standards of criticism, and the human capacities which underlie them which shed light on the nature of objectivity, not the claims about the efficacy of abstract Thoughts. For the nature of the supposed connection between Thoughts and the *phenomenon* of objectivity is one that will never, by the very nature of the case, be revealed to us. Everything useful that we can know about objectivity can be known without recourse to metaphysically real Thoughts.

The theory also offers an unhelpful and even misleading picture of language use. At any rate it did, I believe, mislead Frege in this connection.

In some places Frege is dominated by a conception of Thoughts according to which they make language possible. I have already described how Frege's theory of the nature of ideas led him to the view that 'thinking is the grasping of a Thought' (see above, chapter 6, section (b) (v)). In the same way he was led by his theory of ideas to the view that communication is the bringing about of another person's grasping a Thought. Frege asks, 'What is it that is communicated in language?' One answer — the traditional empiricist answer — is that it is ideas which are communicated. But for Frege ideas are private. An idea is something which cannot stand alone: it can exists only as part of an individual's consciousness. 'It is so much the essence of any of my ideas to be a content of my consciousness that any idea someone else has is, just as such, different from mine ([1918*a*], p. 352 (15)). I cannot therefore communicate an idea to someone else, in the sense of making an idea pass from my mind to his. The same idea cannot pass from one consciousness to another. But perhaps this is too strong a conception of the communication of ideas. Perhaps we should say instead that I communicate my ideas to another when I get him to recognise the ideas which I have, and to have similar ideas himself (in some as yet unexplained sense of similarity). But Frege cannot allow this either, because he does not believe that there can be any genuine comparisons between the ideas of different people. Ideas are private, not only in the sense of being the inalienable property of those who have them, but in the sense of being available to inspection by their possessors only. He says

> . . . it is impossible to compare my sense-impression with that of someone else. For that, it would be necessary to bring together in one consciousness a sense impression belonging to one consciousness with the sense impression belonging to another consciousness. Now even if it were possible to make an idea disappear from one consciousness and at the same time to make an idea appear in another

consciousness, the question whether it was the same idea in both would remain unanswerable... In any case it is impossible for us as men to compare another person's ideas with our own ([1918*a*], pp. 351-2 (15). See also [1879-91], p. 6 (5) and [1892*b*], p. 141 (60)).

On Frege's own view, communication comes about when the speaker grasps a Thought and utters the corresponding sentence. The utterance is perceived by the hearer, who then associates the sentence with a Thought which he grasps. Of course, in order for this to be a case of successful communication, the hearer has to associate the same Thought with the sentence as the speaker associated with it. Somewhat earlier, Frege had written that 'the task of our natural language is essentially fulfilled provided that people communicating with each other connect the same Thought, or at least a very similar one, with the same sentence' ([1896*b*], p. 236 (33)).

The question here is this: is anything being genuinely explained by this account of communication? We are told that we are able to understand each other because we are able to associate the same Thoughts with the same sentences. Yet this account really suffers from the difficulty which worries Frege about the account according to which we communicate our ideas to each other. Frege's claim was that the ideas of one man cannot be compared with those of another. I cannot communicate my ideas to you because you cannot know what my ideas are. But now consider the communication of Thoughts. Suppose I grasp a Thought and associate it with a sentence which I utter. The hearer picks up the sentence I have uttered, but now he must associate it with a Thought which he too grasps. Which Thought is he to associate with it? According to Frege, in the case of successful communication it is the same Thought that is grasped by me. But how is he to know which Thought I have grasped? A Thought itself may be an objective entity, equally available to all, but my grasping of the Thought is not. It is an event which takes place in my own consciousness and, on Frege's own account, it is not available to anyone but me. So if the hearer cannot have access to the contents of my consciousness, he also cannot have access to a knowledge of which Thought I associate with the sentences that I utter. In order to explain intersubjectivity Frege has invoked the causal efficacy of Thoughts, but now it turns out that they cannot serve their intended purpose because their interaction with our minds is, on Frege's own account, not available for intersubjective comparison.

But there is another conception of Thoughts in Frege's work according to which we can see them as derivative from these human activities. Thoughts are the common content of what many different people think and say at different times. In *Negation* Frege says that 'the being [*Sein*] of a Thought may also be taken to lie in the possibility of different thinkers grasping the Thought as one and the same Thought' ([1918*b*], p. 365 (35)). Perhaps this means that Thoughts arise *because* of the existence of linguistic communication. It is because people are capable of understanding each other that Thoughts exist, rather than the other way around. And much of Frege's earlier discussion of objectivity, particularly in the *Foundations*, is concerned simply with there being an objective content of language and Thought, and with the impossibility of identifying this objective content with the human activities from which they arise, or with their concrete representations in symbols. And here Frege sometimes speaks of these abstract entities as if he thought of them as ultimately derivative upon consciousness.

It is possible to identify, therefore, a strand in Frege's work which employs the notion of Thoughts without becoming involved in dubious claims about their power to bring about thinking and communication. And certainly it is Frege's arguments about objectivity which are important and lasting contributions to philosophy. These arguments can very largely be divorced from metaphysical speculation about a 'third realm' (as he calls it) of Thoughts (see below, chapter 6, section (e) (i)). What Frege always insisted on was that an epistemology of mathematics must do justice to the intersubjectivity of mathematics, and that psychologism failed in this. It is then a further question as to whether the postulation of real Thoughts is a sufficient or even necessary way of overcoming the difficulties of explaining intersubjectivity.

It should be clear that the identification of ideas with mental pictures is an important assumption in Frege's thinking about language and communication. Perhaps I should end this section with some remarks about the character of this presupposition. It is this impoverished notion of ideas — one obtained perhaps from a superficial reading of the empiricist thinkers to which he was so much opposed — which made ideas seem inadequate to the task of explaining thinking. Frege never seems to have questioned this identification, yet had he done so it might have become evident that the invocation of causally efficacious Thoughts was not the only way in which thinking could be explained. Frege might have abandoned the mental picture-paradigm, and cast around for some more embracing conception of idea which will allow us to have ideas of, for instance, numbers and planets. Secondly, and perhaps more importantly from Frege's point of view, he might have taken seriously (that is, taken as serious psychological hypotheses) Kantian ideas about the mind's powers of synthesis, and attributed to the mind sufficient internal capacity to make the phenomenon of thought and judgement understandable without needing to invoke something external to it.

(c) Sense

(i) Sense and meaning

I remarked earlier that interpretations of Frege have often been marred by a tendency to view his philosophy in the light of later developments. Nowhere is this tendency more evident than in interpretations of Frege's theory of sense.

Michael Dummett, Frege's most influential commentator, has written extensively on Frege's theory of sense. In these writings the theory of sense is constantly connected with the problem of what it is to understand one's language.[10] Frege's notion of sense is discussed as a contribution to the solution of this problem, and the Fregean solution which Dummett presents is contrasted with answers given by other philosophers, such as Wittgenstein, Quine and Dummett himself. The notion of sense is connected in Dummett's account with the existence of certain human capacities relevant to linguistic competence — the capacity, for instance, to recognise an object as the *Bedeutung* of an expression.

According to Dummett, Frege went beyond the immediate requirements of his mathematical programme to offer a theory of meaning: 'a general account of the workings of language . . . So Frege's philosophy, so far as it is concerned with language generally, rather than specifically with mathematics, is largely constituted by his theory of meaning' (Dummett [1973], p. 83).

There is no doubt that Frege was deeply concerned with the nature of language. It is less clear that this concern can adequately be described as a desire to formulate a general theory of meaning. And here we ought to be careful to examine the problem in a way which does not presuppose an understanding of developments subsequent to Frege's own work. For instance, Dummett describes Frege as having an interest in language which goes beyond the concerns of the logician, and reasons that Frege's interest was therefore in a general theory of meaning. Today logicians usually have a well defined and rather narrow conception of their relation to language. They are concerned with it from the point of view of the formalisation of the notion of validity. But Frege seems to have seen the logician's role in much wider terms, involving, for instance, considerations of an epistemological kind about the nature of objectivity, and about our abilities to recognise the truth of a premise. I should like to suggest, in fact, that Frege's main concern with language was a concern about the implications of language for the objectivity of our knowledge. In this sense it is, I believe, quite wrong to say, as Dummett does, that Frege put the theory of meaning at the centre of philosophy. Though much of what Frege says about sense and reference can be construed as providing the outline of a theory of meaning, the theses he proposed, particularly concerning sense, derive from insights about knowledge which were of central importance to him. If there was a revolution in philosophy which put the notion of meaning at the centre, it came later with Wittgenstein, the Vienna Circle, and perhaps also with Tarski. Frege's thinking is essentially classical in so far as his central problem was the validation of our (mathematical) knowledge. Let me begin by examining some of the most important pronouncements of Frege's concerning the notion of sense. I shall then consider the relation of Frege's notion of sense to the question of our understanding and acquisition of language, for in Dummett's exposition the theory of sense is continually related to these issues. Then I shall say something about the notion of reference. The general theme of the discussion will be continued in the next section concerning Frege's ideas about the relation of language to thinking.

(ii) Sense and objective knowledge

Frege's deep concern with language was not the result of an interest in the problem of how language is understood, but rather the problem of what we are capable of doing with language when it *is* understood. Taking it for granted that people do display linguistic competence, his concern is to examine the implications, as he sees them, of linguistic communication for human knowledge.[11]

We can, in other words, read Frege's pronouncements about sense as contributions to an epistemological theory about the objectivity of knowledge. The sense of an expression is, on this view, the information conveyed by that expression. This is suggested by the many places in which he described the sense of an expression as its *Erkenntniswert* — something like 'knowledge value' — and by the specific problem-situation which he uses to introduce the notion of sense.

I argued above that Frege introduced a notion of sense to solve two rather different problems raised by his attempt to reduce arithmetic to logic. Both these problems concern the nature of our mathematical knowledge. An epistemological reading of sense is also suggested by a passage in which Frege is discussing the possibility of sense-preserving translations. He says

> We must not fail to recognise that the same sense, the same Thought, may be variously expressed; thus the difference does not here concern the sense, but only the apprehensions, shading, or colouring of the Thought, and is irrelevant for logic. It is possible for one sentence to give no more and no less information than another; and, for all the multiplicity of languages, mankind has a common stock of Thoughts ([1892*a*], p. 170, note (46)).

Here Frege seems to be identifying the sense of a sentence with the information which it conveys, and the reference to humanity's 'common stock of Thoughts' again suggests an epistemic notion; something like our accumulated knowledge. Of course false sentences have a sense (express a Thought) as well as do true ones — as Frege is fond of telling us. Perhaps this fact more than any other has made an epistemological reading of sense more implausible, for knowledge seems to have a stronger connection with the truth than with falsity, and this is not the case as regards sense.

I do not wish to deny that Frege would have conceived of genuine knowledge as necessarily connected with the truth; indeed I have been at pains to point out the extent to which he was committed to the principle that mathematical knowledge must be certainly true. But this should not prevent us from recognising that, for Frege, the domain of Thoughts, both true and false, represent something essentially epistemological. Perhaps I can explain this by appealing to a well known distinction in the theory of subjective knowledge. I shall then claim that we can understand the epistemological role of Thoughts by reference to the objective counterpart to this distinction.

It is usual to distinguish between a person's knowledge and his or her beliefs, or at least to distinguish within the class of his or her beliefs a privileged sub-class which count as knowledge because they have properties which his other beliefs lack. I do not want to consider here whether or not it is ultimately possible to do this in a satisfactory way; my concern here is to concede as much as possible to those who look upon truth as an essential ingredient in knowledge. Now in this sense knowledge may be *preferable* to belief, but belief is just as important an epistemic category as knowledge. It is just as much the task of the subjective epistemologist[12] to account for belief as it is to account for knowledge. Now in the terms with which the distinction between knowledge and belief is usually drawn, items of subjective knowledge correspond naturally to true Thoughts, and the wider class of beliefs (or possible beliefs) to the class of Thoughts in general. Thus if we are interested in looking at epistemology from an objective point of view, as I believe Frege was, we shall be concerned to have not just an objective correlate of knowledge (in the sense of certain or 'true' knowledge) but also an objective correlate of belief. And this is just the class of Thoughts.

My point can be reinforced by noting that in several places in his later work Frege uses 'content' as synonymous with 'sense'. Of course, in his early writings, before he had developed the theory of sense and reference, he used 'content' in an ambiguous way, as we have seen (see above, chapter 4, section (c)).

This use of the word 'content' where sense is clearly meant occurs in several places in 'The Thoughts':

> ... two things must be distinguished in an assertoric sentence: the content, ... and assertion. The former is the Thought, or at least contains the Thought. ([1918*a*], p. 346 (7)).

Thus there is evidence that at this late stage Frege still thought of sense as an explication of the intuitive idea of content or information.

(iii) Sense and language learning

Frege's work does not contain answers to certain pressing questions about the way in which our knowledge of language is acquired. In particular it does not contain an account of how our knowledge of the meanings of complex expressions like 'the King of France' derive ultimately from a knowledge of the meanings of expressions which do not have this complexity and which, as a consequence, are associated with what they signify simply by stipulation or convention. For we cannot suppose that a person learns the use of *all* the terms in his vocabulary by being told that they are equivalent in sense to some descriptive phrase; the question would then arise as to where he learnt the senses of the terms which make up the descriptions. Now Frege talks as if the sense of a proper name — a name like 'Aristotle' — was always that of some complex expression which is not just conventionally associated with what it names. A very important passage is the following:

In the case of an actual proper name such as 'Aristotle' opinions as to the sense may differ. It might, for instance, be taken to be the following: the pupil of Plato and teacher of Alexander the Great. Anybody who does this will attach another sense to the sentence 'Aristotle was born in Stagira' than will a man who takes as the sense of the name: the teacher of Alexander the Great who was born in Stagira. So long as the reference remains the same, such variations of sense may be tolerated, although they are to be avoided in the theoretical structure of a demonstrative science and ought not to occur in a perfect language ([1892*b*], p. 144, note (58)).

I suggest that the natural interpretation of this passage involves attributing to Frege the view that the sense of a proper name can, in general, be given by citing a definite description which refers to the same object.[13] That this is a legitimate conclusion is denied by Michael Dummett, according to whom 'it is extremely dubious that he supposed such a thing': Frege is here simply trying to give a 'brief characterisation of sense' through examples which are easily conveyed. He does not, here or anywhere else, say that the sense of a proper name is always the sense of some corresponding description (see Dummett [1973], p. 110).

The question is then, why is it dubious that Frege would have held the thesis that his words naturally suggest? I suspect that Dummett finds it dubious because he thinks that the position is a theoretically unacceptable one, and is unwilling to attribute to Frege a false theory unless compelled to do so by the texts. If we think of the theory of sense as part of a theory of meaning or, more pertinently, as part of a theory about the speaker's knowledge of his language,[14] we would expect it to contain provision for the fact that a person's knowledge of language cannot always be such that it could be given a non-trivial verbal explication. At some level we must understand our language, or some part of it in a way which does not itself presuppose a grasp of other parts of the language. In that case it would be an unwelcome conclusion to suppose that Frege never took this into account. But it is a fact, none the less, that Frege nowhere explicitly deals with this difficulty, and the claim that he either did privately, or would have done so must remain highly conjectural. If, however, we adopt the position that I have been urging here it becomes less problematic to suppose that Frege thought of sense as something which can always be conveyed in words and in particular that the sense of a proper name is that of some corresponding complex description. For on this view Frege is presupposing a knowledge of language and is concerned with the objective information that language can convey. The claim that the sense of a name is the same as that of some complex description can then be interpreted as the epistemological claim that we do not have direct access to individuals, but access to them only in so far as we know something *about* them. Someone who uses a proper name does so in virtue of knowing some identifying feature of the individual named. (At least they suppose that they know such a thing — they may apply the description incorrectly.) Since Frege wants this knowledge to be reflected at the level of language, he quite naturally thinks of proper names as having the senses of descriptions. But this does not amount to saying that the *meaning* of a proper name is that of some definite description.[15]

In the light of this we must, I believe, be very careful in our interpretation of another passage which is often adduced as evidence that Frege thought of sense as an explication of meaning. In 'On Sense and Reference' Frege remarks that

> The sense of a proper name is grasped by everybody who is sufficiently familiar with the language or totality of designations to which it belongs ([1892*b*], p. 144 (57-8).

Certainly this makes it sound as if all that is needed in order to understand the sense of a proper name is knowledge of language. But it is just after this passage that Frege describes the variability of the sense of a proper name like 'Aristotle', and the consequent variability of informativeness associated with statements containing the name. It seems then that we do not always grasp the same sense of a name like 'Aristotle', even when we are all masters of the same language. In the light of this the best way to interpret the remark just quoted would be as an assertion to the effect that the sense of a proper name, or rather any one of its senses, is *objectively available* to anyone who understands the language. Someone who understands the language does not thereby grasp the sense of a proper name, but they are put in a position where the sense can be grasped if they are presented with it under appropriate circumstances.

In view of what I have said here, an historically accurate explanation of Frege's theory of sense will have to include the following points. Frege presented the theory as a contribution to epistemology, and as a result of his struggles with subjectivism; the existence of senses is, for Frege, what underlines the claim that knowledge can be objective. It was also, as I argued in an earlier chapter, a result of his attempt to justify mathematical knowledge by reducing arithmetic to logic. That attempt involved the radical reformulation of mathematical statements, e.g. numerical equalities, and Frege needed to claim that the knowledge contained in the new, logical statements is, objectively speaking no different from that contained in the familiar arithmetical mode of expression. It also involved the claim that arithmetical statements are analytic, thereby provoking the difficulty of explaining their apparent informativeness. And this, again, was solved with the help of the notion of sense.

Commentators have always been troubled by the problem of how to translate Frege's '*Bedeutung*'. It is most naturally interpreted either as 'significance' or 'meaning'; but the use to which Frege puts the notion in his later work has made 'reference' or 'denotation' seem more appropriate.[16] The choice of either of the last two has had the effect of disguising from English readers the fact that Frege does seem to be using the word in a peculiar sense, and the most recent translations have employed 'meaning'. In an earlier part of this chapter I argued that Frege's use of the term *Bedeutung* in the *Foundations* has roughly the force of 'significance' (see above, this chapter 6, section (b) (iii)). Yet I am unwilling to use this term throughout since it would simply be confusing to introduce yet another term for *Bedeutung* when several are in current use. 'Reference' is certainly not a literal translation, but it is, I think, preferable to 'meaning'. Since I have argued that Frege was not concerned to give a theory of meaning, the latter term can create the wrong impression about the nature of Frege's theory. For this reason I use 'reference' except when discussing the Context Principle where it seems important to use 'significance' in order to convey more adequately what I take to be Frege's intentions.

(d) Language and Thought

(i) Introduction

Though I do not think that Frege was a philosopher of meaning, there is still a sense in which he was a philosopher of language. In this section I want to examine some of Frege's views on langauge and their relation to thinking and objectivity. Let me begin by outlining a number of theses which it is tempting to attribute to Frege.

(1) Something is objective only if it can be described in an intersubjective language.

(2) All our thinking involves liguistic expression.

(3) Thinking has a structure which ultimately resists linguistic expression.

I say that it is tempting to attribute all three of these theses to Frege because there are places in which he appears to endorse each of them. Yet (2) and (3) are, if construed in certain ways, inconsistent. It will be one of our tasks to investigate this possible inconsistency in Frege's thought here.

(ii) Language and objectivity

We have already seen that, for Frege, the crucial notion involved in defending the objectivity of knowledge is that of sense. Senses are contrasted with inner mental processes, which are always essentially subjective (see e.g. [1892*b*], p. 146 (59-60)). As I pointed out in an earlier section, senses are objective in two different ways. First of all they are ontologically independent of the thinking subject; they share, as it were, the objectivity of physical objects. But they are objective in a more important sense: they are expressible in language. The idea that whatever is objective must be expressible in language goes back to the *Foundations*: 'what is objective ... is what is subject to laws, what can be conceived and judged, *what is expressible in words* ([1884*b*], p. 35, my italics).

Any account of the objectivity of our knowledge is bound to seize upon language as the mechanism whereby knowledge becomes public. Thus, from the point of view of someone like Frege who wants to advance the thesis that all our knowledge is objective, it is important to establish a close relationship between subjective thought and language.

(iii) Language and thinking

There is, in fact, a tendency in Frege to assimilate all thinking to the use of language. Notice first how this ties in with Frege's theory of cognition, according to which thinking is the grasping of a Thought. As we have seen, Frege did not have a solution to the problem of discovering a mechanism whereby the mind and the Thought which it grasps interact. But he did think that language was involved in the process. 'The Thought, in itself imperceptible, gets clothed in the perceptible garb of the sentence and thereby we are enabled to grasp it' ([1918*a*], p. 345 (5)). Here of course a problem remains.

How does the sensible perception of a sentence put us in touch with an abstract, non-sensible Thought?

If a necessary condition for the grasping of a Thought is to be the perception of a sentence, all our thinking, or at least all such as involves a cognitive content, must be represented to us in sentential form. We can expect, therefore, that Frege will be pushed towards the view that thinking always involves the reading (perhaps an internal reading) of a sentence. In some passages he suggests exactly this. Early in his career he wrote that 'the value of symbols is not diminished by the fact that, after long practice, we need no longer speak out loud in order to think; for *we think in words nevertheless*, and if not in words then in mathematical or other symbols' ([1882*a*], p. 107 (84), my italics). In a paper probably written in the last year of his life Frege returned to the same theme. By that time, as we have seen, he was convinced that the belief in extensions as objects was an error induced by language. Errors in our thinking about logic come about, he says, because thinking is so intimately bound up with language.

> Our thinking is closely bound up with language and thereby with the world of the senses. *Perhaps our thinking is at first a form of speaking which then becomes a representing of speech. Silent thinking would in that case be speech which has become noiseless, taking place in the imagination.* Now we may of course also think in mathematical signs; yet even then thinking is tied up with what is perceptible to the senses. To be sure, we distinguish the sentence as the expression of a Thought from the Thought itself. We know we can have various expressions for the same Thought. The connection of a Thought with one particular sentence is not a necessary one; *but that a Thought of which we are conscious is connected in our mind with some sentence or other is for us men necessary. But that does not lie in the nature of the Thought but in our own nature. There is no contradiction in supposing there to exist beings that can grasp the same Thoughts as we do without needing to clad them in a form that can be perceived by the senses.* But still, for us men there is this necessity ([1924-5*a*], p. 288 (269), my italics).

There are, on the other hand, certain passages in Frege's work where he emphasises the distinction between thought and language, and which involve the view that certain kinds of knowledge cannot be formulated linguistically. This can happen in two different ways for Frege. First of all, he thinks it the case that certain basic logical distinctions, such as that between concept and object, cannot be fully explicated by language, and that all that we can hope for here is a partial 'elucidation' which can give hints to the reader of what is meant, but which depends for its intelligibility on his or her prior understanding of certain basic notions (see e.g. [1892*a*], pp. 167-8 (42-3) and [1914], p. 254 (235)).

Frege's view seems to be then that we are equipped with a knowledge of certain distinctions which can be brought to light, as it were, by a verbal explication, but that the verbal explication will always depend for its effectiveness on a prior understanding, at some deeper level, of what is involved.

The second case concerns knowledge of the self. Frege had always contrasted the objectivity of Thoughts with the subjective privacy of a person's own ideas. But a difficulty arises here. Frege wants to say that a person can have knowledge of himself, knowledge of a kind which is not available to another person. But Frege's model for knowledge consists in a person grasping a Thought and accepting it as true. But in this case the Thought grasped must, because of the privacy of its subject matter, be unavailable to another person.

> Now everyone is presented to himself in a special and primitive way, in which he is presented to no one else. So, when Dr Lauben has the Thought that he was wounded, he will probably be basing it on this primitive way in which he is presented to himself. *And only Dr Lauben himself can grasp Thoughts specified in this way.* But now he may want to communicate with others. He cannot communicate a Thought he alone can grasp. Therefore, if he now says 'I was wounded', he must use 'I' in a sense which can be grasped by others, perhaps in the sense of 'he who is speaking to you at this moment'; by doing this he makes the conditions accompanying his utterance serve towards the expression of a Thought ([1918*a*], p. 350 (12-3) my italics).

Now the idea that there are Thoughts which can be grasped by only one person on the basis of his privileged epistemological status contradicts all Frege's other assertions that Thoughts are essentially objective entities. The difficulty arises because Thoughts fulfill two different functions for Frege, and these functions ultimately conflict with each other. On the one hand they are that which is communicable and therefore objective; on the other they are that which a person grasps when he engages in any cognitive act. And certain cognitive acts, such as thinking about one's own inner experiences, are not, on Frege's view, capable of being communicated. Frege might have tried to avoid the difficulty by saying that thinking about one's private inner experiences does not consist in grasping a Thought. But the difficulty here is that his earlier arguments to the effect that thinking *is* the grasping of a Thought commit him to the view that thinking about inner experiences involves grasping Thoughts. The argument was that having ideas in the sense of mental pictures is insufficient to explain thinking, and this holds equally well in the private case, since one cannot have a mental picture of, for example, one's own pain.

The source of the difficulty is that Frege has two distinct sets of problems about thought and language, and that he is inclined to say things in respect of the one which conflict with what he says concerning the other. Thus when he is dealing with the logical deficiencies of language, and with the problem that certain logical distinctions turn out, on his account, to be ineffable, he is inclined to distinguish between language and thought, saying that language can be only an inadequate vehicle for the expression of thought, or even that certain ideas cannot be properly expressed in language at all, in which case we have to depend upon a meeting of minds, that we have to take each other's explanations with a grain of salt, etc. On the other hand, when he is dealing with the problem of how thinking actually takes place in a human being, he is inclined to appeal to language as the means whereby thinking makes contact with its intellectual object. In general, Frege's objectivism pushes him towards making thought as articulable as possible, while certain difficulties about notions which resist expression require him to stop short of complete expressibility.

(e) Realism and Idealism in Frege's Philosophy

(i) Introduction

The issues which have been discussed in this chapter all relate to a general puzzle about Frege's philosophy: was Frege a platonic realist who believed in the existence of abstract objects like numbers, sets and propositions? This question has been of particular interest to commentators who see Frege's philosophy as essentially a contribution to ontology: the study of the general categories of existence. In line with the interpretation of Frege which I have adopted here, I shall look at the problem from a somewhat different point of view. As I have already said, I do not think that Frege was centrally concerned with ontological problems; his problems were rather of an epistemological nature; problems about existence in general and the reality of abstract entities in particular arose for Frege out of these more basic problems, and to understand his views on existence correctly, I think that we have to see them against the background of his views about objectivity, the epistemological status of mathematics and logic, and about the nature of cognition.

On the face of it, there seems little doubt that Frege was

committed to an extravagant ontology including numbers, sets, functions and propositions, as well as physical and mental entities. In the *Foundations* he says that 'Every number is a self subsistent object', that the mathematicians' task is not to create the numbers but only to discover what is already there ([1884*b*], p. 67). And in later works he tells us that a thinker grasps a Thought, he does not create it; that Thoughts are timeless entities which cannot be affected by events. In 'The Thought' he enumerates three realms of existent things: physical entities, mental entities, and a 'third realm' of entities which are neither physical nor mental. They are like physical things in being independent of our thought processes, but like mental things in lacking corporeal substance. They are timeless and independent from the changing processes of the mental and physical realms, yet some of them — Thoughts — can exert an influence on our thinking and thereby indirectly on events in the physical worlds. Statements like this give the impression of an uncompromising platonism.

It has been suggested, however, that this is a misrepresentation of Frege's position. Hans Sluga has argued that there are strong reasons for interpreting Frege as a follower of Kant's objective idealism, and that, seen in this light, Frege's position is not genuinely platonistic at all (see Sluga [1975], [1976] and [1977]).

Michael Dummett, as we have seen, has a somewhat analagous interpretive proposal to make. If I understand him, his suggestion is that Frege's Context Principle should be seen as a way of rendering unproblematic any reference to abstract objects. What the Context Principle says is that terms referring to abstract objects — terms such as numerals — are legitimated not by our being able to show that there actually is such an abstract object, but by its being the case that the sentence concerned is true. The truth of the sentence imposes reference on the terms occurring in it (see Dummett [1956] and [1973], p. 497). (Modern semantical theories see the situation as the reverse of this. They make it part of what it takes for the sentence to be true to be that the individual terms occurring in the sentence have reference.) To say, on this account, that the term '2' has a reference, is just to say that the term can occur within certain true sentences, such as '2+2=4'. In this way the whole question of abstract objects becomes deflated. It is a mathematical question whether the number 2 exists (i.e. whether '2' has reference) rather than a philosophical question, because the answer is decided not by investigating the philosophical propriety of supposing that there is a realm somewhere containing the number two, but proving certain mathematical results about that number.

Both of these are positions to which I shall frequently refer and draw upon in what follows. But for the sake of simplicity I shall not be concerned with a detailed analysis of either. Instead, I shall simply offer what I take to be the correct account of the matter.

(ii) Frege and Kant

Frege was certainly very strongly influenced by Kant. We saw earlier how the notion of sense seems to have arisen out of the Kantian notion of a concept, and that much of Frege's objection to naturalism is a reiteration of Kant's distinction between questions of fact and questions of validation. Frege adopted Kant's solution to the problem of how to justify geometrical knowledge. We have seen that Frege was very much opposed to Hilbert's programme for proving the consistency of Euclidean axioms, and that the motivation for Frege's critique seems to have been the idea that Euclidean geometry requires no such consistency proof, because it is obviously true, and propositions which are true are thereby consistent with one another. Finally we saw that, after Russell's paradox and Frege's unsuccessful attempts to alter his logical system so as to avoid it, Frege eventually opted for the Kantian view that arithmetical knowledge is synthetic *a priori* rather than analytic (see above, chapter 5, section (c)).

With all this in mind, we can now turn to the rather different question of how to interpret Frege's attitude towards the existence of abstract objects. It soon becomes apparent that there are two distinct ways of taking many of his pronouncements in the *Foundations* about abstract objects like number. One is to suppose that Frege is offering a defence of a platonic ontology. The other is rather more complex, and will require some scene-setting.

First let us remind ourselves of Kant's notion of *objective* idealism. Kant consistently denied that he was an idealist in the sense of believing that the external world is a subjective construction. Space, time, causality and empirical objects are, for Kant, unreal in a certain sense: they are the creation of consciousness. Things-in-themselves, on the other hand, are real in that they exist independently of any consciousness, and are part of the ultimate fabric of the universe. The empirical world which we experience is not like this. It is a construction of our own conceptual apparatus. But the empirical world is not thereby subjective in the sense of being dependent upon the different subjective experience of different men. The empirical world is the same for all men; each confronts it as something given to him, not as something which he individually creates. Thus Kant can claim to have preserved the objectivity of the external world; that world is objective in the sense of being intersubjective.

Now what Frege says about the objectivity of numbers in the *Foundations* can be interpreted in the same way. His claim that the numbers are objective is supported by arguments to the effect that the numbers are the *same for all of us*. In other words, objectivity is being opposed to the idea (implicit in some psychologistic views) that numbers are creations of the *individual* mind. What is objective, as Frege says, is what can be the subject of inter-personal agreement; that which can be subject to laws we can all recognise, and which can be expressed in a publicly available language.

Note that this interpretation chimes in well with the claims I have made concerning the epistemological basis of Frege's project. For the claim that the numbers are objective in this Kantian sense is precisely the claim which one would expect Frege to make if his real concern were with our knowledge of numbers. To see the *Foundations* as a *metaphysical* enquiry into the ontological status of arithmetical objects would be to misunderstand its purpose. Frege's intention was to defend the objectivity (or intersubjectivity) of our knowledge of arithmetic, not to investigate an ontological category of self-subsistent numbers. As he says

> The self subsistence which I am claiming for number should not be taken to mean that a number word signifies [*bezeichne*] something when removed from the context of a sentence, but only to preclude the use of such words as predicates or attributes which appreciably alters their meaning.[17]

Here again we see the epistemological use to which the Context Principle is put. What is significant about number terms is not their referring to self-subsistent platonic objects, but their occurrence within statements which make up the body of our inter-subjective mathematical knowledge.

Some of Frege's later remarks are in the same vein. In 1895 he wrote that

> these objects [the numbers] are neither palpable, visible, nor even real, if what is called real is what can exert or suffer an influence. Numbers do not undergo change, for the theorems of arithmetic embody eternal truths. We can say, therefore, that these objects are outside time; and from this it follows that they are not subjective percepts or ideas, because these are continually changing in

conformity with psychological laws. Arithmetical laws form no part of psychology. It is not as if every man had a number of his own, called *one*, forming part of his mind or his consciousness: there is just one number of that name, the same for everybody, and objective. Numbers are therefore very curious objects, uniting in themselves the apparently contrary qualities of being objective and of being unreal. But it emerges from a more serious consideration that there is no contradiction here.[18]

Some of this has a platonic flavour; the theorems of arithmetic embody eternal truths, numbers are outside time. On the other hand the rest of the passage makes it clear that Frege is concerned to defend the intersubjectivity of numbers, in the sense that numbers conform to arithmetical laws which are the same for everybody.

The last remark of the quotation is a puzzling one: numbers are objective and unreal, but — and Frege does not tell us why — there is no real contradiction here. What he means should be clear from our earlier discussion; reality [*Wirklichkeit*] is a property like any other, which an object may lack or possess; it is not to be confused with existence. As Frege said in the *Basic Laws*, the number two can exist without being real ([1893], p. xxv (24)). And for Frege the bare existence of numbers was something beyond philosophical dispute, since he believed that statements asserting their existence could be derived from wholly logical principles.

(iii) Was existence important for Frege?

Do these considerations show that Frege was not concerned with ontological problems? I do not think so. First of all, he does assert the existence of numbers and other abstract objects like extensions (numbers are just a sub-class of extensions). Indeed the whole purpose of his logistic enterprise was to enable him to do this in an unproblematic way. The argument for their existence is a logical one rather than a metaphysical one, and when Frege gave up the possibility of finding a satisfactory logical argument (as a result of Russell's paradox) he also gave up the claim that numbers are logical objects. But it is still the case that, in a certain sense, the existence of numbers is an important question for Frege, though it was a question he chose to tackle not by traditional metaphysical means, but with the aid of the logical tools he had invented. Frege's first concern was to refute scepticism about arithmetic, and he was therefore centrally concerned with questions about the status of our arithmetical *knowledge*. But that very concern forced him to adopt an ontological position, in the sense that he felt bound to justify our arithmetical knowledge by proving the truth of the things we typically say about numbers. And that involved, among other things, proving that the numbers exist. Thus it has to be admitted that an ontology of abstract objects arises for Frege as a means of solving his epistemological problems, and in this sense he was and remained a platonist as long as he adhered to the logicist thesis.

(iv) The reality of Thoughts

Secondly, as we have seen from our earlier discussion in this chapter, Frege did engage in metaphysical speculation about the 'reality' of certain abstract objects. Thoughts are real in so far as they exert an influence upon events in the mental and physical worlds. Here, similar comments apply as in the preceding considerations about numbers. The ontological question of the reality of Thoughts arose for Frege because of his concern with problems about knowledge — this time, problems about the nature of cognition. But whatever its source, a quite definite ontological doctrine emerges in this connection.

It might be argued, however, that what Frege says about the reality of Thoughts is really quite compatible with the assumption that his position was that of a Kantian idealist rather than that of a platonic realist. What Frege argues in 'The Thought' is that Thoughts are as real as physical things *in the sense that they too are capable of having effects*. Now a Kantian holds that the things of the physical world are real, in the sense that the effects which they have upon us are determined by laws over which we have individually no control and which are the same for everybody. Yet they are not real in the stronger sense of being independent of *all* consciousness. The physical world is the world of appearance, not of ultimate reality. Frege's arguments about the reality of Thoughts could be construed in a similar way: Thoughts are real in the sense that they are given to us in a way which does not depend upon the subjective idiosyncracies of individual consciousness. They affect each of us in the same way. But they need not be looked upon as platonically real in the sense of being independent of *all* consciousness. Thoughts are *as* real as empirical objects, and, for a Kantian, the reality of empirical objects is subject to certain complex limitations.

In this way we could eliminate any conflict between the interpretation of Frege as a Kantian objective idealist and what I have said about his views on the reality of Thoughts. But there still remains a doubt about the extent of Frege's commitment to a generally Kantian way of thinking about philosophical questions, and part of this doubt arises from some other remarks which he makes in 'The Thought'.

(v) The self and the external world

Frege's arguments in 'The Thought' for the reality of Thoughts presuppose that we already have some unproblematic category of existent objects. For Thoughts are real in the sense that they have effects upon other things — mental and physical things — which we already accept as being real. But philosophers have often denied the existence of the physical world; in a certain sense, as we have seen, Kant himself denies its existence, though in another sense he affirms it. The case against the existence of the material world which Frege here considers is similar to that which Descartes tried to deal with; the case according to which the belief in a material world is an illusion engendered by a person's own subjective ideas.

What Frege seems to be arguing against in fact is a doctrine which has been called 'neutral monism', according to which there are no such things as the self or the physical world but rather a single, undifferentiated category of sensations which can be treated sometimes from the point of view of physical science and sometimes from the point of view of psychology, depending upon our purposes. This view was current during the later part of Frege's career, as a result of work by some German thinkers; e.g. Richard Avenarius and, particularly, the great philosopher-scientist Ernst Mach, whose *Analysis of Sensations* appeared in 1902. Mach, an important forerunner of the logical positivist movement of the 1930s,[19] advocated a view according to which the aim of science is not to discover the truth about an independent physical reality, but to formulate 'economical' relations of functional dependence between groups of sensations which would facilitate prediction and technology. Science was to avoid commitment to any dubious ontology and to use as its material the 'given' of experience, the world of sensations. Mach's work has often been interpreted as simply a new version of the sort of subjective idealism which Berkeley constructed out of empiricism, and it is quite conceivable that Frege took it in the same way. Certainly Frege's work contains critical references to 'the sensualism of Locke and the idealism of Berkeley' ([1891-2*b*], p. 115 (105)). I suggest, in fact, that 'The Thought' be seen as an attempt to answer Mach's philosophy, construed as a version of subjective idealism.[20]

Let us look, therefore, at Frege's argument against the view that the world consists only of sensations; without either a substratum of physical substance or a perceiving self.

Is everything an idea? Does everything need a bearer, without which it could have no existence? I have considered myself as the bearer of my ideas, but am I not an idea myself?... It also seems to me as if I see a chair over there. It is an idea. I am not actually much different from this myself, for am I not myself just an association of sense-impressions, an idea?... How do I come to single out one of these ideas and set it up as the bearer of the rest? Why must this idea be the idea which I chose to call 'I'? Could I not just as well choose the one that I am tempted to call a chair? Why, after all, have a bearer for ideas at all? But this would always be something essentially different from merely born ideas, something independent, needing no extraneous bearer. If everything is an idea, then there is no bearer of ideas.... If there is no bearer of ideas then there are also no ideas, for ideas need a bearer without which they cannot exist.... Being experienced is necessarily connected with pain, and someone experiencing it is necessarily connected with it being experienced. ([1918*a*], pp. 356 (21-2)).

Now it follows that if the self cannot be an idea, then since we have an idea of the self, we have an idea of something which is not itself an idea (pp. 356-7 (21)).

Frege then introduces another criticism of the monistic position. Suppose, contrary to what has been said, that the self is only an idea. Then as such it must occupy part of the consciousness. But the idea of the self necessarily contains the idea of consciousness. And since we are conscious of the self, this new consciousness-idea must contain a new self-idea, different from the idea of self first considered. The same argument freshly applied yields another consciousness-idea containing another self-idea, and so on. Hence, the argument runs, there would be infinitely many selves, not one. But this is a *reductio ad absurdum* of the thesis that the self is an idea (p. 357 (22)).

From the assumption that the self exists Frege wants to draw certain conclusions. His method is similar to that of Descartes. Having 'proved' his own existence, Frege proceeds to the outer world of physical objects, persons, and their own conscious selves. But he does not claim certainty for any of these further claims.

By the step with which I secure an environment for myself I expose myself to the risk of error. And here I come up against a further distinction between my inner and outer worlds. I cannot doubt that I have a visual impression of green, but it is not so certain that I see a lime leaf. So, contrary to widespread views, we find certainty in the inner world while doubt never altogether leaves us in our excursions into the outer world (p. 358 (23-4)).

But although our knowledge of the external world is never

certain, it can attain a probability 'no longer distinguishable from certainty'. Frege does not explain why he thinks that this is the case, or whether he thinks that the probability is made great by the existence of empirical evidence in favour of the hypothesis. He asks

> Would there be a science of history otherwise? Would not every precept of duty, every law otherwise come to nothing? What would be left of religion? The natural sciences too could only be assessed as fables like astrology and alchemy (p.358 (24)).

A number of objections, some of them fairly obvious, can be raised against Frege's attempt to refute Mach's position. But my concern here is not to enter into the metaphysical debate itself, but to examine the nature of Frege's own views. For in the passages I have been considering, Frege reveals, I believe, how distant some of his thinking is from a Kantian epistemology.

As I remarked above, Frege's method for dealing with scepticism about the self and the world is similar to that of Descartes; he begins by establishing the existence of the self, and then tries to argue for the existence of the external world.

Now in the second edition of the *Critique of Pure Reason* Kant sought to refute idealism, which he took to be the denial that the physical world is real. He distinguishes the idealism (now using this word in a rather extended sense) of Berkeley, according to which the existence of the physical world is impossible, from that of Descartes. According to the latter, the only thing of which we are immediately aware is the self, and the existence of things external to us is to be inferred from this, perhaps with probability rather than certainty. Kant then tries to show (with what success we shall not concern ourselves here) that it is wrong to suppose that we have no immediate experience of bodies in space, and that in fact our awareness of ourselves implies a knowledge of such objects. Thus for Kant certainty about the external world is inextricably bound up with certainty about the existence of the self (see [1787], pp.274-9).

As we have seen, Frege does not argue in this way for the existence of the material world. He argues instead that, since we have knowledge of ourselves, and since the self cannot be an idea, there can be no objection in principle to our assuming that there are other things of which we have knowledge but which are not ideas, such as physical bodies. And he concludes that it is only with greater or lesser probability that we can go beyond our immediate experience and assume that there are things in space and time outside of ourselves.

I think that we can conclude from this that Frege's conception of the physical world would have been regarded by Kantians as a naively realistic one, likely to fall foul of sceptical objections. If, on the other hand, Frege had been at all impressed by Kant's argument that we can know bodies in space with apodictic certainty, I think that he would have been anxious to use it against subjectivism. To be sure, none of this shows that Frege was a platonic realist, but it does show that, on a very important issue, he was capable of deviating markedly from Kant's position.

It is true that, taken as a whole, the argument we have just been considering embodies certain elements of Kantian thought. Thus Frege insists in Kantian fashion that there cannot be ideas without a bearer; experiences have to be the experiences *of* someone. But at most this illustrates Frege's eclecticism, not his consistent adherence to Kantianism.

(vi) Geometry and the foundations of arithmetic

One further issue which must be considered in relation to Frege's alleged Kantianism is the decision which he took at the end of his life to turn to geometry as the foundation of arithmetic. Does this fact in itself not reveal the strength of Frege's Kantianism? Can we give a more consistent picture of his philosophical development by minimising the extent to which we suppose his philosophical position to have been disturbed by this final change? The stronger we suppose his Kantianism to have been throughout his career, the easier it is to understand his decision to fall back on synthetic *a priori* intuition as the source of arithmetical knowledge.

How genuinely Kantian is Frege's final position on arithmetic? Certainly he claims that arithmetical knowledge is synthetic, but then the paradoxes which had destroyed the system of the *Basic Laws* had shown that arithmetic could not be based on the sort of premises which Frege took to have a clearly logical character. So for this reason, quite apart from any Kantian considerations, arithmetical knowledge would seem to be non-analytic. And furthermore, Frege does not claim, as Kant had done, that arithmetical knowledge comes about through a pure intuition of time: rather he wants to *identify* arithmetical and geometrical knowledge; as he puts it, 'the whole of mathematics is really geometry' ([1924–5*b*], p. 297 (277)).

As for Frege's insistence that we have *a priori* knowledge of (now supposedly synthetic) arithmetic, this is easily explained in terms of

Frege's problem situation. Frege held that the best kind of knowledge is absolutely secure from sceptical doubt; it was to save mathematics from such doubts that he had developed his logicist thesis and elaborated the critique of psychologism. I think that it was this demand for certainty which led the early Frege to formulate his objectivism, and the later Frege to fall back on synthetic *a priori* knowledge of mathematics. Let me explain briefly what I mean by this.

I pointed out much earlier that it was the desire for a secure foundation for mathematics which made Frege oppose psychologism. Psychologism, he felt, leads to relativism, for it involves the actual identification of numbers with ideas in the psychological sense. And since he held that ideas are incommunicable, Frege saw psychologism as entailing the view that everyone carries around with them their own private mathematics, the results of which, however strange they may be, are never criticisable from the outside. Such relativistic consequences would make the justification of mathematics impossible, except in so far as everyone could justify their own mathematics to themselves and to no other person. For this reason Frege held that, in order to give a satisfactory justification to mathematics, we must show that mathematics is objective.

But objectivity, which appears here as a necessary condition for the justification of mathematics, actually raises grave problems for it. By emphasising the distinction between our subjective understanding and objective mathematical truth, we open up the possibility that they diverge, and that we might be wrong in our assessment of the content of objective mathematics. So objectivism must here be supplemented by some guarantee that we are capable of correctly grasping mathematical reality. As long as he could hold that mathematical knowledge is knowledge of logical truths, Frege could solve the problem by making the plausible assumption that we have the ability to recognise those truths which are, as it were, the most general and self-evident laws which underlie all reasoning. (I shall say something about this assumption in the next section.) It seems to be his view that the laws of arithmetic have this character. He says that 'we have only to deny any one of them and complete confusion ensues. Even to think at all seems no longer possible' ([1884*b*], p. 21). As long as we postulate only axioms which have this clear and obvious character, we can say that their truth is clear to our reason.

As we have seen, when Frege came to supplement the axioms of his *Begriffsschrift* with a principle which relates concepts to the corresponding objects (Axiom (V) of the *Basic Laws*) he was uneasy about according it the status of a clear and obvious truth. When Russell's paradox showed that Axiom (V) was false, and even contradictory, Frege's claim that his system of logic was transparent to reason had lost its credibility. If mathematical truth is objective, it seems now that it must be admitted to be highly conjectural.

In his last years Frege sought a new foundation for arithmetic which could invest it with the previously sought certainty, and he thought that this could be found in the discipline which he had always acknowledged to be securely based on *a priori* intuition — geometry. Rather than admit that mathematical knowledge is irredeemably conjectural, Frege sought a non-logical basis for arithmetic. And what more obvious solution could there be than to opt for the view that he had always held with respect to geometry — that it is synthetic *a priori* knowledge?

We can say, then, that what pushed Frege into the position which he finally took concerning the foundations of arithmetic was not any preference for a Kantian solution to his problem, but simply a desire to see mathematics put on a secure footing by *some* means. And the only means left to him seemed to be the appeal to synthetic *a priori* knowledge.

The issue of Frege's ontology is a complex one, not susceptible to a solution based on a straightforward adoption of a category for his thought — 'realism', 'idealism', 'nominalism' etc. Certainly Frege's early work contains strong elements of Kantianism. Later other features emerge: the insistence that all expressions correspond to extra-linguistic entities, and the invocation of Thoughts as part of the causal structure of the world. All I would insist upon is that, whatever entities Frege was prepared to invoke, they were invoked as solutions to problems about the nature of our knowledge.

To underline the last remark, let me offer a conjecture about one possible reason for Frege's increasing sympathy towards platonism in his work after 1890. As I have pointed out, the *Foundations* is written very much from the standpoint of Kantian idealism; it is the intersubjective accessibility of the numbers that he constantly insists upon. But in later works we are presented with an ontology of functions and objects existing timelessly and independently. What brought about this change? One reason was, I believe, connected with the introduction of his Axiom (V). In the *Foundations* Frege had written that

In arithmetic we have to do . . . with objects *which are given directly to reason which sees them, transparently, as its own* ([1884*b*], p. 115. My italics).

This suggests a certain explanation of mathematical knowledge. The numbers are the creation of reason; therefore men, having the faculty of reason, see them transparently. We know arithmetic with apodictic certainty because it is the creation of our most basic cognitive structure. At this time Frege was not committed to the view that numbers must be introduced as objects. He thought that it might be possible to construct arithmetic on a basis of concepts alone. Later he abandoned this position and adopted Axiom (V) as the means whereby we can pass from a concept to a corresponding object, its extension or course of values. Axiom (V) is, moreover, the only source of information that we have about courses of values and, as I have already remarked, it fails to characterise courses of values uniquely. This indeterminacy also affects the numbers, since they are taken to be courses of values. But in that case the numbers do not seem to be transparent to reason, since reason, via Axiom (V), fails to identify them uniquely. In that case, if numbers are determinate objects — and Frege did not at this stage consider denying that they are — they must exist independently from reason. Reason does not determine what they are, so there must be more to them than reason knows. Perhaps considerations of this kind inclined Frege to accept something like a platonic ontology of numbers; that they are autonomous entities to which our access is merely partial; which we can investigate and, perhaps, come to know more about through logical analysis, but whose real nature is inscrutable.

(vii) Logic and knowledge

One important question concerning Frege's attempt to set mathematics on a firm epistemological footing has so far been neglected, and it is appropriate that we deal with it here, following the discussion of Frege's relations to Kant.

The problem is this. If arithmetical knowledge is to be justified by its being shown that arithmetic is really a part of logic, then it must somehow be the case that logical knowledge is secure against sceptical doubt. The difficulty here is that Frege hardly ever discusses the issue of our knowledge of logic. He says only that it is not the task of logic itself to justify a premise; that is the task of epistemology (see [1879-91], p.3 (3) and p.6 (6)). If we are to reconstruct Frege's view we must look for suggestive clues rather than for direct statements of position.

Now Kant held that our knowledge of logical (analytic) truths is knowledge derived from our understanding of concepts: a logical truth is one where the concept of the predicate is contained in that of the subject. 'All bodies are extended' is for Kant a logical truth because the concept of extension is contained in the concept of body. Our knowledge of analytic truths derives from our understanding of concepts. It is our understanding of concepts, an understanding which does not involve any intuition (either pure or empirical), which gives us our understanding of logic. Now Frege thought that there were a number of things wrong with Kant's characterisation of logical truth. But I want to suggest that, none the less, his own view of the source of logical knowledge derives from Kant's. First of all, Frege held Kant's view to be deficient because, as stated, it applies only to a very limited class of propositions — those which fall into the traditional category of 'universal affirmative' propositions (e.g. 'All men are mortal'). Secondly, Frege wants to make the notions of analyticity and logical truth relevant to the way in which a proposition is to be proved, rather than to the content of the proposition itself.

When a proposition is called *a posteriori* or analytic in my sense, this is not a judgement about the conditions... which have made it possible to form the content of the proposition in our consciousness; nor is it a judgement about the way in which some other man has come, perhaps erroneously, to believe it true; rather it is a judgement about the ultimate ground upon which rests the justification for holding it to be true ([1884*b*], p.3).

This means that all the explanatory weight of the notion of logical truth is thrown upon the axioms. For once their logical and epistemological status is clear, the theorems, including the specifically mathematical ones, inherit from them the status of truths of logic (for deduction does not lead us out of the class of logical truths).

Now, in fact, for most of Frege's logical axioms, the question of their justification hardly arises; to deny them leads directly to a contradiction. The axioms from the propositional part of logic follow from the definitions of the truth-functional connectives; they literally cannot be false (relative, that is, to assumptions about classical two valuedness, but I do not believe that it occurred to

Frege that this could seriously be questioned). Two other axioms are in the same position. The first says that if a property holds of everything, it holds of any given thing, while the other says that if a (second order) property holds of all (first order) properties, then it holds of any given such property. What of Axiom (V), governing the relation between a concept and its extension (more generally, a function and its course of values)? Frege never concealed from himself or from his readers that this axiom did not have quite the appearance of self-evidence enjoyed by the other axioms. It is a remarkably powerful axiom in its ability to prove existential propositions, and this might itself have been a source of worry. Yet it seems to state what is involved in the very notion of a concept having an extension, and 'is what people have in mind when they speak of the extension of a concept'. Frege's view seems to have been that if we have any grasp of the extension of a concept, it must be because this axiom is true. Our understanding of extensions proceeds from a prior grasp of concepts, via the recognition of Axiom (V). As he says:

> By means of a logical faculty we lay hold upon the extension of a concept by starting out from the concept ([1906*c*], p. 197 (181)).

So Frege has in mind something like a transcendental argument: a necessary condition for our grasp of extensions is the truth of Axiom (V). In this way we can understand why the refutation of the axiom left Frege with a puzzle about how we apprehend logical objects. In a letter to Russell of 1902 he said

> How do we apprehend logical objects? I have found no other answer to it than this. We apprehend them as extensions of concepts, or more generally as courses of values of functions. I have always been aware that there are difficulties connected with this, and your discovery of the contradiction has added to them; but what other way is there? (p. 223 (141)).

The seriousness of Russell's discovery was thus partly due to the fact that it showed that we do not have a clear grasp of the relation between concepts and their extensions; and this seemed to undermine the objective status of Frege's programme.

All this is, of course, mostly conjecture. It is a puzzle about Frege's work that he nowhere considers in detail the question of what justifies our claim to know the truths of logic. Perhaps his doubts about Axiom (V) made him reticent on the subject. Once, towards the end of his life, Frege did discuss what he describes as the 'logical source of knowledge'. He distinguishes three sources of knowledge; the empirical (sense experience), the geometrical (our intuition of space), and the logical. Language, he says, is the source of our logical knowledge. He tells us that he no longer believes that this source is incorrigible, presumably because of the discovery of the paradox, and that language can lead us astray on the question of whether there exist logical objects. He believed previously that the numbers are logical objects, but now he does not believe that logic alone can provide us with any objects at all (this was Kant's view) ([1924-5*a*]).

This raises a number of questions. It seems, first of all, to imply that at one time Frege *did* hold that logical knowledge is in some way given by language. If I am right about the association between logical truths and the analysis of concepts, this suggests that our knowledge of concepts is given by their linguistic representation. Yet in precisely what sense Frege would have meant this is not clear. Did he perhaps mean that concepts, and the so called 'logical objects' associated with them are by-products of language? This might well have been Frege's early view, since in one place he says that a 'concept gradually frees itself from intuition and becomes self-subsistent' ([1874*a*], p. 50). This suggests that concepts become reified through a process of objectification, perhaps through their coming to be expressed in language. Yet later Frege insisted, sometimes in a tiresomely pedantic way, that concepts have no history, no development (see [1891*a*], p. 122 (204)). This seems to rule out any dependence on language.

One thing, however, is clear. For the Fregean programme in the foundations of arithmetic to be carried through successfully, there must be some way in which we can have indubitable knowledge of the relevant logical truths. It is certainly a weakness in Frege's account that he offers no detailed argumentation on this point.

(f) Conclusions

In this chapter I have been concerned to discover the general character of Frege's philosophical views. Let us recall the points made.

First, Frege's objections to psychologism, empiricism and formalism in mathematics and logic were discussed. Frege has two fundamental objections to these positions. One is that in attempting to make mathematics and logic part of the natural world—by saying, for example, that the laws of logic are the descriptive laws of thinking, or that numbers are physical configurations — the peculiarly secure epistemological status of mathematics and logic is lost sight of. They can no longer be regarded as having a claim to constitute knowledge of greater certainty than that of the inductively based sciences. The other objection is that any naturalistic definition of the numbers will fail to account for the mathematical properties of the numbers, so will be irrelevant. A definition of number must figure significantly in a mathematical theory about numbers. Numbers are of no significance in themselves; they are important to us because we have a particularly precise and well worked out theory in which they figure. A definition of number is valuable only in so far as it helps to strengthen the foundations of that theory, and this is something which naturalistic theories of number fail to do.

An attempt was made to create a coherent picture of Frege's views about cognition. Because his remarks take the form of unsystematic asides, any conclusions drawn must be rather speculative. I have suggested that Frege transformed his thesis that all knowledge is propositional into a psychological hypothesis according to which thinking is the mind's grasping of an abstract Thought or proposition. As Frege's ideas crystallised with his introduction of the distinction between sense and meaning he abandoned his original formulation of the Context Principle in favour of a principle which expressed more directly the epistemological content of that earlier principle and freed it from associations with semantics; the principle according to which 'thinking is the grasping of a Thought'.

The distinction between sense and reference was then discussed and I argued that the notion of sense is best understood against the background of Frege's views about the objectivity of knowledge rather than as a contribution to the problem of how we understand the meanings of expressions in our language.

Finally, I tried to assess the extent to which Frege could be described as a platonist who believed in abstract objections. Here again, I think it unwise to be dogmatic. In many ways Frege was clearly influenced by Kant, and certain of his platonistic-seeming remarks can be interpreted as Kantian assertions about the objectivity rather than the metaphysical reality of entities like numbers. Yet, as I have tried to show, the picture of Frege as a thoroughgoing Kantian is one which fits ill with certain of his texts. What seems clear to me at least is that, whatever Frege's views on the metaphysical status of abstract objects, this question was not his primary concern. For him the main question was the status of our knowledge, and in particular our mathematical knowledge.

The hypothesis on which this book has been based is that Frege's work, both in logic and in philosophy, is best understood as a contribution to epistemology. I have tried to test this hypothesis in two different ways. First, I have tried to show that it is consistent with, and often corroborated by, Frege's own formulations of his problems and theories. Secondly, I have used the hypothesis to shed light on doctrines of his which seem to contain elements of unclarity or which seem otherwise odd and out of place. I do not think that in this way I have achieved absolute consistency with the texts, nor have I avoided a residue of problematic statements. But I hope that my interpretation has to some extent improved our understanding of Frege's thought.

I have tried, in particular, to offer explanations for the ways in which Frege's views developed over time. Most of these explanations have made specific reference to his concern with the justification of mathematical knowledge. The two crucial changes were, I think, both associated with the introduction of logical objects as a way of reducing mathematics to logic. First, some time after the *Foundations* and before the *Basic Laws* Frege introduced courses of values with his Axiom (V). This led to a deepening of his platonism. Before, he had thought that numbers were transparent to our reason; indeed the very creations of reason itself. But Axiom (V), because it tells us so little about the nature of courses of values, encouraged the view that logical objects are independent of us and can be grasped only imperfectly by reason. During the same period Frege introduced his distinction between sense and reference. Again, this can be explained in terms of the needs of his philosophy of mathematics; for Frege required a way of showing that analytic identities can be informative.

The second great change in Frege's views came with the discovery that Axiom (V) is false. Because of the requirements of Frege's philosophical outlook, no adequate alternative to it could be found. Yet Frege clung to the view that we know mathematics with apodictic certainty, and so turned to our intuition of space as the basis both for geometry and for arithmetic.

Notes

1 Frege quotes the formalist Thomae as saying that 'The formal standpoint rids us of all metaphysical difficulties; this is the advantage it affords us' (see Frege [1903*a*], section 89).

2 Theories of arithmetic sometimes combined elements from each of these positions. See the remarks on Helmholz in Frege [1903*a*], section 137.

3 Conversely, in advancing and proving the propositions of arithmetic, the mathematician is simply not offering anything of psychological significance; he is not shedding any light on the structure of or the relations between ideas. As Frege says 'Mathematics is not concerned with the nature of the mind, and the answer to any question whatever in psychology must be for mathematics a matter of complete indifference' ([1884*b*], p. 105).

4 This kind of formalism must be distinguished from the subtler formalism which originated with Hilbert's work at the end of the nineteenth century, though it was some time before the two positions were clearly distinguished. Apparently Frege, in a letter to Löwenheim which has been lost, indicated that a formal theory of arithmetic in this later sense might be possible.

5 Introducing a later discussion of his *Grundlagen* definition of number in terms of extension, Frege says 'The following discussion will show that this explanation gives the right results when applied, by deriving the basic properties of the numbers from it' ([1891-2*a*], p. 81 (72)).

6 See e.g. [1897], p. 150 (138); 157 (145); [1906*e*], p. 210 (185); [1915], p. 271 (251); [1919], p. 273 (253).

7 Frege's use of the term *Wirklichkeit* and its cognates is not always consistent. In the *Foundations* section 26, he uses it as synonymous with 'physically real': 'I distinguish what I call objective from what is handleable or spatial or actual [*Wirchlichen*]'. (See also [1897], p. 149 (137).) But in section 85 he describes numbers as *wirklich*, though they are not perceptual or spatial. Then, in the last sentence of the book he says that numbers are not 'real, or actual or palpable'. Clearly, at this early stage Frege's ideas about *Wirklichkeit* had not yet crystallised. The ascription of *Wirklichkeit* to numbers probably constitutes nothing more than a forceful expression of the view that numbers exist in the sense that we can prove from logical truths alone that there are numbers. Later, Frege distinguished sharply between statements of existence and statements which ascribe *Wirklichkeit* to objects: 'And if I wish to say that the number two acts or is active, this would be false and wholly different from what I mean by "There are square roots of four"' ([1893], p. xxv (24). See also [1895*b*], p. 213 (482).)

8 Frege [1897], pp. 137-63 (126-51). Already in the *Basic Laws* (p. xxiv), Frege likens the mind's grasping of its intellectual object to a causal process: 'If I grasp a pencil, many different events take place in my body; .... But the totality of these events neither is the pencil nor creates the pencil; the pencil exists independently of them. It is essential for the grasping that something be there which is grasped; the internal changes alone are not the grasping'. But no conclusions are drawn from this about the reality of Thoughts.

9 For some criticisms of Frege's view see Armstrong [1981].

10 '... to give an account of the sense of an expression is to give a partial account of what a speaker knows when he understands that expression' (Dummett

[1975], p. 122). See also McDowell: 'The job of a theory of sense should be to fix the content of speech-acts which a total theory of the language concerned would warrant ascribing to speakers' (McDowell [1977], p. 159. McDowell cites Frege [1892*b*], pp. 59 and 62 of the English edition).

11 Here I seem to be in agreement with Hacker (see his [1975], p. 604).

12 I use the term 'subjective epistemologist' to describe a philosopher interested in knowledge as it manifests itself as a subjective state of the knowing subject.

13 Frege certainly expresses himself imprecisely here, when he says that the sense of 'Aristotle' might be taken to be the pupil of Plato and teacher of Alexander the Great, which is to say that the sense of 'Aristotle' might be the *reference* of 'Aristotle'. He clearly means that the sense of 'Aristotle' might be the same as the sense of 'the pupil of Plato and teacher of Alexander the Great'.

14 Dummett identifies the two (see his [1976]).

15 This is how he is interpreted by Saul Kripke in his [1972].

16 Russell employed 'indication' in his [1903]. 'Reference' is used by Geach and Black. Feigl uses *nominatum* in his [1949].

17 Frege [1884*b*], p. 72. Earlier Frege said that 'We understand by a man something self-subsistent, but we do not understand this by a square root of 4' ([— 1884], p. 64 (57)).

18 Frege [1895*b*], p. 213 (482). In 1906 Frege wrote that 'The Thought expressed in Pythagoras' theorem is the same for all men; it confronts everyone in the same way as something objective, whereas each man has his own ideas, sensations, and feelings, which belong only to him' (Frege [1906*f*], p. 214 (198)).

19 The Vienna Circle was officially called the 'Ernst Mach Society'.

20 Frege never refers explicitly to Mach, and I cannot demonstrate that Mach's ideas were the intended object of Frege's criticism. One piece of indirect evidence is, however, instructive. In the course of arguing that there is no essential difference between knowledge of oneself and of other people, Mach provides a drawing of what a person's body looks like to himself, seen out of his left eye (ibid., p. 19). In *Der Gedanke* Frege says, while considering the neutral monist's case, 'It seems to me as if I was lying in a deck-chair, as if I could see the toes of a pair of waxed boots, the front part of a pair of trousers, a waistcoat, buttons, part of a jacket, in particular sleeves, two hands, the hair of a beard, the blurred outline of a nose. Am I myself this entire association of visual impressions, this total idea?' (Frege [1918*a*], p. 356 (21)). This description fits Mach's picture almost exactly.

Glossary of Important Terms

Anerkennung Recognition. Frege says that judgement is the recognition of the truth of a Thought. Possibly Frege sometimes uses *Anerkennung* in the weaker sense of *acceptance* (of a Thought as true).

Anzahl Number. Frege uses this expression instead of the more common *Zahl* for the numbers which are used for counting.

Bedeutung Reference or Significance. Frege uses this term in at least two distinct senses:
(*a*) in the *Foundations* it has the same intuitive sense as 'importance' or 'significance';
(*b*) in his later work it becomes a technical term meaning the entity referred to by an expression. I sometimes use 'reference' as a translation for this word, sometimes 'significance'. Others have adopted 'reference' throughout (Geach and Black), 'indication' (Russell), *nominatum* (Feigl) and, more recently, 'meaning' (Long and White).

Begriff Concept. A function of one argument which takes truth-values as values. Functions of several arguments which take truth-values as values are called 'relations' (*Beziehungen*).

Begriffsschrift Concept-writing. Frege uses this expression sometimes as the name of his book; sometimes as the name of his formal language; sometimes as a name for any formal language similar to his own. I leave the term untranslated in the text.

Funktion Function. An incomplete or unsaturated (*ungesättigt*) entity.

Gedanke Thought. The sense of a sentence.

Gegenstand Object. A complete or saturated entity.

Gleichzahlig Equinumerate. A relation between concepts when the objects falling under the one can be put into a one-one correspondence with the objects falling under the other.

Inhalt Content. Closely related to the notion of sense. In section 8 of the *Begriffsschrift* Frege uses it in a way which corresponds closely to his later *Bedeutung*.

Objektiv Objective. The property of entities in virtue of which they are independent of individual consciousness.

Satz Sentence. In the *Foundations* Frege often uses this word in something like the sense of 'Thought'. Later he distinguishes between the sentence and the Thought which it expresses.

Sinn Sense. The objective information or content of an expression.

Umfang Extension (of a concept). A special case of the course of values of a function.

Urtheil Judgement. The recognition of a Thought as true.

Vorstellung Representation. In his later work Frege distinguished between objective and subjective representations, usually reserving the term for the subjective sense. This word is most often translated as 'idea'.

Werthverlauf Course of values (of a function).

Wirklich Actual or real. Things are actual if they can act (*wirken*) on other things.

(1) *Bibliography of Frege's Writings*

'[1880-81]' means written between 1880 and 1881;
'[-1884]' means up to 1884;
'[1884-]' means 1884 or after.

[1873]: *Über eine geometrische Darstellung der imaginären Gebilde in der Ebene* [On a Geometrical Representation of Imaginary Figures in the Plane], Doctoral dissertation. Jena: Neuenhann. Reprinted in Angelelli (ed): [1967] pp. 1–49.

[1874*a*]: *Rechnungsmethoden, die sich auf eine Erweiterung des Grössenbegriffes gründen* [Methods of Calculation: based on an extension of the Concept of Magnitude], Habilitationsschrift, Jena: Frommann. Reprinted in Angelelli (ed): [1967], pp. 50-84.

[1874b]: Review of H. Seeger: *Die Elemente der Arithmetik, fur den Schulunterricht bearbeitet, Jenaer Literaturzeitung*, 1, p. 722. Reprinted in Angelelli (ed): [1967] pp. 85-6.

[1877*a*]: Review of A. von Gall and E. Winter, *Die Analytische geometrie des Punktes und der Geraden und ihre Anwendung auf Aufgaben, Jenaer Literaturzeitung*, 4, pp. 133-4. Reprinted in Angelelli (ed): [1967], pp. 87-8.

[1877*b*]: Review of J. Thomae, *Sammlung von Formeln, welche bei Anwendung der elliptischen und Rosenhain'schen Functionen gebraucht werden, Jenaer Literaturzeitung*, 4, p. 472. Reprinted in Angelelli (ed): [1967] p. 89.

[1878]: 'Über eine Weise, die Gestalt eine Dreiecks als Komplexe Grösse aufzuffassen' [On a Way of Representing the Shape of a Triangle as a Complex Magnitude], *Jenaische Zeitschrift für Naturwissenschaft*, 12, p. xviii. Reprinted in Angelelli (ed): [1967], pp. 90-1.

[1879*a*]: *Begriffsschrift, eine der arithmetischen nachgebildete Formelsprache des reinen Denkens*. [Concept-Writing. A Formal Language of Pure Thought after the Pattern of that of Arithmetic], Halle: Nebert. Reprinted in Angelelli (ed): [1964], pp. vii-88. Translated into English as *Conceptual Notation*, in Bynum (ed): [1972], pp. 101-203.

[1879*b*]: 'Anwendung der Begriffsschrift'. *Jenaische Zeitschrift für Naturwissenschaft*, 13, pp. 29-33. Reprinted in Angelelli (ed): [1964], p. 89-93. Translated into English as 'Applications of the "Conceptual Notation"' in Bynum (ed): [1972], pp. 204-8.

[1880]: Review of R. Hoppe *Lehrbuch der analytischen Geometrie, Deutsche Literaturzeitung*, 1, pp. 210-11. Reprinted in Angelelli (ed): [1967], pp. 92-3.

[1880-81]: 'Booles rechnende Logik und die Begriffsschrift', in Hermes *et al* (eds): [1969], pp. 9-52. Translated into English as 'Boole's Logical Calculus and the Concept-Script' in Long and White (trs): [1979], pp. 9-46.

[1881]: 'Über den Briefwechsel Leibnizens und Huygens mit Papin', *Jenaische Zeitschrift für Naturwissenschaft*, 15, pp. 29-32. Reprinted in Angelelli (ed): [1964], pp. 93-6.

[1879-91]: 'Logik', in Hermes *et al* (eds): [1969], pp. 1-8. Translated into English as 'Logic' in Long and White (trs): [1979], pp. 1-8.

[1882*a*]: 'Über die wissenschaftliche Berechtigung einer Begriffsschrift', *Zeitschrift für Philosophie und Philosophische Kritik*, 81, pp. 48-56. Reprinted in Angelelli (ed): [1964], pp. 106-14. Translated into English as 'On the Scientific Justification of a Conceptual Notation', in Bynum (ed): [1972]: , pp. 83-9.

[1882*b*]: 'Booles logische Formelsprache und meine Begriffsschrift', in Hermes *et al* (eds): [1969]: , pp. 53-9. Translated into English as 'Boole's logical Formula-language and my Concept-script', in Long and White (trs): [1979]; pp. 47-52.

[1882-3]: 'Über den Zweck der Begriffsschrift', *Jenaische Zeitschrift für Naturwissenschaft*, 16, pp. 1-10. Reprinted in Angelelli (ed): [1964], pp. 97-106. Translated into English as 'On the Aim of the "Conceptual Notation"', in Bynum (ed): [1972], pp. 90-100.

[-1884]: 'Dialog mit Punjer über Existenz', in Hermes *et al* (eds): [1967], pp. 60-75. Translated into English as 'Dialogue with Punjer on Existence', in Long and White (trs): [1979], pp. 53-67.

[1884*a*]: 'Geometrie der Punktpaare in der Ebene', [Geometry of Point Pairs in the Plane], *Jenaische Zeitschrift für Naturwissenschaft*, 17, pp. 98-100. Reprinted in Angelelli (ed): [1967], pp. 94-8.

[1884*b*]: *Die Grundlagen der Arithmetik*. Breslau: Koebner. Translated into English as *The Foundations of Arithmetic* (with German on facing pages) by J. L. Austin. Oxford: Blackwell, 1953.

[1885*a*]: Review of H. Cohen, *Das Prinzip der Infinitesimal-Methode und seine Geschichte, Zeitschrift für Philosophie und Philosophische Kritik,* **87**, pp. 324-9. Reprinted in Angelelli (ed): [1967], pp. 99-102.

[1885*b*]: 'Erwiderung auf Cantors Rezension der *Grundlagen der Arithmetik*'. [Reply to Cantor's review of the *Foundations of Arithmetic*] *Deutsche Literaturzeitung*, **6**, p. 1030. Reprinted in Angelelli (ed): [1967], p. 112.

[1885*c*]: 'Über formale Theorien der Arithmetik', *Jenaische Zeitschrift für Naturwissenschaft*, **19**, pp. 94-104. Reprinted in Angelelli (ed): [1964], pp. 103-11. Translated into English as 'On Formal Theories of Arithmetic', in Kluge (ed): [1971], pp. 141-53.

[1890-92]: 'Entwarf zu einer Besprechung von Cantors *Gesammelten Abhandlungen zur Lehre vom Transfiniten*', in Hermes *et al* (eds): [1969], pp. 76-80. Translated into English as 'Draft towards a Review of

Cantor's *Gesammelte Abhandlungen zur Lehre vom Transfiniten* in Long and White (eds): [1979], pp. 68-71.

[1891*a*]: 'Über das Tragheitsgesetz', *Zeitschrift für Philosophie und Philosophische Kritik*, **98**, pp. 145-61. Reprinted in Angelelli (ed): [1967], pp. 113-24. Translated into English as 'On the Law of Inertia', *Studies in the History and Philosophy of Science*, **2**, pp. 195-212.

[1891*b*]: 'Funktion und Begriff'. Jena: Pohle. Reprinted in Angelelli (ed): [1967], pp. 124-42. Translated into English as 'Function and Concept' in Geach and Black (eds): [1952], pp. 21-41.

[1891-2*a*]: 'Über den Begriff der Zahl', in Hermes *et al* (eds): [1969], pp. 81-95. Translated into English as 'On the Concept of Number', in Long and White (trs): [1979], pp. 72-86.

[1891-2*b*]: 'Eine kritische Auseinandersetzung mit Kerry', in Hermes *et al* (eds): [1969], pp. 96-127. Translated into English as 'A Criticism of Kerry', in Long and White (trs): [1979], pp. 87-117.

[1892*a*]: 'Über Begriff und Gegenstand', *Vierteljahrsschrift für Wissenschaftliche Philosophie*, **16**, pp. 192-205. Reprinted in Angelelli (ed): [1967], pp. 167-78. Translated into English as 'On Concept and Object', in Geach and Black (eds): [1952], pp. 42-55.

[1892*b*]: 'Über Sinn und Bedeutung', *Zeitschrift für Philosophie und Philosophische Kritik*, **100**, pp. 25-50. Reprinted in Angelelli (ed): [1967], pp. 143-62. Translated into English as 'On Sense and Reference', in Geach and Black (eds): [1952], pp. 56-78.

[1892*c*]: Review of G. Cantor, *Zur Lehre vom Transfiniten, Zeitschrift für Philosophie und Philosophische Kritik*, **100**, pp. 269-72. Reprinted in Angelelli (ed): [1967], pp. 163-6.

[1892-5]: 'Ausfuhrung über Sinn und Bedeutung', in Hermes *et al* (eds): [1969], pp. 128-36. Translated into English as 'Comments on Sense and Meaning', in Long and White (trs): [1979], pp. 118-25.

[1893]: *Grundgesetze der Arithmetik*, vol. 1. Jena: Pohle. Reprinted, Hildesheim: Olms, 1962, Partially translated into English in Furth (ed): [1964].

[1894]: Review of E. Husserl; *Philosophie der Arithmetik, Zeitschrift für Philosophie und Philosophische Kritik*, **103**, pp. 313-32. Reprinted in Angelelli (ed): [1967], pp. 179-92. Translated into English as 'Review of Dr. E. Husserl's *Philosophy of Arithmetic*', in *Mind*, **81**, pp. 321-37, 1972.

[1895*a*]: 'Kritische Beleuchtung einiger Punkte in E. Schröders *Vorlesungen über die Algebra der Logik,' Archiv für Systematische Philosophie,* 1, pp. 433-56. Reprinted in Angelelli (ed): [1967], pp. 192-210. Translated into English as 'A Critical Elucidation of some Points in E. Schröder's *Vorlesungen über die Algebra der Logik*', in Geach and Black (eds): [1952], pp. 86-106.

[1895*b*]: 'Le Nombre Entier', *Revue de Metaphysique et de Morale*, 3, pp. 73-8. Reprinted with German translation in Angelelli (ed): [1967], pp. 211-19. Translated into English as 'The Whole Number', *Mind*, **79**, pp. 481-86, 1970.

[1896*a*]: 'Über die Begriffsschrift des Herrn Peano und meine eigene', *Berichte über die Verhandlungen der Königlich Sächsischen Gesellschaft der Wissenschaften zu Leipzig Mathematisch-Physische Klasse,* **48**, pp. 361-78. Reprinted in Angelelli (ed): [1967], pp. 220-33. Translated into English as 'On Herr Peano's Begriffsschrift and my Own', *Australasian Journal of Philosophy*, 47, pp. 1-14.

[1896*b*]: 'Lettera del sig. G. Frege all'Editore *Rivista di Matematica,* **6**, pp. 53-9. Reprinted in Angelelli (ed): [1967], pp. 234-9. Translated into English in 'Peano's Review of Frege's *Grundgesetze*', *Southern Journal of Philosophy*, **9**, pp. 25-37, 1971.

[1897]: 'Logik', in Hermes *et al* (eds): [1969], pp. 137-63. Translated into English as 'Logic', in Long and White (trs): [1979], pp. 126-51.

[1897-8]: 'Begrundung meiner strengeren Grundsätze der Definierens', in Hermes *et al* (eds): [1969], pp. 164-70. Translated into English as 'The Argument for my stricter Canons of Definition', in Long and White (trs): [1979], pp. 152-6.

[1898-9]: 'Logische Mängel in der Mathematik', in Hermes *et al* (eds): [1967], pp. 171-81. Translated into English as 'Logical Defects in Mathematics', in Long and White (trs): [1979], pp. 157-66.

[1899]: 'Über die Zahlen des Herrn H. Schubert'. Jena: Pohle. Reprinted in Angelelli (ed): [1967], pp. 240-61.

[1899-1906]: 'Über Euklidische Geometrie', in Hermes *et al* (eds): [1969], pp. 182-4. Translated into English as 'On Euclidean Geometry', in Long and White (trs): [1979], pp. 167-9,

[1903*a*]: *Grundgesetze der Arithmetik*, vol. 2. Jena: Pohle. Reprinted, Hildesheim: Olm, 1962. Partially translated into English in Furth (ed): [1964] and in Geach and Black (eds): [1952], pp. 137-244.

[1903*b*]: 'Über die Grundlagen der Geometrie I and II', *Jahresbericht der Deutschen Mathematiker-Vereinigung*, **12**, pp. 319-24. Reprinted in Angelelli (ed): [1967], pp. 262-72. Translated into English as 'On the Foundations of Geometry', in Kluge (ed): [1971], pp. 22-37.

[1903-]: 'Notizen Freges zu Hilberts *Grundlagen der Geometrie*', in Hermes *et al* (eds): [1969], pp. 185-8. Translated into English as 'Frege's Notes on Hilbert's *Grundlagen der Geometrie*', in Long and White (trs): [1979], pp. 170-3.

[1904]: 'Was ist eine Funktion?', in *Festschrift Ludwig Bolzmann gewidmet zum sechzigsten Geburtstage*. Leibzig: Barth. Reprinted in Angelelli (ed): [1967], pp. 273-80. Translated into English as 'What is a Function?', in Geach and Black (eds): [1952], pp. 107-16.

[-1906]: '17 Kernsätze zur Logik', in Hermes *et al* (eds): [1969], pp. 189-90. Translated into English as '17 Key Sentences on Logic', in Long and White (trs): [1979], pp. 174-5.

[1906*a*]: 'Über die Grundlagen der Geometrie', I, II und III, *Jahresberichte der Deutschen Mathematiker-Vereinigung*, **15**, pp. 293-309, 377-403, 423-30. Reprinted in Angelelli (ed): [1967], pp. 281-323. Translated into

English as 'On the Foundations of Geometry', in Kluge (ed): [1971], pp. 49-112.

[1906*b*]: 'Antwort auf die Ferienplauderei des Herrn Thomae', *Jahresbericht der Deutschen Mathematiker-Vereinigung.* **15**, pp. 586-90. Reprinted in Angelelli (ed): [1967], pp. 324-8. Translated into English as 'Reply to Mr. Thomae's Holiday Chat', in Kluge (ed): [1971], pp. 121-7.

[1906*c*]: 'Über Schoenflies: *Die Logischen Paradoxien der Mengenlehre*', in Hermes *et al* (eds): [1969], pp. 191-9. Translated into English as 'On Schoenflies: *Die Logischen Paradoxien der Mengenlehre*', in Long and White (trs): [1979], pp. 176-83.

[1906*d*]: 'Was kan ich als Ergebnis meiner Arbeit ansehen?', in Hermes *et al* (eds): [1969], p. 200. Translated into English as 'What may I regard as the Result of my Work?', in Long and White (trs): [1979], p. 184.

[1906*e*]: 'Einleitung in die Logik', in Hermes *et al* (eds): [1969], pp. 201-12. Translated into English as 'Introduction to Logic', in Long and White (trs): [1979], pp. 185-96.

[1906*f*]: 'Kurtze Übersicht meiner Logischen Lehren', in Hermes *et al* (eds): [1969], pp. 213-18. Translated into English as 'A Brief Survey of my Logical Doctrines', in Long and White (trs): [1979], pp. 197-202.

[1908*a*]: 'Die Unmöglichkeit der Thomaeschen formalen Arithmetik aufs neue nachgewiesen', *Jahresbericht der Deutschen Mathematiker-Vereinigung*, **17**, p. 52-5. Reprinted in Angelelli (ed): [1967], p. 329-33. Translated English as 'Renewed Proof of the Impossibility of Thomae's Formal Arithmetic', in Kluge (ed): [1971], pp. 132-7.

[1908*b*]: 'Schlussbemerkung', *Jahresbericht der Deutschen Mathematiker-Vereinigung*, **17**, p. 56. Reprinted in Angelelli (ed): [1967], p. 333. Translated into English as 'Concluding Remarks', in Kluge (ed): [1971], p. 138.

[1912]: 'Remarks on P. Jourdain, "The Development of the Theories of Mathematical Logic and the Principles of Mathematics"', *Quarterly Journal of Pure and Applied Mathematics*, **43**, pp. 237-69. Reprinted in Angelelli (ed): [1967], pp. 334-41.

[1914]: 'Logik in der Mathematik', in Hermes *et al* (eds): [1969], pp. 219-70. Translated into English as 'Logic in Mathematics', in Long and White (trs): [1979], pp. 203-50.

[1915]: 'Meine grundlegender logischen Einsichten', in Hermes *et al* (eds): [1969], pp. 271-2. Translated into English as 'My Basic Logical Insights', in Long and White (trs): [1979], pp. 251-2.

[1918*a*]: 'Der Gedanke: Eine logische Untersuchung', *Beiträge zur Philosophie des Deutschen Idealismus*, **1**, pp. 58-77. Reprinted in Angelelli (ed): [1967], pp. 342-62. Translated into English as 'Thoughts', in Geach (ed): [1977], pp. 1-30.

[1918*b*]: 'Die Verneinung: eine logische Untersuchung', *Beiträge zur Philosophie des Deutschen Idealismus*, **1**, pp. 143-57. Reprinted in Angelelli

(ed): [1967], pp. 362-78. Translated into English as 'Negation' in Geach (ed): [1977], pp. 31-53.

[1919]: 'Aufzeichnungen für Ludwig Darmstaedter', in Hermes *et al* (eds): [1969], pp. 273-7. Translated into English as 'Notes for Ludwig Darmstaedter', in Long and White (trs): [1979], pp. 253-7.

[1922-]: 'Logische Allgemeinheit', in Hermes *et al* (eds): [1969], pp. 278-81. Translated into English as 'Logical Generality', in Long and White (trs): [1979], pp. 258-62.

[1923]: 'Logische Untersuchungen, Dritter Teil: Gedankengefüge', *Beiträge zur Philosophie des Deutschen Idealismus*, **3**, pp. 36-51. Reprinted in Angelelli (ed): [1967], pp. 378-94. Translated into English as 'Compound Thoughts', in Geach (ed): [1977], pp. 55-77.

[1924*a*]: 'Tagebucheintagungen über den Begriff der Zahl', in Hermes *et al* (eds): [1969], pp. 282-3. Translated into English as 'Diary Entries on the Concept of Number', in Long and White (trs): [1979], pp. 263-4.

[1924*b*]: 'Zahl', in Hermes *et al* (eds): [1969], pp. 284-5. Translated into English as 'Number', in Long and White (trs): [1979], pp. 265-6.

[1924-5*a*]: 'Erkenntnisquellen der Mathematik und der mathematischen Naturwissenschaften', in Hermes *et al* (eds): [1969], pp. 286-94. Translated into English as 'Sources of Knowledge of Mathematics and Mathematical Natural Sciences', in Long and White (trs): [1979], pp. 267-74.

[1924-5*b*]: 'Zahlen und Arithmetik', in Hermes *et al* (eds): [1969], pp. 295-7. Translated into English as 'Numbers and Arithmetic', in Long and White (trs): [1979], pp. 275-7.

[1924-5*c*]: 'Neuer Versuch der Grundlegung der Arithmetik', in Hermes *et al* (eds): [1969], pp. 298-302. Translated into English as 'A New Attempt at a Foundation for Arithmetic', in Long and White (trs): [1979], pp. 278-81.

(2) *Collections and Translations of Frege's Work*

Angelelli, I. (ed): [1964]: *Begriffschrift und andere Aufsätze.* Hildesheim: Olm.

Angelelli, I. (ed): [1967]: *Kleine Schriften.* Darmstadt: Wissenschaftliche Buchgesellschaft.

Bynum, T.W. (ed): [1972]: *Conceptual Notation and Related Articles.* Oxford: Clarendon Press.

Furth, M. (ed): [1964]: *The Basic Laws of Arithmetic.* University of California Press.

Gabriel, G., Hermes, H., Kambartel, F., Thiel, C. and Veraart, A. (eds): [1976]: *Wissenschaftlicher Briefwechsel.* Hamburg: Meiner.

Geach, P.T.(ed): [1977]: *Logical Investigations.* Oxford: Blackwell.

Geach, P.T. and Black, M. (eds): [1952]: *Translations from the Philosophical Writings of Gottlob Frege.* Oxford: Blackwell.

Hermes, H., Kambartel, F. and Kaulbach, F. (eds): [1969]: *Nachgelassene Schriften.* Hamburg: Felix Meiner.

Kluge, E.H.W. [1971]: *On the Foundations of Geometry and Formal Theories of Arithmetic.* Yale University Press.

Long, P. and White, R. [1979]: *Posthumous Writings.* Oxford: Blackwell.

McGuinness, B. (ed) and Kaal, H. (trs): [1980]: *Philosophical and Mathematical Correspondence.* Oxford: Blackwell.

(3) *Bibliography of Secondary Material*

Angelelli, I. [1967]: *Studies on Gottlob Frege and Traditional Philosophy*. Dordrecht: Reidel.

Anscombe, G. and Geach, P. [1961]: *Three Philosophers*. Oxford: Basil Blackwell.

Armstrong, D. M. [1981]: 'Frege's Thoughts', in L. Chipman (ed): *Reason, Truth and Theory*. Amsterdam: Nijhoff. *Forthcoming*.

Arnauld, A. and Nicole, P. [1724]: *The Art of Thinking (Port Royal Logic)*. New York: Bobbs-Merrill, 1969.

Benacerraf, P. [1965]: 'What Numbers could not be', *Philosophical Review*, **74**, pp. 47-73.

Boehner, P. [1952]: *Mediaeval Logic*. Manchester University Press.

Bolzano, B. [1837]: *Wissenschaftslehre*. Aslen: Scientia. Partially translated into English as *Theory of Science*, by B. Terrell. Dordrecht: Reidel, 1973.

Boole, G. [1854]: *An Investigation of the Laws of Thought*. New York: Dover.

Cantor, G. [1885]: Review of Frege [1884], *Deutsche Literaturzeitung*, **6**, pp. 728-9. Reprinted in E. Zermelo (ed): *Gesammelte Abhandlungen*. Hildesheim: Olms.

Carnap, R. [1963]: 'Intellectual Autobiography', in P. A. Schilpp (ed): *The Philosophy of Rudolf Carnap*. La Salle: Open Court.

Coder, D. [1974]: 'The Opening Passage of Frege's "Über Sinn und Bedeutung"', *Philosophia*, **4**, pp. 339-43.

Descartes, R. [1628]: *Rules for the Direction of the Mind*, in E. S. Haldane and G. R. T. Ross (eds): *The Philosophical Works of Descartes*, vol. 1, pp. 1-77, Cambridge University Press, 1911.

Descartes, R. [1637]: *Discourse on the Method of Rightly Conducting the Reason*, in E. S. Haldane and G. R. T. Ross (eds): *The Philosophical Works of Descartes*, vol. 1, pp. 81-130.

Descartes, R. [1644]: *Principles of Philosophy*, in E. S. Haldane and G. R. T. Ross (eds): *The Philosophical Works of Descartes*, vol. 1, pp. 203-302.

Dirichlet, P. L. [1837]: 'Über die Darstellung Ganz Willkürlicher Functionen durch Sinus- und Cosinus-Reihen', in H. W. Dove and L. Moser (eds): *Repertorium der Physik*, **1**, pp. 152-74.

Dudman, V. H. [1970]: 'Frege's Judgement Stroke', *Philosophical Quarterly*, *Philosophy*, **47**, pp. 119-22.

Dudman, V. H. [1970]: Frege's Judgement Stroke', *Philosophical Quarterly*, **20**, pp. 150-61.

Dudman, V.H. [1972]: 'The Concept Horse', *Australasian Journal of Philosophy*, **50**, pp. 67-75.

Dudman, V.H. [1976]: 'From Boole to Frege', in Schirn (ed): [1976], vol. 1, pp. 109-38.

Dummett, M. [1956]: 'Nominalism', *Philosophical Review*, **65**, pp. 491-505. Reprinted in *Truth and Other Enigmas*, pp. 38-49. London: Duckworth.

Dummett, M. [1973]: *Frege. The Philosophy of Language*. London: Duckworth.

Dummett, M. [1975]: 'What is a Theory of Meaning?', in S. Guttenplan (ed): *Mind and Language*. Oxford: Clarendon Press, pp. 97-138.

Dummett, M. [1976]: 'What is a Theory of Meaning? (II)' in G. Evans and J. McDowell (eds): *Truth and Meaning*, pp. 67-137.

Feigl, H. [1949]: Translation of Frege's [1892*b*], in H. Feigl and W. Sellars (eds): *Reading in Philosophical Analysis*, pp. 85-102. New York: Appleton-Century-Crofts.

Fraenkel, A., Bar-Hillel, Y. and Levy, A. [1973]: *Foundations of Set Theory*. 2nd revised edition. Amsterdam: North Holland.

Furth, M. [1965]: 'Two Types of Denotation', in N. Rescher (ed): *Essays in Logical Theory*. American Philosophical Quarterly Monograph.

Geach, P.T. [1961]: 'Frege', in Anscombe and Geach [1961].

Geach, P.T. [1962]: *Reference and Generality*. Cornell University Press.

Grossmann, R. [1969]: *Reflections on Frege's Philosophy*. Evanston: Northwestern University Press.

Hacker, P.M.S. [1975]: 'Frege and Wittgenstein on Elucidations', *Mind*, **84**, pp. 601-9.

Hacker, P.M.S. [1979]: 'Semantic Holism: Frege and Wittgenstein', in C.G. Luckhardt (eds): *Wittgenstein. Sources and Perspectives*, pp. 213-42. Hassocks: Harvester Press.

Halmos, P. [1960]: *Naive Set Theory*. New York: van Nostrand.

Heijenoort, J. van (ed): [1967]: *From Frege to Gödel*. Cambridge, Massachusetts: Harvard University Press.

Heijenoort, J. van [1977]: 'Frege on Sense Identity', *Journal of Philosophical Logic*, **6**, pp. 103-8.

Jevons, W. [1874]: *The Principles of Science*. New York: Dover, 1958.

Kant, I. [1787]: *Critique of Pure Reason*. Second edition. Translated into English by Norman Kemp Smith.

Kant, I. [1800]: *Logic*. New York: Bobbs-Merrill, 1974.

Kenny, A. [1968]: *Descartes. A Study of his Philosophy*. New York: Random House.

Klemke, E.D. (ed): [1968]: *Essays on Frege*. Urbana: University of Illinois Press.

Kline, M. [1972]: *Mathematical Thought from Ancient to Modern Times*. Oxford University Press.

Kneebone, G.T. [1963]: *Mathematical Logic and the Foundations of Mathematics*. London: Van Nostrand.

Kolakowski, L. [1975]: *Husserl and the Search for Certitude*. Yale University Press.

Korselt, A. [1903]: 'Über die Grundlagen der Geometrie', *Jahresbericht der deutschen Mathematiker-Vereinigung*, **12**, pp. 402-7.

Kripke, S. [1972]: 'Naming and Necessity', in D. Davidson and G. Harman (eds): *Semantics of Natural Language*. Dordrecht: Reidel.

Lakatos, I. [1976]: *Proofs and Refutations*. Cambridge University Press.

Lakatos, I. [1978]: 'Cauchy and the Continuum', in J. Worrall and G. Currie (eds): *Mathematics, Science and Epistemology*, pp. 43-60. Cambridge University Press.

Linsky, L. [1967]: *Referring*. London: Routledge and Kegan Paul.

Locke, J. [1700]: *An Essay Concerning Human Understanding*. Edited by J. W. Yolton. London: Everyman's Library, 1961.

McDowell, J. [1977]: 'On the Sense and Reference of a Proper Name', *Mind*, **86**, pp. 159-85.

Mach, E. [1902]: *The Analysis of Sensations*. New York: Dover, 1959.

Mill, J. S. [1879]: *A System of Logic*. London: Longmans.

Moody, E. [1953]: *Truth and Consequence in Mediaeval Logic*. Amsterdam: North Holland.

Moore, E. H. [1902]: 'On the Foundations of Mathematics'. *Science*, **17**, pp. 401-16.

Musgrave, A. E. [1972]: 'George Boole and Psychologism', *Scientia*, **107**, pp. 1-16.

Nusenoff, R. B. [1978]: 'The Closing Passage of Frege's "Über Sinn und Bedeutung"'. *Notre Dame Journal of Formal Logic*, **19**, pp. 282-401.

Nusenoff, R. B. [1979]: 'Frege on Identity Sentences', *Philosophy and Phenomenological Research*, **39**, pp. 438-42.

Passmore, J. [1953]: 'Descartes, the British Empiricists, and Formal Logic', *Philosophical Review*, **62**, pp. 545-53.

Peano, G. [1895]: Review of Frege [1893], *Rivista di Matematica*, **5**, pp. 122-8.

Quine, W. O. [1955]: 'On Frege's Way Out', *Mind*, **64**, pp. 145-59. Reprinted in Klemke (ed): [1968], pp. 485-501.

Ray, R. [1977]: 'Frege's Difficulties with Identity', *Philosophical Studies*, **31**, pp. 219-34.

Resnik, M. D. [1976]: 'Frege's Context Principle Revisited', in M. Schirn (ed): *Studies on Frege*, vol. 3, pp. 35-50.

Ringer, F. K. [1969]: *The Decline of the German Mandarins*. Harvard University Press.

Robinson, A. [1966]: *Non Standard Analysis*. Amsterdam: North Holland.

Robinson, A. [1967]: 'The Metaphysics of the Calculus', in I. Lakatos (ed): *Problems in the Philosophy of Mathematics*, pp. 28-40. Amsterdam: North Holland.

Russell, B. [1903]: *The Principles of Mathematics*. Cambridge University Press. Second edition, 1937. London: Allen & Unwin.

Russell, B. [1908]: 'Mathematical Logic as based on the Theory of Types', *American Journal of Mathematics*, **30**, pp. 222-62. Reprinted in R. Marsh (ed): *Logic and Knowledge*, pp. 59-102.

Russell, B. [1959]: *My Philosophical Development*. London: George Allen & Unwin.

Russell, B. and Whitehead, A. N. [1910]: *Principia Mathematica*, vol. 1. Cambridge University Press.

Sluga, H. [1970]: Review of Klemke (ed): [1968], *Philosophy*, **45**, p. 75.

Sluga, H. [1971]: Review of Hermes *et al* (eds): [1969], *Journal of Philosophy*, **68**, pp. 265-72.

Sluga, H. [1975]: 'Frege and the Rise of Analytic Philosophy', *Inquiry*, **18**, pp. 471-86.

Sluga, H. [1976]: 'Frege as a Rationalist', in M. Schirn (ed): *Studies on Frege*, 1, pp. 27-47. Stuttgart-Bad Canstatt: Frommann.

Sluga, H. [1977]: 'Frege's alleged Realism', *Inquiry*, **20**, pp. 227-42.

Smiley, T. [1973]: 'What is a Syllogism?', *Journal of Philosophical Logic*, **2**, pp. 136-54.

Sternfeld, R. [1966]: *Frege's Logical Theory*. Carbondale: University of Southern Illinois Press.

Stoothoff, R. H. [1963]: 'Note on a Doctrine of Frege', *Mind*, **72**, pp. 406-8.

Thiel, C. [1965]: *Sense and Reference in Frege's Logic*. Dordrecht: Reidel.

Tichy, P. [1979]: 'Existence and God', *Journal of Philosophy*, **76**, pp. 403-20.

Tugendhat, E. [1970]: 'The Meaning of "Bedeutung" in Frege', *Analysis*, **30**, pp. 177-89.

Wittgenstein, L. [1921]: *Tractatus Logico-Philosophicus*. London: Routledge & Kegan Paul.

Zermelo, E. [1908]: 'Investigations in the Foundations of Set Theory I', in Heijenoort (ed): [1967], pp. 199-215.

Index